THE PERAMBULATION
DARTMOOR'S GREATEST LONG DISTANCE WALK

DESCRIBING THE MEDIEVAL ROUTE
FOR THE MODERN-DAY WALKER

Roland Ebdon

HALSGROVE

DEDICATION

This book is dedicated to my wife Rosamond and my seven grandchildren: Lucy, Philippa, Daisy, Beatrice, Isaac, Sebastian and Albert. Most of them have been to the moor with me and at least two now actively seek more visits to the 'misty mountains'.

First published in Great Britain in 2016

British Library Cataloguing-in-Publication Data
A CIP record for this title is available from the British Library

ISBN 978 0 85704 281 1

HALSGROVE
Halsgrove House,
Ryelands Business Park,
Bagley Road, Wellington, Somerset TA21 9PZ
Tel: 01823 653777   Fax: 01823 216796
email: sales@halsgrove.com

Part of the Halsgrove group of companies
Information on all Halsgrove titles is available at:
www.halsgrove.com

Printed and bound in China by
Everbest Printing Investment Ltd

PART ONE

FOREWORD

England in AD1204 was a land in turmoil. The king, John, who must have hoped to reap the rewards from the years his family had ruled found that he had inherited a crumbling empire. In a desperate attempt to raise funds for an army to carry war to Philip of France, he gave up his control over Devon but retained the heights of Dartmoor and Exmoor for himself. This action was the start of a little known but fascinating story about what is now a major part of one of our national Parks – the Forest of Dartmoor.

Land owned by the Crown has the official title of 'Forest' and at that time anyone infringing the Royal rights was subject to draconian laws. The 'Forest of Dartmoor' changed hands often in its first one hundred years but has been in the possession of the Duke of Cornwall, the heir to the throne, since it was first given to the Black Prince 1337. The present Duke of Cornwall is also the Prince of Wales – HRH Prince Charles.

A forest boundary is important as the owner derives revenue from activities within the forest such as when animals graze. However, King John failed to follow both Norman and Saxon tradition in that he did not order a perambulation to fix the boundary of the Forest. Perhaps this was just not high on his list of priorities remembering that he faced trouble both at home and abroad throughout his reign. For example, during his reign, the English Barons revolted and forced the sealing of the first Magna Carta in 1215 that severely limited his authority – including that relating to the Forests he retained.

The Dartmoor Forest boundary was first perambulated on the orders of his successor, his son, King Henry III in 1240. The return from that first perambulation has never been identified but several copies were made at key moments over the next five centuries. Nine of these have been traced and examined. They were written in medieval Latin shorthand and have been subject to many reinterpretations.

The Dartmoor Forest boundary has been disputed since its first recognition. Since the boundary has never been fenced, it has always been open to reinterpretation. In 1608/9, a major attempt was made to clarify the boundary. In the 19th century, the Ordnance Survey both mapped Dartmoor as a whole and defined the Forest boundary as explained to them by local 'witnesses'. At the same time, many scholars attempted to justify their understanding of the boundary and relate the data in the return to the ground named on the new maps.

This new examination based on scholarly work and practical application reveals that, in the past, misunderstandings of the boundary might well have been made – most often to the detriment of the Crown. Furthermore, it is now suggested that the very start point of the perambulation has been mis-understood by all.

Is the boundary important today? Whilst the Duke of Cornwall still owns the forest, he did allow it to be registered as common land in 1967. Because of the Dartmoor Commons Act of 1985, graziers and others accessing the Forest for recreational purposes have the right of free access on foot or horseback in perpetuity. Thus, the boundary is of no financial relevance today. However, the uncertainty about where exactly it was intended to be when it was first perambulated makes it worthy of re-examination.

Roland Ebdon
2016

ACKNOWLEDGEMENTS

I wish to thank all those who have supported or contributed in any small measure in the production of this book. First and foremost my thanks go to my wife who has patiently seen me off to the moor more times than she can probably remember and often catches me in a near dream like state as I have wrestled with getting the words for this text down on paper.

Mike Rice was with the project from the outset and provided photographs, advice and support and accompanied me during my first perambulation of the boundary.

Many geocachers have been involved and provided advice, some possibly unknowingly, and in that list I include Ian and Caroline Kirkpatrick (Ochico), Matt Prior (MuddyPuddles), Dave Martin (DartmoorDave) and Margaret Batten (BrentorBoxer).

The staff of the Duchy of Cornwall offices in Princetown and London who have provided data and advice.

Many librarians have aided me in my search and my thanks go to staff members of the Surrey (Guildford, Woking and Dittons) and Devon (Exeter and Honiton) libraries, the British Library and the Lincoln's Inn Library.

The National Archives staff members at Kew, the Devon Heritage Centre and the West Devon Record Office all offered advice and gave freely of their knowledge and experience.

Professor Ian Mercer late of the Dartmoor National Park Authority kindly put me right about more recent events.

Many others around the globe whom I have contacted by e-mail and who all added a little to the sum of my knowledge.

Simon Butler of Halsgrove Publishing who offered advice over the many years of the gestation of this text.

A FEW WORDS OF CAUTION FOR MOOR WALKERS

Any book advocating walking on Dartmoor must necessarily point out some of the dangers and suggest suitable precautions. Here are a few.

The maps offered here are sketches. Walkers should use them to plan their routes using proper maps such as sold by the Ordnance Survey. They should also be able to read them whilst on the moor and navigate with a compass if the weather becomes inclement.

The weather is not always sunny. Suitable attention should be paid to forecasts and the clothing worn and equipment carried should be sufficient for all members of the party to cope with rapid changes. As well as food and drink for consumption, carry some emergency reserves.

Let someone know where you are going and when you expect to be off the moor. Also let them know what they should do if you fail to return at the planned time. Stick to your planned route. Take a whistle to raise attention and nowadays a mobile telephone - albeit you might need to make for high ground to get a signal and do not wait too long (i.e. not until dark!) before asking for advice and possibly assistance.

If you have not walked on Dartmoor before, it is useful to know that covering two miles in an hour is a good pace. Thus you can plan how long each trip should take but do allow for refreshment stops and time to take photographs and for further exploration.

If you are lost, admit it. Start taking action to find out where you are. Climbing in good weather could bring you to a suitable viewpoint. In really bad weather and if it really is necessary, find a stream and follow it downhill. You will eventually reach the edge of the moor but possibly miles from your car.

Military training, including live firing, takes place on parts of Dartmoor – but not normally at weekends. If you anticipate crossing into a military training area (marked on the Ordnance Survey maps) check on the military website that training will NOT be in progress. Do not enter range areas that are marked with red and white poles if red flags are flying from the prominent tors.

Observe the country code – shut gates behind you, keep dogs under control, take care with fires, do not leave litter.

The routes suggested are mainly over goodish country with plenty of sheep trails or better to follow but bad weather can change the going and, of course, if you get lost you could meet all sorts of difficult ground. When walking observe this piece of old moorland wisdom – 'If you encounter a bog and your first step results in your foot sinking to your ankle and your second results in you sinking to your knee make sure your third is backwards'. On Dartmoor, the quickest and safest route between two points is not always the shortest. Be prepared to divert around bad ground.

Do not leave valuables in your car.

CONTENTS

SOURCES OF INFORMATION

Historians unravel their stories by interpreting ancient artefacts and often use the work of their forebears. Both involve a lot of subjective interpretation. Determining exactly what happened in the past is invariably time consuming when sources are difficult to decipher or possibly incomplete and even documents created to meet the express wishes of monarchs are subject to the ravages of time. In this study we rely upon five primary surviving sources of information

One - The Pipe Rolls held by the National Archives, sometimes called the Great Rolls, are a collection of financial records maintained by the English Exchequer (Treasury) and its successors. The earliest date from the 12th century and the series extends, mostly complete, from then until 1833. They form the oldest continuous series of records concerning English governance kept by the English, British and United Kingdom governments. They were originally records of the yearly audits performed by the Exchequer of the accounts and payments presented to the Treasury by the sheriffs and other Royal officials and owed their name to the shape they took, as the various sheets were affixed to each other and then rolled into a tight roll, resembling a pipe, for storage. Their form and purpose developed over the centuries and the Rolls are now considered under at least four headings – Fine Rolls, Close Rolls, Patent Rolls and Charter Rolls. A *'fine'* was essentially a promise of money to the king in return for a concession or favour and the first purpose of the Fine Rolls was to record the money so offered. The Close Rolls are an administrative record created in order to preserve a central record of all *'letters close'* issued by the Chancery in the name of the Crown. The first Close roll was started in 1204 (in the reign of King John). Records of King John's order creating the Forest of Dartmoor and of King Henry III ordering the first

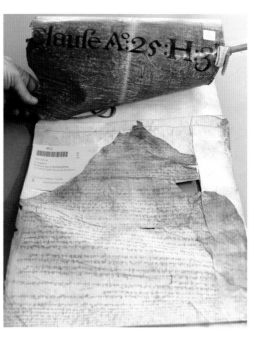

Example of a damaged Pipe roll.

perambulation of the Forest of Dartmoor are still retained in the Pipe Rolls. Damage has occurred to many of the Pipe Rolls and we are fortunate that so much material has actually survived.

Two - Ancient copies of documents made for other purposes later in history. Although the original return from that first perambulation has never been identified, copies of it have been found on documents from as early as 1335 and subsequently at points in history that were important for those affected by the boundary of the Forest.

Three – The work of two noted recorders of the families of Devon (and Cornwall) - Sir William Pole (1561-1635) and Tristram Risdon (1580-1640) who drew on Pole's earlier work.

Four - Earlier work by historians, especially in the 19th century. As cheaper means of transportation became freely available from early in the 19th century, more and more people began to visit previously remote places such as Dartmoor. Many, including local clergymen, took a scholarly interest in the history of the area and in particular the actual boundary of the Forest of Dartmoor. Their work included early attempts to translate the copies of the return, which were written in Latin and shorthand, and also to relate what they read to the names on the maps being created at the time by the Ordnance Survey.

Five - Modern storage and retrieval systems such as the world-wide-web. The Internet contains a mass of information but much of which has to be treated with caution, as not everything recorded is accurate and sections might not 'pass' a peer review. Its usefulness grows by the day - for example, during the period of researching the material for this book, all of the Fine Rolls of King Henry III's reign have been photographed and translated and are now available on line. Also of interest to us are both the results of recent research and analysis by learned bodies and copies of earlier material previously only found in private libraries or archives. More and more books are appearing almost daily in digitised form on the www. Whilst not making the need for trips to archives or libraries less necessary, it does allow quick, focused searches of far more material than was previously possible. However, one has to be careful as another hurdle when using the www for research is that early documents contain names spelt in a variety of fashions. Interestingly, during this research the Artificial Intelligence based tool 'Google translate' arrived and proved invaluable.

INTRODUCTION

This book has been written and illustrated to encourage further academic study and practical moorland exploration. Those who might wish to follow the trail of clues about this early Plantagenet mystery could be historians, puzzle sleuths, existing Dartmoor Forest boundary perambulators, those who already know and love Dartmoor, other walkers who perhaps need a spur to encourage them to venture a little further and armchair admirers of wild landscapes.

In studying the history of the creation of the forest and noting the arguments about its exact boundary over the centuries, ancient documents have been located, medieval Latin shorthand translated, libraries and repositories scoured for other writings and the forest boundary and parts of the moor overlooking it, walked many times. Here is a presentation of the findings to date with the hope that they may be the start point for further study. As well as encouraging scholarly endeavour, there are descriptions, maps and photographs of sixteen excursions that can be undertaken to examine portions of the boundary – most of which include visits to historic and beautiful sites on Dartmoor.

Here is an attempt to answer questions with relation to four separate events: firstly - the 'sale' of Devon and Cornwall, less the Forests of Dartmoor and Exmoor; secondly - the issuing of the writ for a perambulation of the Forest of Dartmoor in 1240 and its promulgation; thirdly – the first perambulation, the participants and their route, i.e. the intended boundary; and fourthly – the worth of subsequent perambulations.

We know that the Forest was created in 1204 and we know who has owned it since and who owns it now. We do not know why John chose to retain these forests but can guess.

Although Forest Law was not formally promulgated until 1217, when that law was formalised it would have been on the basis of precedent. We know that under both Saxon and Norman custom a perambulation of any new boundary would have been expected. Thus we know why a perambulation was expected but we can find no evidence that John ordered one. We do know when the first recorded perambulation was ordered – 13 June 1240 – and by whom – King Henry III. How and by whom the instruction was transmitted to Devon can also be deduced from court records.

We know when the perambulation occurred – 23/24 June 1240. We know who were the official perambulators and can guess who else might have been involved. Where they might have started is fairly self-evident – Okehampton – but the route they took and hence the boundary itself is unclear in several sections. There are multiple copies of the 1240 perambulation return dating from as early as or before 1335. They are all hand written on vellum in a personalised form of Latin shorthand and contain names of key points on the boundary. These names were obviously spoken in the local dialect and written down phonetically and have been subject to re-interpretation ever since. The copies vary one from another showing how different scholars interpreted the writing of the original recorder and the place names. The contents of these documents create a source of uncertainty about the exact route taken by those first perambulators and hence the boundary itself. It is clear that the line of the boundary now generally accepted has been influenced by the self-interests of adjacent landholders.

Hoping to encourage people to get out to explore the natural beauty of Dartmoor.

That the boundary was open to doubt is clear from the need in succeeding centuries for further perambulations in order to resolve disputes. These were in response to claims by adjacent landholders. The most significant one for this study is that of 1608/9. Scholars in the 19th century uncovered the return from that perambulation. It is significant in that it added many more boundmarks and was based upon evidence gathered from local experts - there being no accurate maps at that time. It represented a summation of the inroads that local custom and practice had made into the area of the Forest.

Today we have the benefit of detailed maps, aerial photographs, Google Earth etc to plot our walks on Dartmoor. There was nothing like this in the 12th century. The Ordnance Survey created the first accurate maps of Dartmoor, its topographical features and boundaries, in the 19th century. The surveyors relied heavily upon local knowledge when it came to ascribing names to features and boundary lines. Records show us that in the six hundred years between the first perambulation and the mapping of the moor, many disputes arose as to the line of the boundary. Indeed, one local landowner actually constructed a 'tor' of his own – Little Hound Tor – to try to extend his lands. Therefore simply relating the names of hills and features shown on today's maps to those recorded in that first perambulation return may have given rise to misinterpretation.

Further study is encouraged as the author is of the firm belief that the boundary that has been accepted for many years, has, in parts, been misinterpreted - in some places by wide margins. These discrepancies are explained and can be examined on the ground by those prepared to make the effort. Further walking is encouraged as the moor offers so many beautiful vistas and the opportunity for healthy recreation.

POPULAR AND PROPOSED BOUNDARY

The route that most modern walkers follow assuming it to be the route the early perambulators took is as follows (the name given on the 1240 return is shown first):

Hoga de Cossedonne – Cosdon (SX636915), hoga de Hundetorre – Hound Tor (SX628890), Thurlestone – Watern Tor (SX629868), Wotesbrokelakesfote – Hew Lake Foot (SX639860), Heigheston – Shovel Down Longstone (SX660856), Langestone – the Heath Stone (SX671837), Turbary of Alberysheved – Metherall Marsh (SX673832), Furnum Regis – King's Oven (SX674812), Wallebrokeshede – Wallabrook Head (SX675810), Along the Wallabrook to its confluence with the East Dart (SX672747), Dartmeet (SX671731), Okesbrokesfote – O Brook confluence (SX662724), la Dryeworke – Dry Lake's tin streams (SX660710), Dryefeld Ford – intersection of Dry Lake and the Sandy Way (SX659697), Battyshull – Ryder's Hill – (SX659690), Wester Wellabroke – Wellabrook Head (SX665683), down the Wellabroke to its confluence with the river Avon (SX664661), Ester Whyteburghe – Eastern Whittabarrow (SX665651), la Redlake – Red Lake Foot (SX635661), Grymsgrove – Erme Head (SX621668), Elysburghe – Eylesbarrow (SX599685), Syward's Cross – Syward's Cross (SX601699),Ysfother – South Hessary Tor (SX597723), another Ysfother – North Hessary Tor (SX578742), Mystor – Great Mis Tor (SX562769), Mewyburghe – White Barrow (SX568793), Lullingesfote – Limsboro Cairn (SX565805), Rakernesbrokyfote – Rattlebrook Foot (SX560837), up the Rattlebrook to its head (SX559869), la Westolle – Stenga Tor (SX567880), Ernestorre – Yes Tor (SX580901), Ford near Chapel of St Michael de Halgestoke – Halstock Chapel – Cullever Steps (SX605921), Cossedonne – return to original starting point.

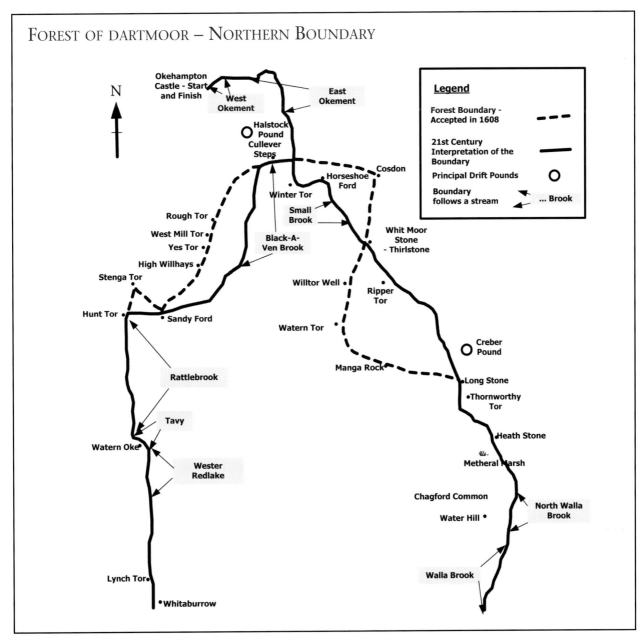

FOREST OF DARTMOOR – NORTHERN BOUNDARY

Legend

Forest Boundary - Accepted in 1608

21st Century Interpretation of the Boundary

Principal Drift Pounds

Boundary follows a stream ... Brook

The boundary that is now being suggested as the one that the 1240 perambulators actually intended is as follows – the differences from that above are highlighted:

Hoga de Cossedonne – **Belstone Ridge** (SX610914), hoga de Hundetorre – **ridgeline near Whitemoor Circle** (SX632896), Thurlestone – **White Moor Stone** (SX633894), Wotesbrokelakesfote – **confluence of Walla Brook and North Teign river** (SX654870), Heigheston – Shovel Down longstone (SX660856), Langestone – the Heath Stone (SX671837), Turbary of Alberysheved – Metherall Marsh (SX673832), Furnum Regis – King's Oven (SX674812), Wallebrokeshede – Wallabrook Head (SX675810), along the Wallabrook to its confluence with the East Dart (SX672747), Dartmeet (SX671731), Okesbrokesfote – O Brook confluence (SX662724), la Dryeworke – Dry Lake's tin streams (SX660710), Dryefeld Ford – intersection of Dry Lake and the Sandy Way (SX659697), Battyshull – Ryder's Hill – (SX659690), Wester Wellabroke – Wellabrook Head (SX665683), down the Wellabrook to its confluence with the river Avon (SX664661), Ester Whyteburghe – **Western Whittabarrow** (SX653654), la Redlake – Red Lake Foot (SX635661), Grymsgrove – **Grim's Grave** (SX612664), Elysburghe –

The northern part of Dartmoor showing the original Forest boundary and the modern boundary as interpreted and described in this book.

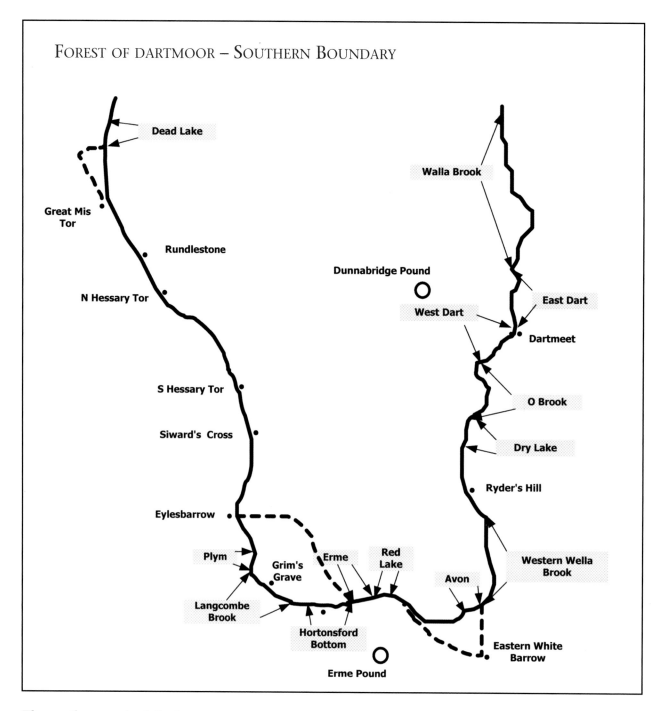

FOREST OF DARTMOOR – SOUTHERN BOUNDARY

The southern part of Dartmoor showing the original Forest boundary and the modern boundary as interpreted and described in this book.

Eylesbarrow (SX599685), Syward's Cross – Siward's Cross (SX601699), Ysfother – South Hessary Tor (SX597723), another Ysfother – North Hessary Tor (SX578742), Mystor – Great Mis Tor (SX562769), Mewyburghe – White Barrow (SX568793), Lullingesfote – Limsboro Cairn (SX565805), Rakernesbrokyfote – Rattlebrook Foot (SX560837), up the Rattlebrook to its head (SX559869), la Westolle – **Sandy Ford** (SX574878), Ernestorre – **Black-a-Ven brook** (SX596904), ford near Chapel of St Michael de Halgestoke – Cullever Steps (SX605921), Cossedonne – return to original starting point.

Chapter 1

Birth of the Forest and the 1240 Perambulation

Dartmoor, one of the fifteen National Parks in Britain, contains within its border the 'Forest of Dartmoor'. This was not an area of trees but an area reserved as a Royal hunting ground. It was established as such by King John in 1204 and thus may be regarded as a Plantagenet (or Angevin) legacy.

The size and extent of the Forest has been the subject of controversy since its creation. The boundaries of such forests have under both Saxon and Norman tradition been fixed and promulgated by means of a perambulation. King John failed to order such an event and the first known perambulation of the Forest of Dartmoor occurred in 1240 when ordered by his son and successor, King Henry III, in response to a request from those in Devon and to appease his brother. Whilst a copy of the writ ordering that perambulation still exists, the original return from the perambulation has never been identified.

Edward, the Black Prince, first Duke of Cornwall. Much of Dartmoor still remains in Duchy hands 700 years after Edward held it.

DEVON , CORNWALL, DARTMOOR AND EXMOOR

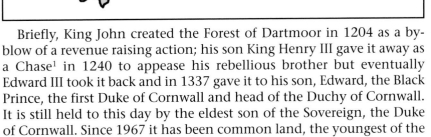

Location map showing Dartmoor and Exmoor in relation to the counties of England and Wales.

Briefly, King John created the Forest of Dartmoor in 1204 as a by-blow of a revenue raising action; his son King Henry III gave it away as a Chase[1] in 1240 to appease his rebellious brother but eventually Edward III took it back and in 1337 gave it to his son, Edward, the Black Prince, the first Duke of Cornwall and head of the Duchy of Cornwall. It is still held to this day by the eldest son of the Sovereign, the Duke of Cornwall. Since 1967 it has been common land, the youngest of the Dartmoor Commons.

---

[1]Only a sovereign can hold a 'Forest'; if it passes to a prince or other noble it should properly be regarded as a 'Chase'.

THE NORMAN AND THEN
THE ANGEVIN EMPIRE

LEGEND

☐ The Norman Conquests

☐ Angevin Territories

☐ Eleanor's 'Dowry' for Henry II

☐ Taken from France, Louis VII, by Henry II

☐ Territories Conquered with Papal Consent

Cornwall Devon LONDON

NORMANDY
BRITTANY
MAINE
ANJOU
TOUR-AINE
PARIS
AQUITAINE
TOULOUSE

Plantagenet Lands.

THE HISTORICAL SETTING

At the time of interest to us here, namely the reigns of Richard, John and King Henry III, these early Plantagenets were losing lands in France and support within England as the tax burden to fund the growing infrastructure and dynastic wars became more and more resented.

The creation of the Forest of Dartmoor was but one by-blow as in 1204 John raised 5000 Marks from the 'people of Devon and Cornwall' by giving up his rights in those two counties – in disafforesting them, he gave up control and the income derived. This was not a new idea. In 1072, William the Conqueror began the practise of 'selling' areas but also of retaining Forests for his personal pleasure and hunting. Forest Law derives from that time. John did not give up all his rights in Devon and retained the Forests of Dartmoot and Exmoor for himself. Perhaps he did this out of spite. Such an action would certainly be in line with part of his nature. But he had much to be bitter about. He came to rule at a time when the autocratic rights of the King that had been enjoyed for nearly two hundred years were being challenged, land was being lost abroad and revolt was fomenting at home. England in the period 1204 to 1240 was not a realm at peace.

Today, we live in a land shaped by the Plantagenets. The dynasty lasted for over three centuries and is considered to have begun when King Henry II took the throne in 1154. The first Plantagenet kings were French and for a long time there was little cultural difference between the two realms although conflict within and between them was commonplace. In such tumultuous times, the Normans and then the Plantagenets built many keeps as fortresses as they fought to maintain control of the land they had conquered and to protect its borders. In England, the massive stone fortresses such as Dover Castle, the Tower of London and Caernarfon Castle were expanded and still stand today. Westminster Palace, Westminster Abbey and St Paul's Cathedral rose in their first great forms during the 13th and 14th centuries – as did magnificent cathedrals such as Winchester, Salisbury, Lincoln and York. The dynasty split into the two branches of Lancaster and York in 1399 and was eventually replaced by the Tudors after Richard III lost the battle of Bosworth in 1485.

The Plantagenet rise to prominence was almost by accident as a result of William the Conqueror having no immediate heir. In need of an energetic ruler, those seeking a worthy successor to secure the Conqueror's realm chose one of his great-grandsons, the ambitious Count of Anjou and Duke of Normandy, an Angevin. He became King Henry II and displayed the energy needed in this time of great flux where the expansionist desires of the Normans/Plantagenets were countered both internally and internationally.

In their 331 years, the Plantagenets laid many of the foundations of today's Britain and especially the basic principles of law, justice and parliamentary rule. The first Plantagenets, the Angevins, oversaw much of the groundwork. The first Angevin, King Henry II, was the 'father of the common law'. His son, King John, was the unwilling grantor of the first version of the Magna Carta in 1215; to this charter the kingdom owes the principles of government restrained by law, habeas corpus and trial by one's own peers. During the reign of John's son, King Henry III, the first parliaments were summoned. Over the next two hundred years Parliament would claim the right to approve taxation and impeach ministers.

Such strides forward and changes indicate the tremendous energy displayed by the leaders of the dynasty, especially the Angevins, generally set against a sea of foment from those governed.

King John.

THE RISE OF THE ANGEVINS

Whilst William the Conqueror, the first Norman king of England, spent his life successfully consolidating and maintaining his hold over his continental possessions and England, he failed to secure a smooth succession. After his death in 1087, his kingdom was split. Normandy went to his eldest son Robert Curthose and his second surviving son, William Rufus, received England – he reigned as King William II. Henry, the Conqueror's third son was given a 'chest of gold'. This split of possessions would lead to decades of dispute within this troubled family.

In England, King William II proved to be unpopular, greedy, self-centred and a poor administrator. Although, he ruled following Saxon traditions to try to keep peace at home, he also continued the family tradition of trying to increase his power base. Henry, being unsatisfied with his inheritance, tried to gain and keep lands in Normandy against his brother Robert's wishes and subsequently allied himself with William. He was accepted and was actually present when William was accidentally killed whilst hunting in 1100. As William II had no heir, Henry being on the scene took his chance and seized the throne – King Henry I.

Robert disputed this power grab and invaded in 1101. The two armies that met were of comparable sizes and their leaders recognised the stalemate. Subsequently a negotiated settlement was agreed and Henry confirmed as king and so it seemed peace might reign. But, this peace was to be short lived. Henry counter-invaded the Duchy of Normandy, defeated Robert at Tinchebrai in 1106 and kept him imprisoned for the rest of his life. This would seem to have settled the succession within this family as Henry had a son, William Adelin. But this was not to be the case as this sole direct heir was drowned in 1120. Henry took a second wife but that marriage was childless. Perhaps in desperation, Henry declared that his daughter Matilda would be his heir.

In order to improve Matilda's power base, when her first husband, Henry V the future Holy Roman Emperor died, he arranged for her to marry a young man whose talents he admired, Geoffrey of Anjou. Geoffrey, who was to become the fifth Count of Anjou, Touraine and Maine, was known by a nickname derived from his habit of wearing a sprig of Broom blossom in his hat. In France, the Broom shrub (planta genista) is known as gênet and Geoffrey was known as Geoffrey Plantagenet. It was not a happy marriage but Matilda needed his support as when her father died in 1135, both Normandy and England chose Stephen of Blois (a grandson of the Conqueror) as the successor. She was not going to accept this and a period of civil war – the 'Anarchy' – existed from 1135 to 1153. During this period, Matilda claimed the throne of England and Geoffrey seized the Duchy of Normandy. Their son, Henry, actively supported his mother and at seventeen was

Matilda, daughter of Henry I.

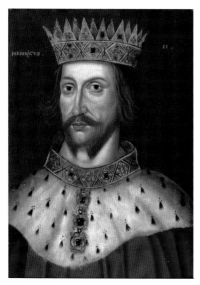

Henry II.

rewarded and made Duke of Normandy. He led a military expedition to England in 1153 and through treaty with Stephen agreed a peace whereby he, Henry, would inherit the throne of England on Stephen's death. This happened in 1154 and Henry II, a great-grandson of William the Conqueror and head of the Angevin family, became the first Plantagenet king of England.

William the Conqueror would have regarded Henry II as a worthy successor and he is regarded as one of England's greatest kings. He was an energetic and sometimes ruthless ruler driven by a desire to restore the lands and privileges of his Royal grandfather, Henry I. During the early years of his reign he restored the Royal administration in England, re-established hegemony over Wales and gained full control over his lands in Anjou, Maine and Touraine. Henry's desire to reform the Crown's relationship with the third great power in the land, the church, led to conflict with his former friend Thomas Becket whom he had made Archbishop of Canterbury. This controversy lasted for much of the 1160s and resulted in Becket's death in 1170. Henry soon came into conflict with Louis VII of France and the two rulers fought what has been termed a 'cold war' over several decades. Henry expanded his empire, often at Louis's expense, taking Brittany and pushing east into central France and south into Toulouse. Despite numerous peace conferences and treaties no lasting agreement was reached. By 1172, he controlled England, large parts of Wales, the eastern half of Ireland and the western half of France. This area of power, later described as the Angevin Empire, was probably at its zenith at this time.

THE START OF THE DEMISE OF THE ANGEVIN EMPIRE

Henry II had taken the reins of his family's original holdings and those bequeathed to him by the Conqueror and by marrying Eleanor of Aquitane added further territory. However, like the Conqueror, he failed to nominate a successor powerful enough to rule absolutely. Whilst he was regarded as a worthy successor and a fair and just king, his sons were regarded as a 'nest of vipers'. Of his eight children, five were male. The eldest, William, died aged just three. In 1183, Henry, the next in line, died whilst arguing with his father over his inheritance. When this happened, Henry II decided that Richard (later more commonly known as 'the Lionheart') was to be made King of England but without any actual authority until his father's death – which did not please the ambitious Richard.

Richard was widely regarded as an outstanding leader and knight and was very popular in England – which is odd as despite being born in England and living there until he was eight, he probably only visited it briefly twice as an adult. He spent most of his life fighting battles in France or on Crusade.

The next in line, Geoffrey, had been made Duke of Brittany but was not content with this and sided first with his elder brother Henry in battles with his father and then with Richard. He eventually accepted his appointed lands but died in a tournament in Paris in 1186.

John the youngest son became Henry II's favourite despite making a poor job of exerting authority on an expedition to Ireland in 1185. He became known by the nickname John Lackland (lacking in land) that clearly did not endear his father to him. These four adult sons who all bore grudges and some of whom had openly rebelled and made plays for power became known in popular mythology as the 'devil's brood'. When Henry II eventually died in 1189 he had two surviving sons – Richard and John. Richard successfully claimed his father's lands but then soon departed on the Third Crusade. Whilst he was absent his brother John, Richard's regent, lost control of the original Angevin territories and Philip of France captured all of the continental possessions except Gascony.

Richard the Lionheart's statue outside the Houses of Parliament.

The next blow for the family and the one that probably dealt the most severe damage to any hope of a revival of their dynastic fortunes was the capture of Richard near Vienna in 1192 as he returned from Crusade. He was held for ransom for over a year. Eleanor, Richard's mother, and John managed to raise the fee to release Richard, an enormous amount that was about two to three times England's annual income. On his return he now had to start rebuilding the family's French empire almost from scratch. He started in Normandy and in the next few years defeated Philip on numerous occasions and spent a fortune establishing elaborate and sophisticated castles to defend his lands. But then in 1199, whilst besieging a minor castle in the Limousin, he was struck by a crossbow bolt and subsequently died. He left no legitimate heirs and his French territories rejected John as a successor. This left John as King of England but with no possessions on the Continent. This really can be seen as the beginning of the end of the 'Angevin Empire' but the start of the Plantagenets regarding England as their main seat of power.

Much of Richard the Lionheart's life was spent at war, either in France or on Crusade.

A SUMMARY OF THE ANGEVIN'S RULE

The three kings that ruled England whilst still directly tied to their Anjou based empire were Henry II, Richard (the Lionheart) and John. When Henry II came to rule, England was but a northerly province of that empire. He expanded the family's sphere of influence to include Wales, Scotland and Ireland to varying degrees of success and ruled over the Angevin empire at the peak of its growth. He established law and order, ruling with a firm hand and introduced a measure of control through the creation of a bureaucracy that may be seen as the birth of today's civil service. He did not dismiss the barons but ensured that they recognised him as their ruler. He adopted the Anglo-Saxon rules of the forest – later described by Manwood and Coke. He also sought to reduce the power of the church by ensuring that law-breaking clerics were subject to civil and not just ecclesiastical law. His rule has been described as an excellent one for Great Britain. Richard spent little time in England after his childhood and probably primarily regarded it as a source of income to fund his territorial ambitions in France and for crusading. Somehow though with his aura he imbued in the English a sense of rightness in a cause and in common myth is regarded as a great king. John ruled over the last of the continental family territories but eventually lost them. He also created uproar amongst the barons to such a degree that they revolted and forced him to seal the Great Charter – Magna Carta. This 'bill of rights' brought about a major reduction of the power of the king as an individual but left the monarchy intact. As today's National Anthem reminds us in a line in the second verse, 'May she/he defend our laws', note – not 'my laws' – reminding all that the monarch is not above the law as had previously been the case. By the end of their rule, England had adopted the Angevin three lions as one of its symbols and become a nation content within itself – one with a monarch that looked on the continental countries as 'abroad'. As far as this study is concerned, it left Dartmoor as a Forest but without boundaries fixed in the traditional fashion.

King John spent much of his time hunting. A comprehensive body of laws and administrative machinery protected the royal forests where kings could enjoy this recreation.

Also of note for this study is the fact that many of the historical documents we can still see survive because of the efforts of King Henry II and John in particular. King Henry II's army of bureaucrats noted his commands, wishes and communicated these in writing. John continued this practice and also ordered that such documents be bound up in Rolls. These Rolls, Pipe Rolls, are now kept in the National Archives. These records were made up of pieces of vellum (cured animal hide) stitched together in a long series ('Exchequer Style') and then rolled up and stored in a waterproof sheath – looking like a pipe. Primarily they were a financial record – moneys paid by or to the Crown, or debts

William Marshal Ist Earl of Pembroke

owed. Actions such as the disafforestation of Devon and Cornwall or the ordering of a perambulation were also recorded as they had financial implications.

At this point it is worth noting the influence throughout this period of an Englishman of great note – William Marshal (1147–1219). William the Marshal (Norman French: Williame le Mareschal) was an English (or Anglo-Norman) soldier and statesman. He has been eulogized as the 'best knight that ever lived.' He served four kings – Henry II, Richard the Lionheart, John (Lackland) and King Henry III – and rose from obscurity to become a regent of England for the last of the four and so one of the most powerful men in Europe. Before him, the hereditary title of 'Marshal' designated the head of household security for the King of England. By the time he died, people throughout Europe (not just England) referred to him simply as 'the Marshal'. He received the title of '1st Earl of Pembroke' through marriage during the second creation of the Pembroke Earldom. Known for his prowess as a knight he was also always seen to be calm, fair, trustworthy and dedicated to the English monarchy. Fortunately, the Angevins seem to have taken much of his diplomatic advice throughout this turbulent period. So perhaps John did not exclude Dartmoor and Exmoor from the 'sale' out of spite but rather to keep a foothold in a large and wealthy but remote part of his kingdom, perhaps at the suggestion of the Marshal. We can but wonder.

1204 – KING JOHN DISAFFORESTS DEVON

We could possibly sympathise with John even though he was such a widely reviled figure. He came from a great family but had seen the actions of his father, his mother and his elder brothers leave him with far less than his father had enjoyed. He rallied support and carried the fight to Philip of France over the next fifteen years. Eventually his efforts proved unsuccessful and having lost at the battle of Bouvines in 1214, his control of any of the Angevin continental lands was lost forever. Shortly after this of course, the English Barons revolted and forced the sealing of the Magna Carta one aspect of which was to reduce the king's authority.

As well as having to treat with his barons, John was also at odds with another major power in the land in this period – the church. This feud must have been bubbling in 1204 but came to a head in 1208. The Archbishop of Canterbury, Hubert Walter, had served under Henry II and Richard. On his death in 1205, John chose his preferred replacement, John de Grey, Bishop of Norwich. The church made its disfavour known as both the monks and the Pope rejected him. This ongoing rift eventually led to the imposition of the Interdict on England in 1208 that lasted for five years. This was no mean slight. During an Interdict, church services were forbidden and the populace were terrified of dying in sin and enduring eternal damnation. Also, John was excommunicated in 1209 – for four years. For John this was a serious blow to his ability to rule the country as it absolved his subjects from their oaths of allegiance, gave the Barons reason to revolt and allowed the King of France to invade England to remove John from power.

Any sympathy we might feel should be tinged with knowledge of his less favourable character traits. He was far from popular amongst his subjects and had a nasty nature. Whilst he was considered a hardworking administrator, an able man and an able general, nonetheless, modern historians agree that he also had many faults as king. These included his distasteful, even dangerous, personality traits, such as pettiness, spitefulness and cruelty. One action of his surely demonstrates such a trait and is of direct significance to this study. In 1204, in the midst of the Anglo-French war (which included the loss of

Normandy) and the start of the Fourth Crusade, John gave up his rights in Devon and Cornwall. He did this in return for a *'fine'* of 5,000 marks. He disafforested *Devon 'up to the metes of the ancient regardes of Dertemore and Exmore, as these regardes were in the time of King Henry the First.'* Such an act of disafforestation was not new. His brother Richard before him had disafforested many parts of Britain in return for funds to continue the fight with the French. By 1215, there were at least 143 forests in England. What we have to question is why John excluded the two areas of Dartmoor and Exmoor from the 'sale'. There is no record of him ever having visited the West Country and perhaps never having got even as far as or beyond Exeter. True the two moors still afforded him an income but why not ask those in Devon to pay a larger *'fine'* in the first place and turn his back on the West Country. No, it was probably done to spite someone as he retained a toehold in a large area that would otherwise be ruled by his nobles. Certainly John gave it little attention. He did not order a perambulation at the time to clarify the boundary – as had been both a Saxon and Norman custom for centuries – but as we have noted above, he had other matters of grave importance to occupy his time. It was left to the reign of his son (King Henry III) before the first known perambulation occurred, in 1240.

Although John was the last ruler of the Angevin Empire he was also a Plantagenet, as was Henry his son. So the disafforestation of Devon except for Dartmoor and its first perambulation were both ordered by Plantagenets.

Map describing the notional borders of the moor and Dartmoor Forest within it.

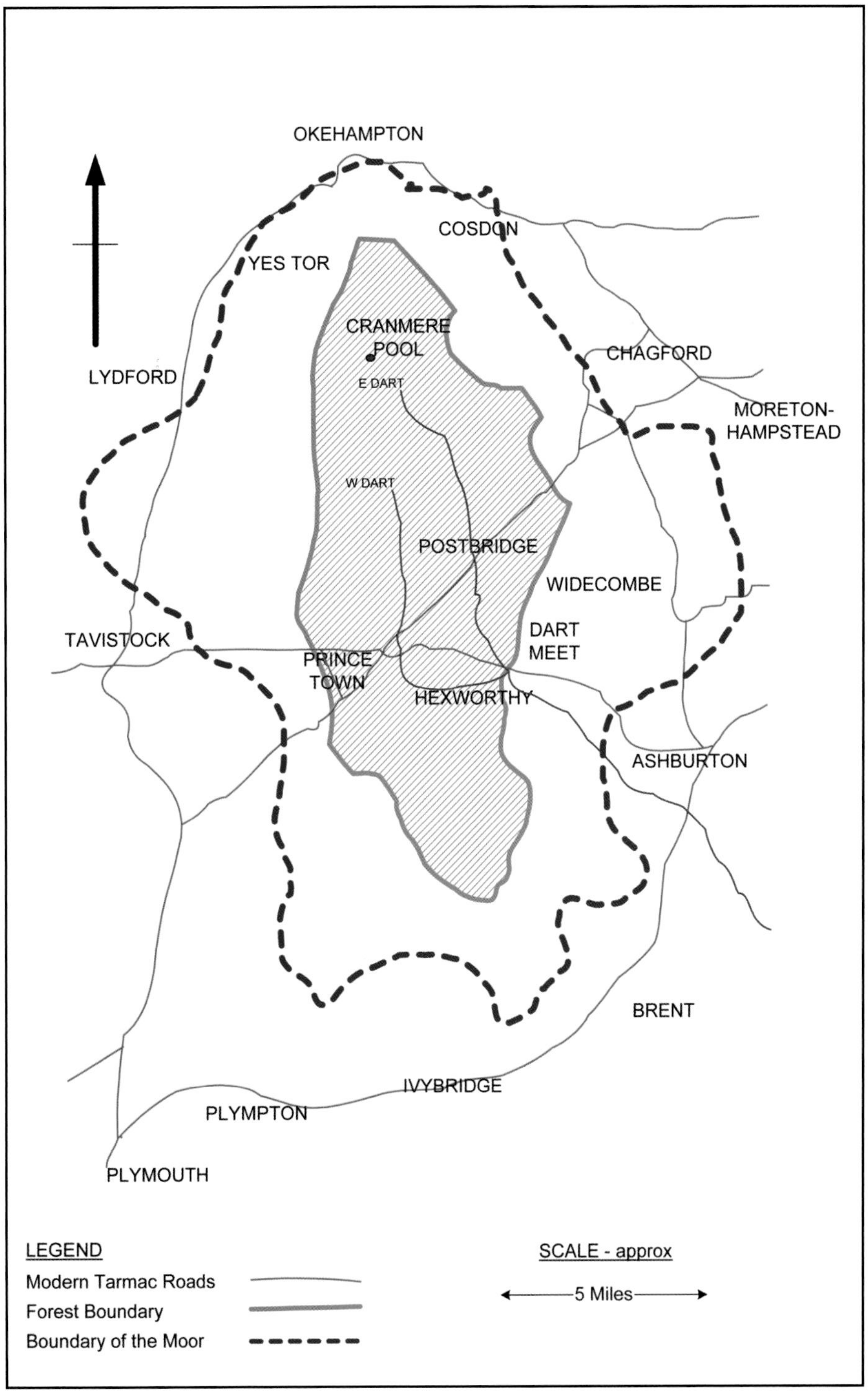

What is the 'Forest of Dartmoor'?

As you can see from the map here, there is more than one border on Dartmoor. There are no physical boundaries at the edges of Dartmoor for as a whole it has never been fenced. Portions of moorland itself have been taken as 'newtakes' and enclosed, most commonly using walls – but that is a whole other story.

The boundary of the area for which the Dartmoor National Park Authority (DNPA) holds responsibilities, the 'Park', extends well beyond the open moor. The Park includes many farms and towns that may no longer abut open moorland. If a walk is planned along a route across what might be privately owned land, one should check the relevant DNPA web page first.

Most people regard the start of the open moor as 'Dartmoor' proper. This area of open land was previously known as the 'Commons of Devonshire'. Most Devonians had the right to graze them until the last century. Excluded were the inhabitants of Totnes and Barnstaple. It is not certain why this was so but as they, with Lidford, were the only Royal Boroughs in the West, perhaps they had the privilege under another authority. Now only those who have undisputed registrations under the 1965 Act have that right. This open moor lies inside the enclosed farmland and geographically includes the area properly known as the 'Forest of Dartmoor'. The approximate edge of the open moorland is shown on this map as the 'Boundary of the Moor'. Trying to draw it accurately would reveal a very wiggly line and would probably upset a few landholders if errors were included. It is fairly obvious on the ground where open moor ends and enclosed land begins because of the many fences, walls and cattle grids that exist.

Finally, the inner portion is the 'Forest of Dartmoor' – on this map it is etched in green. It has little practical significance today as in 1967 the Duchy decided not to object to the registration of the Forest as 'common' under the Commons Registration Act of 1965.

THE IMPORTANCE OF FOREST LAWS

William the Conqueror and succeeding rulers took all conquered territories as theirs to dispose of as they wished. Thus after the invasion of 1066, the whole of England could be regarded as a 'Royal Forest'. Selling or giving away tracts of land brought income or bought loyalty for the monarch and over the next few hundred years, lands were disposed of but tracts retained as stand-alone forests. There might have been as many as 143 at one time. Laws concerning these forests were introduced by the Conqueror in 1072 (although they were not formally promulgated as 'Forest Law' until 1217). This made all parts of the forest, from animals to the leaves on the trees, the property of the King. Anyone found killing or taking part of any part of the forest would be guilty of taking the King's property. Punishments were harsh and could include mutilation or death.

Manwood gave the first accepted definition of a Royal Forest in his 'Treatise of the Forest Laws' first published in 1598:

Hunting was the preserve of Kings and laws protecting game were harsh.

'A Forest is a certain territory of woody grounds and fruitful pastures, privileged for wild beasts[2] and fowls of forest, chase, and warren, to rest and abide there in the safe protection of the King, for his delight and pleasure; which territory of ground so privileged is meered and bounded with unremovable marks, meers and boundaries, either known by matter of record, or by prescription; and also replenished with wild beasts of venery or chase, and with great coverts of vert, for the succour of the said beasts there to abide; for the preservation and continuance of which said place, together with the vert and venison, there are particular officers, laws, and privileges belonging to the same, requisite for that purpose, and proper only to a forest, and to no other place.'

Though they were not enclosed in the physical sense, it was important that the forest boundaries were clearly delineated because the statutes of the Forest Law could only be applied to those guilty of trespass on land within the forest.

'Tis necessary that every forest should be bounded, for 'tis very requisite that the boundaries should be generally known, especially by those who are Officers of the Forest; for if a man is presented for killing a beast it is very material that it should be distinctly known where the same was killed; for though it might be a wild beast of the forest, yet if it was killed out of the limits thereof, it may be no offence against the Forest Laws.'

[2]The beasts of the forest were the hart, the hind, the hare, the wild boar and the wolf. The beasts of the chase were the buck, the doe, the marten, the roe deer, and the fox, while the beasts and fowl of the warren were the *cony* (rabbit), the pheasant and the partridge.

Grazing animals of course do not know what is forest and what is not and just go to where the pasture is suitable. Where owners of flocks or herds of animals had land abutting the forest, they would and could use the forest for their own benefit. Monarchs recognised that this was happening and charged for the right to allow animals to graze within the forest. This made it even more important that the forest boundary was known and accepted. Indeed, the first recorded perambulation in 1240 occurred to satisfy claims made by four landowners with 'grievances'. There are further instances recorded in the Close Rolls where owners of land adjoining Dartmoor Forest sought clarification of the boundary by a perambulation in later centuries.

Local Implications

On creation, the boundary of the Forest had fiscal implications for its 'stakeholders'. Grazing within the Forest was not free and the holder was paid '*fines*' by those with grazing animals – these were not fines as we know them but fees. Those with tenancies within the Forest, e.g. at Brimpts and Pizwell, obviously paid rent. Those with land outside the Forest but who grazed it fell into two categories of '*Fenfield* ' men. The first were those whose land abutted the Forest, e.g. at Babeny. They had the right of pasture free to the extent of their winter holding ('*levancy*' and '*couchancy*') and other rights ('*Rights of Common*') on payment of '*fines villarum.*' For more animals, they paid the same as a '*stranger*' to graze in the Forest day and night, namely payment per head of a single fee or '*fine.*' Others from within Devonshire without land abutting the Forest – '*strangers*' – could graze their animals in the Forest but had to pay pasturage per head and did not have '*Rights of Common.*' Already we can see that whenever the perambulators set out to ride the boundary of this new forest, they would have had to balance the desire of the sovereign to maximise his income with the largest forest possible against the supposed historic rights of those who also used it for grazing.

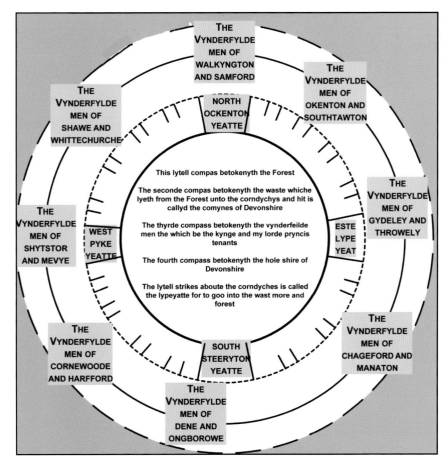

Copy of a sixteenth century cartogram of the Commons, Forest and Venville of Dartmoor.

The concept of having a Forest within an area of common land within the County of Devon with several categories of holders of rights obviously taxed the minds of earlier scholars. A 1541 cartogram made for a commission inquiring into the land and rights of Buckfast Abbey after its dissolution has been re-drawn here to illustrate this.

Let us examine each of the circles in a little more detail. The inner-most one is the boundary of the Forest that we shall be examining in depth further in this book. The next ring, shown dotted, represents the extent of the Commons of Devonshire up to the corn ditches. These ditches would have enclosed an area that was used for grazing by both the local Fenfield landholders and others in the County entitled so to do. The upkeep of the corn ditches – designed to be a barrier for grazing animals – and the gates through them, called here *'yeatte'* or *'leaps'* (perhaps because deer could leap them but cattle would not) would have been the responsibility of the owners of the land abutting the common area, i.e. the Fenfield men. No obvious evidence of any corn

Dartmoor Forest and parish boundaries 1905.

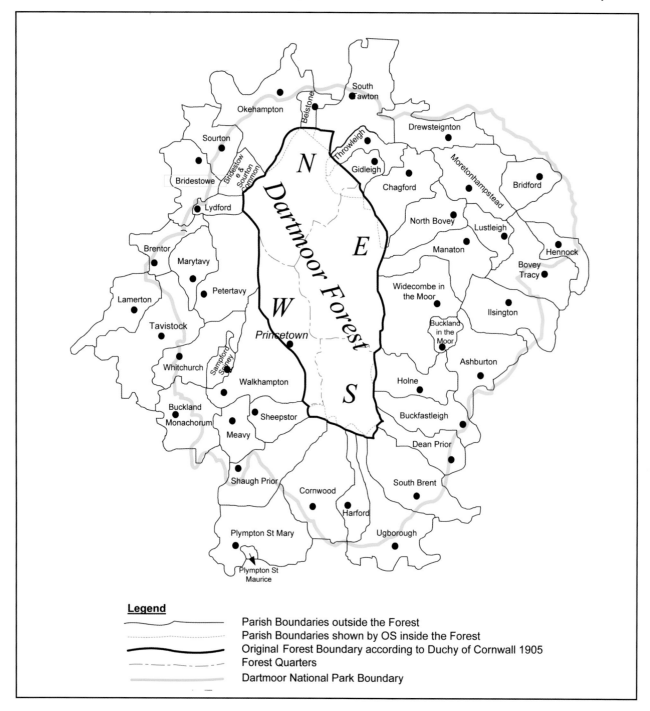

Legend

———	Parish Boundaries outside the Forest
·········	Parish Boundaries shown by OS inside the Forest
▬▬▬	Original Forest Boundary according to Duchy of Cornwall 1905
—·—·—	Forest Quarters
———	Dartmoor National Park Boundary

ditches remains or of any *'lypeyattes'* and so perhaps the drawer of the cartogram was showing what he considered to be the ideal state rather than the actual one. The next solid circle shows the extent of the manors and *'vills'* held by the local lords and, of course, beyond that is Devon itself.

The manors held by the Fenfield men have changed size and hands over the centuries. These days the farms abutting the Commons of Devonshire are all fenced or their extents are known in detail. This has not always been so simple.

For example, an added complication in our study has been the increasing influence of the church throughout the history of the Forest. In 1240, parishes were only just starting to be recognised and the requirement to 'feed the poor' still rested mainly with the lord of each manor. This role slowly passed more and more to the church. The income that a parish derived was directly linked to the farming activity of the parishioners.

Therefore, both the Fenfield men and the church had, or have had, a direct interest in the amount of land taken into the Forest as they would have to pay to utilise it rather than have free access to the Commons. Today there are twenty-two parishes abutting the Forest boundary.

On the map opposite we can see where parish boundaries and one interpretation of the Forest Boundary overlap.

The division of the Forest into Quarters was linked to the appointment of overseers. These four men were employed by the Crown to police their areas and make sure fees were paid where appropriate. Also, once a year drives (known locally as 'drifts') were (and still are) organised to ensure that the ownership of all animals grazing the moor are known.

THE ACCEPTED FOREST BOUNDARY AND SOME EARLIER ALTERNATIVES

Shown here is a sketch of the boundary accepted by the Duchy. Also shown are some of the suggestions made by others of alternative lines for the boundary. As is clear, each alternative would decrease the size of the Forest and benefit others.

Some of the features en route are easily identifiable today, e.g. 'Siwards Cross' but others less so, e.g. Thirlstone and Sandy Ford. The incursions are described briefly here, shown in red numerals on the map.

1 The largest would be to exclude from the Forest the Galaven Mire near Wild Tor Well. If accepted this would obviously increase the holding of one of those named as having a grievance – William Le Prous of Gidleigh.

2 The incursion below Thornworthy Tor is now under the waters of the Fernworthy Reservoir.

3 The probable route over Asacombe Hill will be examined further later.

The boundary accepted by the Duchy and variations.

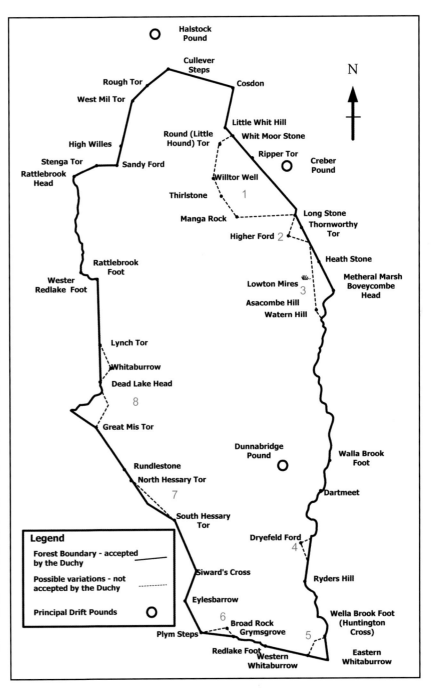

4 Dryefeld Ford could be anywhere and no easily identifiable feature retains this name.

5 In the south of the moor, local landowners would have exerted pressure in 1240 and later the Church (in the form of the monks at Buck-fastleigh) disputed the boundary. Whether or not the perambulators visited Eastern Whitaburrow will also be examined later.

6 The location of the feature called 'Grymsgrove' is still open to conjecture.

7 The direct route from South Hessary Tor to North Hessary Tor is only just possible today as the outskirts of Princetown now press up against the boundary line.

8 The route past Great Mis Tor could take several lines as the riding here is easy. The perambulators may well have passed White Barrow but if it was as indistinct then as it is now, it is no wonder it received no direct mention.

PEADINGTON'S ESTATE

Here is a rather curious earlier idea about where it was thought the boundary between the Forest and the Fenfield men's holdings might have been.

There is an ancient Saxon record held in Exeter that lists a series of points that would make a boundary. This seems to describe the boundary of the lands held by the Peadington family. Quite who they were is unknown. The list reads as shown below, on the right.

The famous Devonshire archaevist John Hooker/Vowell[3] must have seen this list as in the 16th century he appears to have misinterpreted it and used it to describe what he called 'the bounds and limits of the Fenfield men's tenures'. He transcribed it in the form of a diagram – on which, for reasons unknown, he placed north at the bottom of the page. As best as we can read his hand writing (there are two copies, one

Hooker's map of Peadington's Land and (right) the legend.

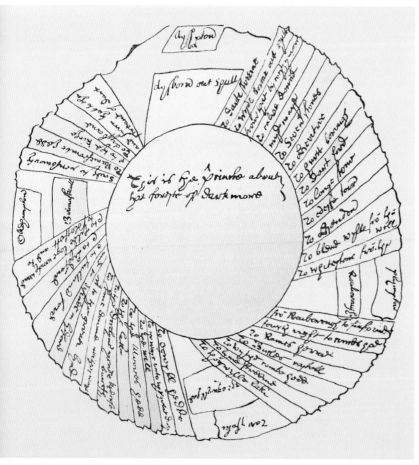

This is Peading tunes landscaro thær Æscburne utscyt.
On Dertam stream o Wedeburne utscyt.
Up an Wedeburnan oth Wi imor.
Up an Wi imore on Cealfa dune middewearde.
Of Cealfa dune on Sofon stanas.
Of Sufon stanum on Hyfan treow.
On Hyfan treowe on Hord burh.
Of Hordbyrg on Deorford.
Of Deorforda on Langastan.
Of Langa Stane on Eofede tor.
Of Eofede torre on Hean dune forewearde.
Of Hean dune on thone blindan wille.
Of am wille on Writelan stan.
Of tham stane on Ruwa beorh.
Of Ruwan beorge on Fyrspenn.
Of Fyrspenne on Wyrt cumes heafod.
Of Wyrtcumes heafde on Rammeshorn.
Of Rammeshorne on Lulca stile.
Of Lulca stile on Wice cumes heafod.
On Lymenstream oth Woggawill lacu utscyt.
On tha lace o Wocgawilles hafod.
Of Woeggawilles heafde on thone weg o tha greatan dic.
Of thær dic on thone wille on thæs mores heafod.
On tha lace to thære sweliende.
Of ære speliende on Yederes beorh.
Of Jederes beorge on Standune [nithe]wearde oth tha gretan linde
Of thæ linde on Dyra snæd midde wearne.
Of Dyra snæ on Hwita ford.
Of Fulan forda on Hildes ford.
Of Hildes forda on Hildeslege nor ewearde oth Sole get.
Of Sole gete to Brynes enolle su e weradum on Puneces wurdi.
Of Puneces wurthige on Hremnes cumes heafod.
Of Hremnes cumbe on tha ri e o Æseburnan.
Thanone on stream to Dertan.

 [3]Another famous member of this family was Richard Hooker of whom there is an imposing statue in Exeter's Cathedral Close.

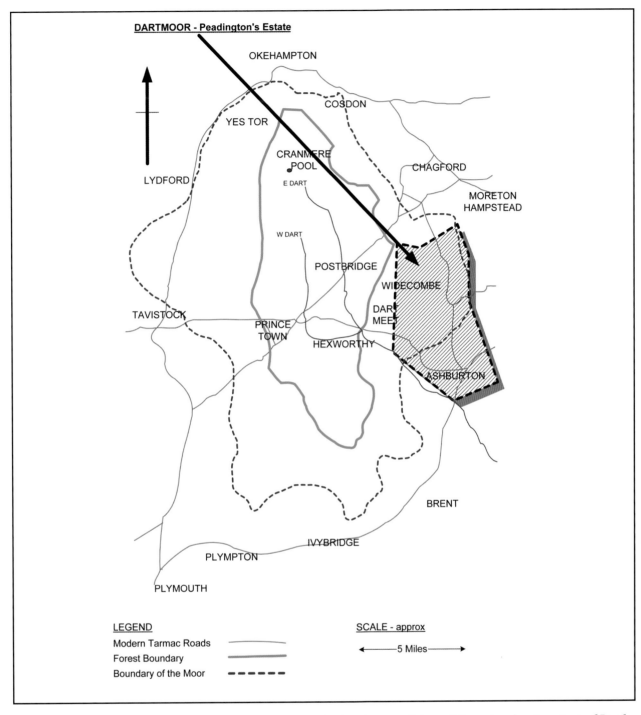

The approximate extent of Peadington's Estate shown against modern Dartmoor boundaries.

in Devon and one in London and both are identically hard to read) he lists the tenures as follows: Podaston Lake; Ashburton; in Dart Stream to Widborne and Shipstop; Whitmore; Calstone Midicays; Seven Stones; Heavitree; Herborough; Doreford; Longstone; Effedator; Hyndon; Blundell; Writeston; Roborough; Furzpen; Ramshorn; Lustleigh; Withecombe-Head; Lime Stream; Voghill Lake; Voghill's Head; Ditch; Well in Moreshead into the lake; Smely; Jeredsborough; Standon; Great Lynd; Dyersnade; Lidford northwards; Seliot; Gurnadsknoll; southward unto Poncartsworth; Ramscombe-Head; the right stream; Ashborn; and from thence in stream of Dart.'

If we plot this boundary on our modern maps, as far as we can tell it is to the south east of the Forest and although certainly large, it is not what we understand to have been the area of the Forest.

So what have we learnt? Perhaps the most fundamental thing is that deciding where the Forest boundary was meant to be has perplexed scholars, some eminent, for centuries. We are now going to join the debate by not only examining the records that exist and interpreting them for ourselves but also try to learn about the practicalities, situations and motives of those involved.

Henry III.

1240 – THE ISSUING OF THE WRIT TO UNDERTAKE THE PERAMBULATION

In the Pipe Rolls known as the Close Rolls there are many records of King Henry III ordering that perambulations be undertaken to clarify boundaries within his kingdom. This can be seen as part of his role as a peacekeeper. In 1240, four knights with land abutting the Forest of Dartmoor petitioned the king asking that the border be clarified. These four are mentioned in the writ and are – William Le Pruz (of Gidleigh), William Hamlyn (of Widecombe), Robert de Hellion (of Ashton, near Chudleigh – who also had an estate near Buckfast Abbey called Hawson) and Henry de Merton (of Moreton Hampstead). The writ itself was recorded and issued at Westminster on 13th June 1240.

Although the King was often asked to order a perambulation, they would have been for his own Forests. Here it was slightly different. Earlier, Henry had given the Forest of Dartmoor to his younger brother, Richard, Earl of Cornwall. Richard had been supportive of Henry in major campaigns but also sometimes rebelled against him and often had to be bought off with such lavish gifts. In 1225, as a birthday present, Henry gave Richard the county of Cornwall, making him its High Sheriff and 1st Earl of Cornwall. This was no small gift as the returns from the county made Richard one of the wealthiest men in Europe. In 1238, Richard rose in rebellion against Simon de Montfort – one of Henry's favoured court. He was once again placated with rich gifts and in 1239 Henry also gave him the Forest of Dartmoor. The Forest itself, which should more properly be called a 'Chase' as only a King can hold a Forest, was not closed but its use by others was limited by a set of stringent rules (later to be termed 'Forest Law') and was a source of further income for its new owner. By ordering a perambulation, King Henry III was obviously trying to keep the peace between his fractious brother and other nobles in the West Country.

TRANSMISSION OF THE ORDER TO DEVON

The successful government of medieval England depended on the king employing an efficient body of messengers, an indispensable link between central authority and its main local agents – the sheriffs. When a writ was issued, it had to be endorsed with a statement of what action the sheriff had taken within three weeks.

We know that the writ for the perambulation was issued on 13th June and that it was carried out on 23/24th July. The writ was signed at 'Westmonasterium' that today we know as Westminster. The sheriff would have gathered the perambulators at his castle at Okehampton and set off from there. Of course there were no methods of instant communication in those days. A member of the Royal Messenger Service would have carried the writ to Devon. These messengers were expected to cover 30-35 miles per day whether on foot or on horseback. Those on horseback would be used to carry heavier loads, the foot messengers lighter loads such as written missives. The Sheriff of Devon probably received the message on or around 18/19th June.

We cannot be sure who actually carried the message or by what route they travelled. We know who were the messengers in the Service at the time and they included one Cornwaleis (or Le Cornwaleys or Cornubiensis), Walter; i.e. 'Walter the Cornishman' who served from 1226 to 1251. Messengers were drawn from across the realm and each would know the main thoroughfares they needed to travel to their part of the kingdom. He would surely have known the routes into Devon and

Cornwall and would probably have followed the surviving Roman roads to the West Country – such as the most noticeably straight stretch from Micheldever to Salisbury (the modern A30).

THE PERAMBULATORS

The Sheriff – although one might infer from the writ that King Henry III expected the Sheriff personally to undertake the perambulation, there is no record that he actually did. At the time the sheriff was Walter of Bath (Walter Bathon, Walter de Bathonia, Bada). He certainly played his part in events in that he would have ordered the perambulation and he would have used knights gathered at his castle at Okehampton at the time.

The Complainants – there were four knights with a grievance named in the writ. We can learn a little about them from the Pipe Rolls and other records although searches are painstaking as spellings vary from document to document.

William le Pruz, (Prouz, Preuz, Priuz, de Preus) held land at Gidleigh. Examination of the records is made tricky as he named his son William after himself – a not uncommon custom in those days. It appears from an entry in the Fine Rolls of 1242, that one William passed his holdings to another William, i.e. the perambulator might have died soon after unless the son undertook the task for his father.

The parishioners proudly display a board showing the patrons of their parish, including William Prous, in the lovely church in Gidleigh right next to the ruins of the old manor house.

There are several entries in the Fine Rolls in the reign of King Henry III mentioning the family and their disputes, e.g. for taking livestock or with other neighbours, e.g. the men of Cadeleigh.

We do know that Henry de Merton (Henry of Merton, Merthon) was wealthy and held three 'knights fees' including a fifth part of the barony of Great Torrington. One knight's fee would be a portion of land deemed sufficient to support one knight. This area would provide sustenance for himself, his family, esquires and servants and also the means to pay to furnish himself and his retinue for war. He died in 1245.

Of Robert de Hellion and William Hamlyn there are no mentions in the Fine Rolls. A 'Robert de Hilion' is mentioned by Risdon as having lands in 1251 on the edge of Dartmoor at Ashton and a Walter Helion became a Justice in 1260.

The 'Jury' – Of the twelve knights named in the perambulation return, little can be found in the Fine Rolls. There are minor mentions. In 1230, Hugo Bellay had a disagreement with a tenant in Sheldon (near Honiton) and was fined for his actions. A family called 'Belet' also had lands in Dorset and Somerset. A 'Henry, the son of Henry' might be Henry de la Pomeray of whom two entries are noted in 1269.

This lack of data is possibly not surprising as the lot of a landless knight was of little consequence. They spent their days honing their warlike skills – their horsemanship, practising with sword, lance, shield and other weapons. They owed everything to whichever Lord they were sworn to serve. They would have hoped to earn favour by acts of valour or service and their first aim, after serving their lord and, of course, survival in what was a brutal age, would be to be given land and the income it generated. They would each expect to ride and would hope to have a good destrier or courser (a war horse) or at least a rouncey or palfrey (a lighter 'all-purpose' horse) and, of course, pack animals. For the perambulation a palfrey or perhaps a local pony would have been the compromise between looking warlike or workmanlike on the terrain involved.

Two noted recorders of the families of Devon (and Cornwall) are Sir William Pole (1561–1635) and Tristram Risdon (1580–1640) who drew

The ruins of Okehampton castle as depicted by John Swete in 1801. Originally granted to Baldwin de Brionis by William the Conqueror, it later came into the hands of the Courtenays.

The ruins of Gidleigh manor, land held by William le Pruz.

A list of rectors and patron in Gidleigh church records names of the Prous and le Pruz family.

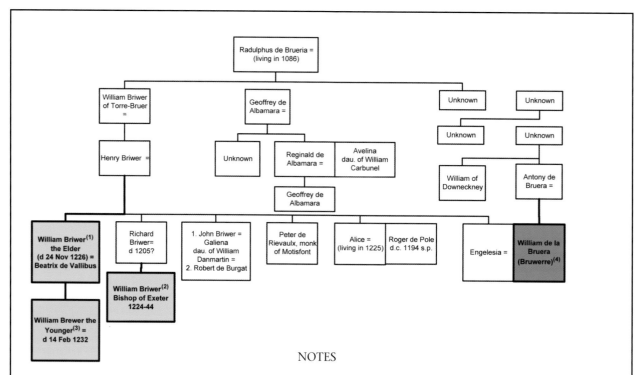

NOTES

1. A very influential man in the Norman Court with land holdings all over England. Known as "premier judge and first commoner in the realm". He had "unswerving loyalty to the lawful king" and crowned Henry III. Earlier, was a hunting companion of Henry II, judge under Richard 1 and hunting companion of John. He was credited with breaking the deadlock over ransoming Richard 1 from Leopold, Duke of Austria. John held him in high regard and William travelled widely with him both in England and France. He was often a sole witness of charters. Was Sheriff of Devon (1180–1189) and at times sheriff of 8 other counties. Witnessed the charter disafforresting the whole of Cornwall save the 2 moors – Foweymoor and Gundince (1204 and again in 1215). Witnessed the charter disafforesting the whole of Devon save Dartmoor and Exmoor (18th May 1204). Given custody of Lydford Castle and hence Lydford Parish which included the whole of the forest of Dartmoor (31st July 1216). Retired to Devon, Dunkeswell, 1224. Buried at Dunkeswell.
2. A crusader and very influential churchman – Bishop of Exeter.
3. Was influential at Court in his own right before inheriting from his father. Sheriff of Devon and of Cornwall. Was taken prisoner by K of France in 1204 and ransomed 6 months later. Witnessed the "Great Charter of Liberties" (1225) – a follow up to the earlier Magna Carta. Was buried at Torre Abbey.
4. This was probably the "William Brewer" who undertook the Perambulation in 1240. A "poor relation", on marriage he was given land such as at Grindle (now Greendale) at Woodbury, Devon, by William Briwer the Elder. Later, he received further land from William the Younger (1229). He was a witness to the charter founding Torre Abbey ('Willielmus de Briwera').

Geneaology of parts of the Briwer family.

on Pole's earlier work. They mention some of the perambulators. Further information can be gleaned from the research of others now available on the www. When searching for this kind of data, one has to be prepared to try different spellings of the names.

Much attention has been focused on William Brewer as there are several famous men with that name in this period. Earlier, one was Sheriff of Nottingham from 1194–1199. Another was Bishop of Exeter (1224–1244). It is doubtful that such a nobleman would have undertaken the ride. A short chart showing the probable relationship between the perambulating William (highlighted in green) and some of the more famous ones is shown above.

Guy Breteville might have been noted as 'Britvile' by Risdon. In which case knights of this family served from King Stephen's time to the reign of Edward III (1135 – 1377). In Henry II's time, they held five knight's fees at Totenays (today's Totnes).

William Wydeworthy is not mentioned by Risdon but a possible successor, Hugh Widworthy is noted in 1263. He was from Widworthy (near Honiton).

Hugo Bellay is not noted by Risdon, but a 'Willelmus Belet' from Frome in Somerset is mentioned. He was knight in the reigns of Kings Henry I and Stephen.

Of Richard Giffard there is no mention in Risdon. He must have come from a large family as records of Giffards pop-up in many places and some held positions of authority in the West Country. The family was possibly most associated with Weare Giffard, a village in north Devon. Also, Roger Giffard is recorded as a knight from 'Aulescombe' (today's Awliscombe near Honiton, Devon) in 1258 a Johell Giffard of 'Bukenton' (possibly today's Bickington, a village on the edge of Dartmoor, west of Newton Abbot) is similarly recorded.

Odo (or Otho) Treverbyn (or Treverbin) may well have been a member of Richard of Cornwall's family. He is mentioned by Risdon as a knight without 'arms'. Another researcher claims that he might be the greatx20 grandfather of the present Duke of Cornwall! His family appeared to have held lands near Kingsbridge in Devon at West Alvington.

William Trenchard would probably have been a member of the Trenchard family of Collacomb (in the parish of Lamerton, near Tavistock) and Lywetrenchard (today's Lewtrenchard, near Okehampton).

No further trace of Philip Parrer has been found.

Nicholas Heamton seems to have disappeared from the records. Risdon notes a family called Hidon from Hemyock, (near Honiton) but not a son with that forename.

William Mor(e)leghe may be related to the family that eventually owned Morleys Hall near Liverpool but no further record of a William has been found.

Quite who Durant, the son of Boton was lost in the mists of time.

We may learn more about these knights as more and more records come to light and researchers turn their attention to them. But for now, we will just regard them as a group of probably landless knights just starting out on their lives from near the bottom of the chivalric ladder.

Of course, the perambulation party would have been greater than just the twelve knights and those with grievances or their representatives. Each would have had a squire and/or other servants. Also, they would have needed guides from the local areas. As the distance to be covered exceeded that which even the King's Messengers could be expected to cover on good roads in a day, the whole event probably took at least two days. Therefore pack animals and their handlers might well have been included in the party to bring bedding and food.

KEY DATES RELATING TO THIS STUDY

With a story spanning several centuries, it is thought worth tabulating, in chronological order, some of the key events relating to the Forest and the records that still exist and which have led to the preparation of this book.

1066 – Since the successful conquest in 1066, the sovereign retained whole areas of land, including the counties of Devon and Cornwall. Such areas being owned by a king were called 'Forests' and strict rules, 'Forest Law' applied for those actually living in or near them.

1199 – King John succeeded his brother Richard 'the Lionheart' amidst the start of the loss of the Angevin possessions in France.

1204 – Needing to raise money for his Exchequer (a continuing story for the kings at this time with debts from the crusades and expensive wars to fight in France trying to retain or regain Angevin territory lost to the French King) King John gave up or disafforested Devon for the sum of 5,000 marks – with the exception of Dartmoor and Exmoor. This event is noted on a Close Roll held by the National Archives

1215 – John's rule was beset with trouble. He lost further lands in

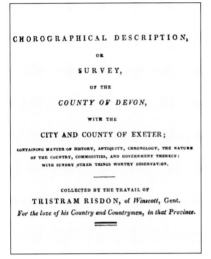

Title pages of Tristram Risdon's Survey of the County of Devon.

France and his English barons revolted leading to a major moment in English history – the sealing of the first Magna Carta at Runnymede, beside the River Thames near Windsor. There were many clauses in this charter seeking to reduce the sovereign's rights in relation to Forests. Most of these were removed in the re-writes of the charter in 1216 and 1217 and included in a new Charter – the 'Charter of the Forests'. One clause that did survive was number forty-seven – *'All forests that have been created in our reign shall at once be disafforested'*. This might lead one to suppose that the newly proscribed Dartmoor Forest should have disappeared but, as we know, it survived.

1216 – At the age of only nine, King Henry III succeeded from his father, John, in the midst of the First Great Barons' war. His reign was one dominated by turmoil both abroad and at home. At this time, a major influence on policy making would have been the guidance of William Marshall.

1225 – King Henry III reissued the Great Charter (a revised version of the Magna Carta) at which point it is considered to have entered into English law.

1225 – Henry's younger brother, Richard, was supportive of the king in major campaigns but also rebelled against him three times and had to be bought off with lavish gifts. In 1225, as a birthday present, Henry gave Richard the county of Cornwall, making him its High Sheriff and 1st Earl of Cornwall. This was no small gift as the returns from the county contributed to making Richard one of the wealthiest men in Europe. King Henry III still retained the Forest of Dartmoor.

1239 – In 1238, Richard rose in rebellion against Simon de Montfort, one of Henry's favourites. He was once again placated with rich gifts and in 1239 King Henry III gave him the Forest of Dartmoor. The Forest itself, which at this point should more properly be called a 'Chase' as only a King can hold a Forest, was set aside for the pleasure of hunting. It was not closed but its use by others was limited by a set of stringent rules.

1240 – To ratify who owned what and settle disputes between Richard, Earl of Cornwall, the Forest's owner, and four knights with neighbouring lands, the bounds of the Forest of Dartmoor were perambulated on the King's order for the first recorded time in 1240. Whilst the writ ordering the perambulation still exists – in the National Archives at Kew – whatever original return was made has not yet been identified.

1256 – An indication of just how important a man Henry's brother, Richard, 1st Earl of Cornwall, had become, was that he was elected King of Germany.

1272 – Following a stroke, Richard died. At this point, the Forest of Dartmoor passed to his son Edmund.

1300 – On the death of Edmund with no heir in 1300, the Forest reverted to the Crown.

1308 – King Edward II granted the Forest to a favourite, Piers Gaveston, but when they fell out and Piers was beheaded in 1312 it reverted to the Crown, by this time held by King Edward III.

1335 – The Earl Of Devon, a position first created in 1141, would have had a great and continuing interest about the limits of the Forest throughout this period. In 1335 the earldom passed to the 9th Earl, Hugh de Courtenay, and it is fortunate that his Feodary and Cartulary[4] has recently passed into public ownership. This volume, held by the British Library, is important in that it contains the earliest known copy of the return from the 1240 perambulation – indeed it might well be the original!

1337 – Edward III created the first English Duke in 1337 – the Duke of Cornwall – and conferred the title upon his son Edward, the Black

Simon de Montfort.

---

[4] A Feodary is a compilation of feudal duties and services and a Cartulary is a medieval manuscript volume containing transcriptions of original documents relating to the foundation, privileges and legal rights, of amongst others, private families. The term is sometimes also applied to collections of original documents bound in one volume – as is this one. It may be considered to be an 'audit' of duties, rights and privileges.

Prince. Since that first such investiture, the Duchy of Cornwall, including the Forest of Dartmoor, has been the possession of the sovereign's eldest son.

1478 – During the reign of Edward IV, a coloured map was created showing the boundary of the Forest of Dartmoor in pictorial form as well as repeating the words of the 1240 perambulators' return seen in the 1335 cartulary. It shows more detail of the south of the Moor and may well have been created during the ongoing disagreement with the monks of Buckfastleigh Abbey. This map is held in Exeter.

1502 – Henry, later to be King Henry VIII, became Duke of Cornwall. A scrap of vellum with a copy of the 1240 perambulators' return is held in the National Archives at Kew and is thought to date from this time.

1599 – During the reign of Elizabeth I, a noted Devon historian, John Hooker, wrote a study of key personnel in Devon and included a copy of the 1240 perambulators' return. At least two copies exist, one in Devon and one in London.

1609 – King James I ordered another perambulation. The Duchy holds the oldest documents relating to this event but herein the work of 19th-century scholars will be used. They gave a clear description of the boundary as it was understood to be at that time. This description of the boundary includes additional points compared to that of 1240. It also suggests significant reductions in the size of the Forest in places.

James I.

1624 – Towards the end of the reign of King James I (1603–1625), there appears to have been a disagreement about the boundary between Brent Moor and the south of the Dartmoor Forest. The land here belonged to the Cistercian monks of Buckfastleigh Abbey. The British Library holds a crowded volume of documents including a copy of the 1240 perambulators' return.

1650 – Oliver Cromwell seized power in 1649 and in 1650 the King's Serjeant, John Maynard a court official, included a copy of the 1240 perambulators' return in a volume of documents now held at the Inns of Court, London.

1699 – The Plymouth and West Devon Record Office holds a 1699 copy of the 1240 perambulators' return possibly created when someone was researching the possessions of the Count of Mortain – one of King John's lost titles.

1793 – The Duchy Office holds just one hand written copy of the return of the 1240 perambulation. This was created for one Thomas Lane in 1793 but quite who he was and why it was made is unknown.

1809 – The Ordnance Survey printed the first one-inch to the mile maps of Devon (Old Series). They would have obviously used old maps and local sources to identify and name the various features on Dartmoor.

1826 – NT Carrington published a book entitled 'Dartmoor – a Descriptive Poem'. Within that book, a Devonian scholar by the name of W Burt describes in great detail much of the history of the various perambulations that have been conducted over the centuries.

1848 – On starting a study of the first perambulation of the Forest of Dartmoor, one finds oneself immediately drawn to a book first printed by Samuel Rowe in 1848 entitled 'A Perambulation of the Antient (sic) and Royal Forest of Dartmoor and the Venville Precincts'. It would be easy to take the work to be a definitive study of the first perambulation but the title is misleading. The book does not introduce any new material, relying on repeating much of what W Burt had previously uncovered and is actually a guide to walks in and around Dartmoor as a whole. (It is especially worth viewing a copy of the third edition of this book first printed in 1896 by J Brooking Rowe as it includes two dozen excellent pictures created by F J Widgery. These paintings are now held by the Royal Albert Memorial Museum in Exeter).

1872 – A member of the Devonshire Association described in their Transactions (TDA) of 1872 a map now held at the Devon Heritage Centre, Sowton (see the entry for 1478 above). Over the next twenty-six years or so, other members worked intermittently to explain the route taken by the first perambulators using the documents to hand.

1881/2 – Royal Engineer surveyors working for the Ordnance Survey examined the boundary and recorded their findings in a Boundary Remark Book.

1967 – The Duchy decided not to object to the registration of the 'Forest' as common under the Commons Registration Act of 1965. The commons that abut the Forest are called the Commons of Devon and most Devonians had the right to graze them until the last century. Now only those who have undisputed registrations under the 1965 Act have that right.

2007/Present – I undertook my first perambulation of the boundary (as described by Rowe) in 2007/8 (in stages!). Since then I have conducted further documentary research and walked many of the boundary legs and possible alternatives again and again.

*   *   *

Early in the morning – a group of youngsters training for the Ten Tors expedition on Prewley Moor heading for Meldon.

Now it is your turn to share this examination of the surviving records and by study and practical expeditions, to form your own opinion of the route the perambulators might have taken in 1240. May you have good luck and enjoy fine weather.

Chapter 2

Ancient Documents and Their Present Locations

HANDWRITTEN RECORDS RELATING TO THE FOREST OF DARTMOOR

The earliest records relating to this research are hand-written. Therefore, one of the tasks facing historians is the interpretation of these handwritten texts. Assuming the texts have been preserved without damage, are complete and are legible, there are also the challenges of knowing which language(s) was/were used (mainly Latin but some words with Celtic or Anglo-Saxon backgrounds), expanding any shorthand that might have been employed and where proper nouns are used, such as the names of places or objects, imagining how they might have been reinterpreted over the centuries.

A copy of the record of the original writ ordering the disafforestation of Devon and Cornwall still exists. This disafforestation is relevant to our research as it is really the start point. When this occurred, the sovereign, King John, whilst giving up Devon and Cornwall in exchange for 5,000 marks, retained Dartmoor and Exmoor as 'forests', i.e. land subject to Forest Law.

The writ ordering the 1240 perambulation still exists.

Whilst the original return from the 1240 perambulation has not been found, nine hand-written copies, written in the period 1335 to 1793, have been found in modern repositories.

In addition to these documents relating to major events in the history of the Forest, others exist indicating that there were disputes about the Forest boundary over the centuries. Some relate just to a portion of the boundary, for example where the complainants land abutted the Forest.

Other requests for a complete perambulation were made at various points. The King(s) agreed some requests, refused others and some seemed just not to happen.

It was not until 1608/9 that another full perambulation was made and a return created. Strangely though, whilst the text of that return has been quoted in text-books, I have not found a single original copy in any of the repositories visited.

The National Archives at Kew which holds the record of the ordering of both the 1204 disafforestation and the 1240 perambulation.

THE ORDER TO DISAFFOREST DEVON

1204 – King John ordered the disafforestation of Devon and Cornwall in 1204. He did this in return for the sum of 5,000 marks. The Close Roll (5 John M2 C54-1) on which Devon's disafforestation is recorded is kept in a safe at the National Archives located in an impressive new building beside the river Thames at Kew. It can be viewed by anybody with a reader's ticket but only in a locked room where white cotton gloves are worn.

Fortunately for us, Sir Thomas Duffus Hardy, an English antiquary, made the Rolls, previously held in the Record Office in the Tower of London and other locations, more

An example of Hardy's work.

Carta hōīū Devoñ de foresta.
Joħ's Ði gřa ℞c. Sciatis nos deafforestasse totā Devoniā de omibȝ q̃ ad forestā ℞ ad forestarios ptinent, usqͺ ad metas antiquoȝ regardoȝ de Dertemora ℞ Exemora, que regarda fūnt tempe Reg̃ Henř p'mi, ita q̃d tota Devonia, ℞ hōīes ī ea manentes, ℞ ħedes eoȝ sint deafforestati omĩo, ℞ q'eti ℞ soluti de noꝗ ℞ ħedibȝ nřis, ī ppetuū, de omibȝ q̃ ad forestā ℞ ad forestarios ptinent, exceptis duabȝ moris p̃nōiatis, sclȝ, Dertemoȝ ℞ Exemoȝ p p̃dc̃as metas. Volum⁹ ℞ ℞ concedim⁹ q̃d p̃dc̃i hōīes Devoñ ℞ ħedes eoȝ ħant çsuetudines infra regarda morař illař, sic̃ hře çsuev̄ant ī̃pe p̃dc̃i Regis Henř, faciendo iñ çsuetudines

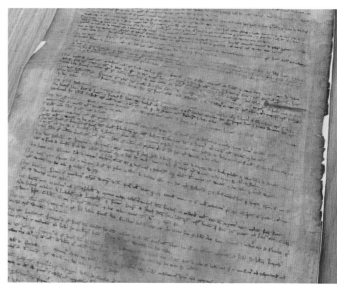

Close Roll in its protective sheath and (right) an example of the Close Roll text.

easily readable for other scholars. His first book in a series gives a useful introduction to the Close Rolls before printing their contents. Here, Hardy whetted historians' appetites by calling up examples he had already found. This included a transcription of the ordering of the writ disafforesting Devon.

THE WRIT FOR THE 1240 PERAMBULATION

1240 – The Close Roll containing the record of the ordering of the 1240 perambulation (King Henry III's 24th year since his accession in 1216) is held at the National Archives at Kew (C54/50 m11). Many of the Rolls have become damaged over the centuries and so we are lucky that the part relevant to the ordering of the perambulation, the 'writ', is still intact. The text is as follows:

'Rex vicecomiti Devonie Salutem. Sciatis quod dilectus frater noster Ricardus Comes Pictavie et Cornubie pro parte sua et Henricus de Mereton, Hamelinus de Eudon, Robertus de Halyun et Willelmus le Pruz, pro parte militum et libere tenencium habencium terras et feoda juxta forestam ejusdem comitatus de Dertemore posuerent se coram nobis in perambulacionem inter terras eorem et predictam forestam ejusdem comitatus faciendam et ideo tibi precipimus quod si alii de comitatu tuo habentes terras Juxta forestam predictam cognoverint coram te et coram custodibus placitorum corone nostre quod predicti quatuor milites de consensu aliorum omnium posuerint se in perambulationem illam pro omnibus aliis tunc assumptis tecum duodecim legalibus militibus de comitatu tuo in propria persona tua accedas ad forestam et terras predictas et per eorum sacramenta fieri faciatis perambulationem inter predictam forestam et terras predictas; ita quod perambulatio illa fiat

Close Roll from 1240 and (right) part of the text including the writ for the perambulation.

per certas metas et divisas. Et scire nobis facias ubicumque fuerimus distincte et aperte sub sigillo tuo et per quatuor milites ex illis qui perambutioni illi interfuerint per quas metas et divisas perambulatio facta fuerit et habeas ibi nomina militum et hoc breve. Teste Rege apud Westmonasterium die Junii.'

This translates as follows: *'The king to the Sheriff of Devonshire greeting. Know ye that our well beloved brother Richard Earl of Poiteau and Cornwall on his part and Henry de Mereton, Hamel de Eudon, Robert de Halyun and William le Pruz on behalf of the knights and free tenants holding lands and fees near the Forest of Dartmoor in the same County have submitted themselves unto us for making a perambulation between their lands and the aforesaid Forest in the same county and therefore we warn you that if others from your county holding lands have enquired before you and before the keepers of the pleas of our crown that the aforesaid four knights by the consent of all others have submitted themselves to that perambulation for all the others then choose to yourself 12 loyal knights in your county. Go in your own proper person to the Forest and the aforesaid lands and by their oath cause the perambulation to be made between the aforesaid Forest and the aforesaid lands. So that, that perambulation may be made by certain meets and divisions and inform us where ever we shall be distinctly and plainly under your seal and by four knights out of those who have joined in that perambulation by what meets and divisions the perambulation has been made and have the names of the knights and this writ. Witness the king at Westminster the 13 June.'*

NINE COPIES OF THE RETURN FROM THE 1240 PERAMBULATION

1335 – The Feodary and Chartulary of the Courtenay Family, Earls of Devon, held by the British Library (Add. 49359 Folio 54), is an impressive leather bound volume closed with a heavy brass clasp. This document, probably originally compiled in connection with the recognition of Hugh de Courtenay as Earl of Devon in 1335 with the issue of letters patent, contains a copy of the return from the 1240 perambulation written on vellum – now stuck onto a paper page. It is beautifully presented with red highlighting of some key letters but is rather indistinct and difficult to decipher in places. However, it can be photographed easily and the subsequent picture subjected to modern enhancement techniques.

Folio 54 of the Feodary held at the British Library. An enlargement of this document is included as Appendix 1 on page 146.

The entrance to the British Library.

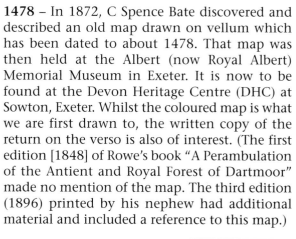

1478 – In 1872, C Spence Bate discovered and described an old map drawn on vellum which has been dated to about 1478. That map was then held at the Albert (now Royal Albert) Memorial Museum in Exeter. It is now to be found at the Devon Heritage Centre (DHC) at Sowton, Exeter. Whilst the coloured map is what we are first drawn to, the written copy of the return on the verso is also of interest. (The first edition [1848] of Rowe's book "A Perambulation of the Antient and Royal Forest of Dartmoor" made no mention of the map. The third edition (1896) printed by his nephew had additional material and included a reference to this map.)

Above: *Copy of the return that appears on the verso of the ancient map (below) discovered by C. Spence Bate. An enlargement of the map itself is included in Chapter 16 on page 116.*

Devon Heritage Centre, Great Moor House, Exeter.

1502 – The National Archives at Kew hold a single copy of the return from the 1240 perambulation (E32/9). It is estimated that it was created at the time of King Henry VIII. It is badly water damaged.

A copy of the 1240 perambulation return held at Kew. An enlargement of this document taken under ultra violet light is included as Appendix 3 on page 150.

1599 – John Hooker (or Volwell) created a work called "Synopsis Chorographical or An Historical Record of the County of Devon". Actually, two copies of this handwritten book are known to exist. One is kept in the DHC, Exeter (folios 208–209) and another in the Harleian[5] Collection housed in the British Library (Harleian MS 5827, folio 92 verso). They both include a description of the perambulation writ and a copy of the return that was later quoted by Samuel Rowe. The main aim of the work with regard to Dartmoor seems to have been to describe the extents of the parishes with ancient venville rights (i.e. an explanation of how the Normans adopted rights existing from Saxon times). The volumes were probably written before 1599 as Hooker was in poor health in later life and died in 1601. The text of the copy at Exeter is much clearer and easier to read than the one in the British Library that is almost illegible. However both copies miss out individual words compared to the 1335 text, the one in Exeter has the most missing – four complete bounds – and so can have added little to early research.

Copy of John Hooker's perambulation return held at the Devon Heritage Centre and (left) a legible portion of the text.

1624 – There is another old badly written copy of the return in the British Library that is in a volume so tightly packed that it cannot be opened easily to photograph. It is a "Register of records of the manors of South Brent and Churchstow, Devon, formerly held by Buckfastleigh Abbey" (British Library Add 37640). At folio 15 it describes the boundaries of the moors of Brent and Buckfastleigh and of the Forest of Dartmoor as at 24th July 1240 'for Richard, Earl of Cornwall'.

Buckfastleigh Abbey ruins from a 1734 print by Samuel and Nathaniel Buck.

This copy is unusual in that whilst the scribe has followed the familiar pattern of the other 1240 perambulation returns, interestingly he writes several of the names of metes in forms not see in any other copy. Quite why he used lettering not repeated anywhere else is a mystery. He starts off by offering two possible names for the first bound. Whilst the second is recognisable as 'Costdonne' the first is composed of some most odd lettering. He also missed out three bounds in the northern

[5]The Harleian Collection (or Harley Collection) is one of main collections of the British Library, London. The manuscript collection of more than 7,000 volumes, more than 14,000 original legal documents and 500 Rolls was formed by Robert Harley (1661–1724) and his son Edward Harley (1689–1741). In 1753, it was purchased for £10,000 by the British Government and together with the collections of Robert Bruce Cotton (1571–1631) and Hans Sloane formed the basis of the British Museum library (after 1973 – British Library).

quarter altogether. Perhaps this was of less importance to the monks of Buckfastleigh as their lands would not have been on the border of the Forest there.

Where the land of the monastery would have been on the border of the Forest, namely on the modern White Barrow ridge, the scribe appears to indicate that the mete should be taken as the West White Barrow rather than the East White Barrow that the other copies seem to indicate. Of course, this could just be an example of the scribe's rather eccentric penmanship rather than an attempt to influence the interpretation from even earlier copies of the return. The word before the recognisable word meaning White Barrow is really hieroglyphic in nature. If accepted, it would have meant that a disputed part of the Forest should have been acknowledged as church land rather than being inside the Royal forest.

Sir John Maynard's copy of the 1240 perambulation return held at the Inns of Court Library (above).

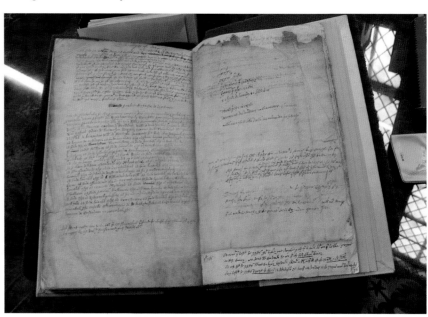

1650 – Sometime during his life in London, Sir John Maynard[6] made a copy (see above) of the 1240 perambulation return – 'Perambulatio forestae de Dertmore'. This is now held in the Lincoln's Inn Library, London (Maynard MS 63, Part 2 folio 329). Although it is indistinct, it can still be read. It was written on parchment. The records show that it was copied from a 'Leiger Book of my Lord of B sometime in the reign of Edward III (1327–1377)'. This was probably the Earl of Bedford's Leiger Book or Cartulary of Tavistock Abbey.

1699 – Part of the National Archive is held in Plymouth at the Plymouth and West Devon Record Office. The repository there contains a scroll wherein are 'details of the disafforestation of Devon and Cornwall (1204); confirmation of the same for King Henry III (original dated 1252); and a copy of the return from the first perambulation (1240)'.

Copy of the perambulation return (right) held at the West Devon Record Office, Plymouth (above).

[6]Sir John Maynard King's Serjeant (1602 – 9 October 1690) was an English lawyer and politician, prominent under the reigns of Charles I, the Commonwealth, Charles II, James II and William III.

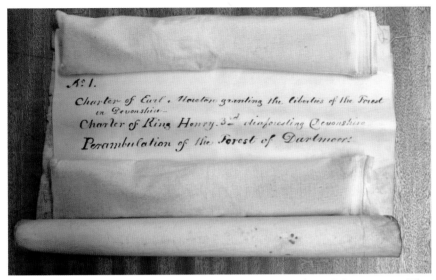

Earl Mortain's scroll held at the West Devon Record Office.

The archivists date the copy of the return to the 17th century. The scroll is marked as 'Charter of Earl Moreton'. Perhaps this refers to a title King John had from 1189 to 1199 before it was lost to France, namely 'Count of Mortain'.

1793 – Duchy Office, London. The Duchy of Cornwall was first created in 1337. It holds a volume containing transcriptions from earlier archival documents that was put together over a number of years and prepared for binding in 1793. It is entitled "Lidford (sic) Manor and Castle and Dartmore Forest: collections of Records and Office Papers etc from 1203 to 1735 by Richard Gray and Robert Gray Dated 1793". This volume contains one short document that it says has been transcribed from the papers of Thomas Lane. Quite who this was is not clear.

OTHER RECORDS RELATING TO THE FOREST BOUNDARY

Although the main two perambulations to pass into recorded history occurred in 1240 and 1609 there are other records of activities indicating that interest in Dartmoor often surfaced.

1279 – In the seventh year of the reign of Edward I (1279), a 'file of perambulations' was made before Walter Scamel [Dean of Salisbury, later Bishop of Salisbury] and Matthew de Columbariis [Chamberlain to the King – a position that included overseeing the sovereign's private estates] at Salisbury on 4th January. The first manuscript mentions the forests of Exmoor and the Mendips. The second has a writ dated 28th April ordering the return of the perambulations. The third refers to Selwood, Neroche and North Petherton forests. The fourth has a fragment of a forest perambulation. The fifth has a note on the forest of Dartmoor – '*Dertemore*'. This document is held at Kew (E32/154).

Copy of the perambulation return held by the Duchy Office, London.
© HRH The Duke of Cornwall 2014

1279 note relating to Dartmoor.

The spoilt return of 1300.

The 1316 request.

The 1316 rebuff.

1300 – A return of a perambulation held in 1320 has been found (Kew - C 47/12/14) which the archivists deduce was a 'fragment from the end of a roll of evidences of charters etc, produced for John Lovel [one of Edward's Barons] and others, justices of the perambulation of 1300 in Som(erset), Dors(et) and Devon'. Quite how they can read this is a mystery as the parchment is so completely spoilt now as to be virtually unreadable – even under ultra-violet light.

1316 – On a parchment fragment held at Kew (SC 8/107/5348) is a record of the 'Community of Devon' requesting that 'King and council order the king's ministers in Devon to carry out a perambulation of the Forest of Dartmoor'. They noted that a previous decision made in the parliament at Lincoln had not been implemented – as there was 'no official being prepared to undertake this work'. The file is endorsed – 'the king is not inclined to do this'.

1320 – On another manuscript fragment (below) held at Kew (SC 8/108/5368) is a request from the 'Commonalty of Devon' asking the 'King and council to order his commissioners to make a perambulation of Dartmoor, which the parliament of Lincoln ordered to be done by Foxle and Bourne and the last parliament at York ordered to be done by Bourne and Henry'. The request is endorsed – 'Let the justices assigned to the matter make the perambulation as required by their commission'. In the same year, another request (Kew SC 8/258/12891) was made and this time the king 'exhorted' his officials to carry out a perambulation. There are records of similar requests for clarification of the Forest Boundary over the next few centuries. These call for decisions about specific points on the boundary rather than seeking a full perambulation. That occurred in 1608 and a jury examined its findings in 1609.

The 1320 request.

The 1320 second request.

The 1320 Exhortation.

Chapter 3

Copies of the 1240 Perambulation Return
and Their Interpretation

It has generally been accepted that the original return from the perambulation of 1240 has been lost. Of course, it is by no means certain that it is lost, just that it has not yet been found!

Here is an analysis of the nine handwritten copies of the return dated on or before 1793 that have been found in this search. Scholars in the 19th century also tracked down several copies of the return. The copies now examined probably include those documents, one in the same place as reported years ago, the Lincoln's Inn Library, but the rest held in new repositories. Most excitingly is the finding of the as yet oldest known copy – created on or before 1335 but not available for study in the 19th century. The British Library only recently bought the feodary and cartulary containing this copy from a private family collection held in Cornwall. This document is also probably the most important as it is written clearly and has been well preserved.

Some of the copies are in poor condition but with modern equipment and methods what remains can generally be enhanced enough to read the lettering. Seven copies have been photographed. Two are unfortunately bound in such a way that they would probably be badly affected by any attempt to photograph them. Commercial software has been used to make the writing more legible. Information on the internet about medieval scripts and the common forms of shorthand has also helped in the process of rendering the scripts into recognisable Latin. These have then been translated using on-line software. Problems still remain with proper nouns of course. It also appears in places as if the original recorder was trying to write down what he heard but in the following centuries others have written the same 'sound' but using different letters.

It must also be remembered that whilst a return was expressly requested in the perambulation writ, in the days before maps and before most people could write, a written record was of little practical use. Therefore the perambulators would most likely have been accompanied along each section of the route by local landowners wherever their land abutted the Forest. Today's regular beating of parish bounds is a continuing example of this ancient Anglo-Saxon custom. It is a simple means by which those with an interest learn about a boundary.

The analysis of the documents found begins with an examination of the script used and it has been transcribed into its most likely modern equivalent. Also, the various shorthand forms used have been interpreted. This has been revealing as whilst the return is written in Latin, previous scholars have assumed that some French words were used. This would not have been the case and might have introduced misunderstandings.

THE SCRIPT USED

The script most commonly used is called Anglicana – this is revealed by the use of the distinctive forms of the letters 'a', 'g' and 'W'. This cursive script was derived from an earlier more formal script called Textura and allowed letters to extend above and below the writing line. Anglicana was in common use from about 1260 for several centuries for the purposes of copying documents and letters. The writers did allow themselves some personal freedom of expression – for example,

Examples of medieval script A–F

Script G–R

Script S–Z

in the way the letter 'e' at the end of a word often has a flourish – and this with the use of shorthand can be confusing.

Some examples of the many variations of Anglicana lettering used throughout the period under consideration are shown on the previous page. Here are some of the letters as they appear in these documents: The fact that some letters are interchangeable, e.g. 'u' and 'w' and 'i', 'j' and 'y', has also to be taken into account when transcribing the script.

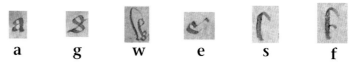

| a | g | w | e | s | f |

THE SHORTHAND USED

A further challenge is to understand the forms of shorthand that the first scribe used and subsequent copiers generally followed.

Having identified the script, it is then necessary to inspect it for: truncation; abbreviation indicated by truncation; contraction; abbreviation marks – both those significant in themselves and those significant in context; superscript letters; and conventional signs. The writers use the following glyphs.

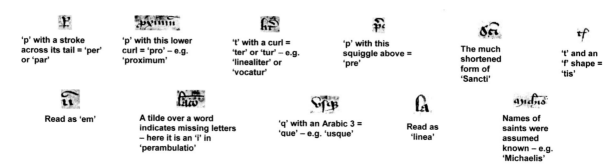

'p' with a stroke across its tail = 'per' or 'par'

'p' with this lower curl = 'pro' – e.g. 'proximum'

't' with a curl = 'ter' or 'tur' – e.g. 'linealiter' or 'vocatur'

'p' with this squiggle above = 'pre'

The much shortened form of 'Sancti'

't' and an 'f' shape = 'tis'

Read as 'em'

A tilde over a word indicates missing letters – here it is an 'i' in 'perambulatio'

'q' with an Arabic 3 = 'que' – e.g. 'usque'

Read as 'linea'

Names of saints were assumed known – e.g. 'Michaelis'

On the following pages, the text is taken line-by-line from the 1335 document (illustrated on page 33), expanded (when the shorthand forms can be identified) transcribed and translated. It is assumed that an earlier scholar introduced the ticks on the script. Later each bound will be treated as if it were written on a new line, even though none of the copies are written in this fashion – presumably to save space on an expensive commodity (vellum).

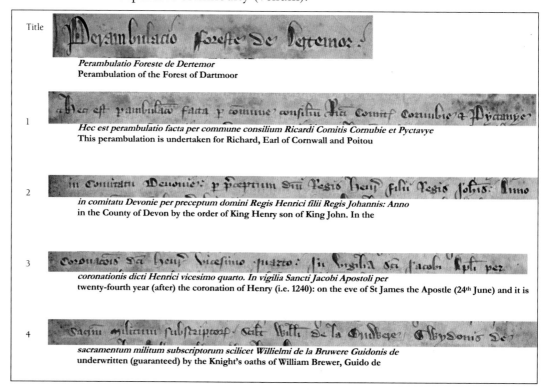

Title

Perambulatio Foreste de Dertemor
Perambulation of the Forest of Dartmoor

1

Hec est perambulatio facta per commune consilium Ricardi Comitis Cornubie et Pyctavye
This perambulation is undertaken for Richard, Earl of Cornwall and Poitou

2

in comitatu Devonie per preceptum domini Regis Henrici filii Regis Johannis: Anno
in the County of Devon by the order of King Henry son of King John. In the

3

coronationis dicti Henrici vicesimo quarto. In vigilia Sancti Jacobi Apostoli per
twenty-fourth year (after) the coronation of Henry (i.e. 1240): on the eve of St James the Apostle (24th June) and it is

4

sacramentum militum subscriptorum scilicet Willielmi de la Bruwere Guidonis de
underwritten (guaranteed) by the Knight's oaths of William Brewer, Guido de

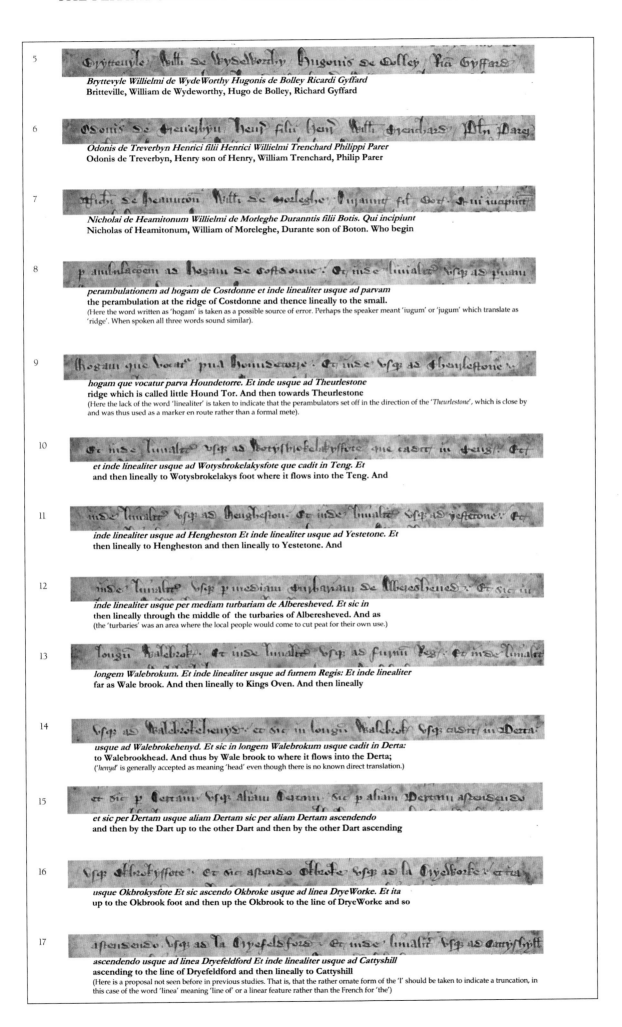

5

Bryttevyle Willielmi de WydeWorthy Hugonis de Bolley Ricardi Gyffard
Britteville, William de Wydeworthy, Hugo de Bolley, Richard Gyffard

6

Odonis de Treverbyn Henrici filii Henrici Willielmi Trenchard Philippi Parer
Odonis de Treverbyn, Henry son of Henry, William Trenchard, Philip Parer

7

Nicholai de Heamitonum Willielmi de Morleghe Duranntis filii Botis. Qui incipiunt
Nicholas of Heamitonum, William of Moreleghe, Durante son of Boton. Who begin

8

perambulationem ad hogam de Costdonne et inde linealiter usque ad parvam
the perambulation at the ridge of Costdonne and thence lineally to the small.
(Here the word written as 'hogam' is taken as a possible source of error. Perhaps the speaker meant 'iugum' or 'jugum' which translate as 'ridge'. When spoken all three words sound similar).

9

hogam que vocatur parva Houndetorre. Et inde usque ad Theurlestone
ridge which is called little Hound Tor. And then towards Theurlestone
(Here the lack of the word 'linealiter' is taken to indicate that the perambulators set off in the direction of the 'Theurlestone', which is close by and was thus used as a marker en route rather than a formal mete).

10

et inde linealiter usque ad Wotysbrokelakysfote que cadit in Teng. Et
and then lineally to Wotysbrokelakys foot where it flows into the Teng. And

11

inde linealiter usque ad Hengheston Et inde linealiter usque ad Yestetone. Et
then lineally to Hengheston and then lineally to Yestetone. And

12

inde linealiter usque per mediam turbariam de Alberesheved. Et sic in
then lineally through the middle of the turbaries of Alberesheved. And as
(the 'turbaries' was an area where the local people would come to cut peat for their own use.)

13

longem Walebrokum. Et inde linealiter usque ad furnem Regis: Et inde linealiter
far as Wale brook. And then lineally to Kings Oven. And then lineally

14

usque ad Walebrokehenyd. Et sic in longem Walebrokum usque cadit in Derta:
to Walebrookhead. And thus by Wale brook to where it flows into the Derta;
('henyd' is generally accepted as meaning 'head' even though there is no known direct translation.)

15

et sic per Dertam usque aliam Dertam sic per aliam Dertam ascendendo
and then by the Dart up to the other Dart and then by the other Dart ascending

16

usque Okbrokysfote Et sic ascendo Okbroke usque ad linea DryeWorke. Et ita
up to the Okbrook foot and then up the Okbrook to the line of DryeWorke and so

17

ascendendo usque ad linea Dryefeldford Et inde linealiter usque ad Cattyshill
ascending to the line of Dryefeldford and then lineally to Cattyshill
(Here is a proposal not seen before in previous studies. That is, that the rather ornate form of the 'l' should be taken to indicate a truncation, in this case of the word 'linea' meaning 'line of' or a linear feature rather than the French for 'the')

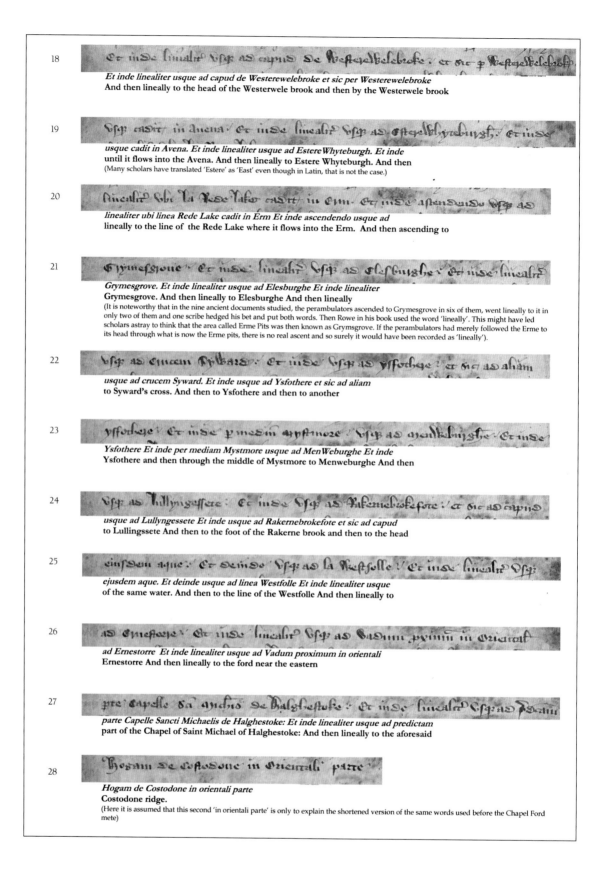

18

Et inde linealiter usque ad capud de Westerewelebroke et sic per Westerewelebroke
And then lineally to the head of the Westerwele brook and then by the Westerwele brook

19

usque cadit in Avena. Et inde linealiter usque ad Estere Whyteburgh. Et inde
until it flows into the Avena. And then lineally to Estere Whyteburgh. And then
(Many scholars have translated 'Estere' as 'East' even though in Latin, that is not the case.)

20

linealiter ubi linea Rede Lake cadit in Erm Et inde ascendendo usque ad
lineally to the line of the Rede Lake where it flows into the Erm. And then ascending to

21

Grymesgrove. Et inde linealiter usque ad Elesburghe Et inde linealiter
Grymesgrove. And then lineally to Elesburghe And then lineally
(It is noteworthy that in the nine ancient documents studied, the perambulators ascended to Grymesgrove in six of them, went lineally to it in only two of them and one scribe hedged his bet and put both words. Then Rowe in his book used the word 'lineally'. This might have led scholars astray to think that the area called Erme Pits was then known as Grymsgrove. If the perambulators had merely followed the Erme to its head through what is now the Erme pits, there is no real ascent and so surely it would have been recorded as 'lineally').

22

usque ad crucem Syward. Et inde usque ad Ysfothere et sic ad aliam
to Syward's cross. And then to Ysfothere and then to another

23

Ysfothere Et inde per mediam Mystmore usque ad Men Weburghe Et inde
Ysfothere and then through the middle of Mystmore to Menweburghe And then

24

usque ad Lullyngessete Et inde usque ad Rakernebrokefote et sic ad capud
to Lullingssete And then to the foot of the Rakerne brook and then to the head

25

ejusdem aque. Et deinde usque ad linea Westfolle Et inde linealiter usque
of the same water. And then to the line of the Westfolle And then lineally to

26

ad Ernestorre Et inde linealiter usque ad Vadum proximum in orientali
Ernestorre And then lineally to the ford near the eastern

27

parte Capelle Sancti Michaelis de Halghestoke: Et inde linealiter usque ad predictam
part of the Chapel of Saint Michael of Halghestoke: And then lineally to the aforesaid

28

Hogam de Costodone in orientali parte
Costodone ridge.
(Here it is assumed that this second 'in orientali parte' is only to explain the shortened version of the same words used before the Chapel Ford mete)

Chapter 4
The 1608 Perambulation and 1609 Survey Court

Although we are studying the 1240 perambulation, the result of another perambulation held in the early 17th century throws some extra light on the subject. In 1608, in the fifth year of the reign of King James I, a survey of the lands, manors, forests and chases etc (i.e. all revenue earning assets) belonging to the Duchy of Cornwall took place. The Forest of Dartmoor was the first estate to be perambulated. For some reason, twenty-five jurors were appointed not the usual twelve – perhaps they undertook a section each around the moor. They presented their findings at a Survey Court in Okehampton on 16th August 1609. (Some authors referred to this perambulation as that of 1608 and others as of 1609 – a small difference).

The Duchy held (and possibly still hold) the records of this perambulation and presentation. Thomas Westcote (1845) and Samuel Rowe (1848) saw those records and so their notes have been used here. As the report was written in an early form of English, it should be easier to understand.

The jurors reported that *'they fynde partlie by the coppies of auncient recordes ptlie. upon the evidence of other p'sons and ptlie. upon their own knowledge but especiallie as the boundes have been and are used and accustomed to be as follows:*

Okehampton castle. By the time of the survey court in 1609, the castle had been abandoned and left in ruins.

'Beginning at a high hill lying in the north quarter of the said fforest called at this date Cosdon, al's Cosson, and in the old records written Hoga de Costdonne and from thence linealie eastward by estimacon one mile or more unto little houndetorr wch. in the said records is called (hoga de parva houndetorr) and from thence lineallie to a place named in the said records Thurleston, now as they suppose called Waterdontorr being about three quarters of a myle from Houndtorr aforesaid, and from thence near a myle to Wotesbrookelake foote wch. falleth into Teynge and wch. lake they thincke to be the same wch. is now called Whoodelake, at wch. place they accompt the North Quarter to end; and thence nere one mile to Hingeston, al's Highstone, in the east quarter lyinge near ffernworthie hedges, and from thence lineallie nere one mile to Yeston, al's Geston, now commonly called Hethstone, and from thence lineallie through a fennye place now called Turfehill, but named in the old records per mediam tubarium de Albereeheved to a place called Kinge's Oven, and in the said record namely Furnum Regis and from thence to Wallebrookeheade and so alonge by Wallebrooke until it fall into Easter Dart and so downwards by the said easter Dart to another Dart called Wester Dart and from thence ascendinge by the said west Dart unto Wobrookefoote wher the east quarter endeth; and from thence linyallie ascendinge to Drylake, al's Dryewoorke and from thence ascendinge by Drylake unto Crefeild fford or Dryefeild ford and thence to Knattleburroughe, wch. they take to the same that is called in the old records Gnatteshill, and so by the same Wester Wellebrooke until it falleth into Owne, al's Aven, and from thence linyallie to Easter Whitaburrowe and from thence liniallie to Redlake foot whir it falleth into Erme, and from thence liniallie ascendinge unto Arme headd, wch, they take to a place named in the same records Grimsgrove and from thence to Plimheadd, where the South quarter endeth; and from thence linyallie to Elisboroughe and thence linyallie to Seward's Crosse and

from thence linyallie to little Hisworthie and so from thence linyallie to another Hisworthie and from thence linyallie through the midst of Mistorr moore to a rocke called Mistorpann and from thence linyallie to Dedlakeheadd wch. They thincke to be the next bound wch. is called in the old records Meuborough and from thence linyallie northwardes to Luntesborowe, wch. they think to be the same that is called in the records Lullingesete and from thence linyallie to Wester Redlake between wch. said two bounds the wester quarter endeth; and from thence north-ward to Rattlebrooke foote and soe from thence to the headd of the same Rattlebrooke and so from thence linyallie unto Steinegtorr and from thence linyallie to Langaford, al's Sandyford and so thence linyallie to the ford wch. lyeth in the east syde of the chapple of Halstocke and so from thence linyallie unto the said hill called Cosdon, al's Cosson wher they did begin.'

If we take these details and write them out in the form of one bound per line as we did in the previous chapter for the 1240 perambulation returns, we see that four extra metes and hence bounds have been introduced whilst two have been missed.

1609 PERAMBULATION RETURN

1   Beginning at a high hill lying in the north quarter of the Forest, called at this day Cosdon alias Cosson and in the old records Hoga de Costdown
2   and from thence lineally eastward by estimation one mile or more unto Little Houndetorr which in the said record is called Hoga de parva Houndetorr
3   and from thence lineally to a place named in the same record Thurleston, now, as we suppose, called Water Donter being about three-quarters of a mile from Houndetorr aforesaid
4   and from thence near a mile to Wates Brook head (foot, as corrected in the margin) which falleth into Teigne, and which lake they now think to be the same which is now called Hood Lake at which place they account the north quarter ends.
5   and from thence near one mile to Hengeston alias Heighstone, in the east quarter, lying near Fernworthy Hedges
6   and from thence lineally near one mile to Yelston alias or Gesstone now commonly called Hethstone
7   and from thence lineally through a fenny place now called Turshill, but named in the records per mediam Turbarium de Aberesheved …
8   (—— Missed and hence no mention of the Walla Brook)
9   to a place called, and in the said records named Furnum Regis
10   and from thence to Wallbrook head
11   and so along by Wallbrook until it falls into the East Dart
12   and so downwards by the said East Dart to another Dart called West Dart
13   and from thence ascendinge by the said West Dart to Wobrook foot, where the east quarter endeth.
14   and from thence lineally ascending to Drye Lake, alias, Drywork
15   and from thence ascending by Dry Lake to Creyselford or Drydelford
16   and from thence to Knattleborough, which they take to be the same which, in the old records, is called Gnattishill
17   and from thence ascending lineally to Wester Wellbrook head
18   and so by the same Wester Wellbrook until it falleth into Owen or Avon
19   and from thence lineally to East Whitaborough
20   and from thence lineally to Red Lake foot, where it falleth into Erme
21   and from thence lineally ascending unto Erme Head, which they take to be the place in the same record named Grimes Grove
21a   and from thence to Plym head, where the south quarter endeth
22   and from thence lineally to Ellisborough

continued...

23	and from thence lineally to Sewards Cross
24	and from thence lineally to Little Hisworthy
25	and so from thence to Another Hisworthy
25a	and so from thence through the midst of Mistermoor to a rock called Mistorpann
26	and from thence lineally to Due Lake head, which they think to be the next bound, and which is called in the said records Mewborough
27	and from thence lineally northwards to a place called Luntesborough, which they think to be the same that is called in the records Lullingsett
27a	and from thence lineally to the Wester Red Lake, between which two bounds the west quarter endeth.
28	and from thence northward to Rattlebrook foot
29	and so from thence to the head of the same Rattlebrook
29a	and from thence lineally unto Steynchatorr
30	and from then lineally unto Langford, alias, Sandiford
31	(—— Missed completely)
32	and so from thence lineally to the Ford which lieth in the east side of Saint Michael's Chapel of Holstock
33	and so from thence lineally to the said hill called Cossdon, alias, Cosston where they began.

From this record, we learn much of how the view of the boundary had altered over the intervening centuries. We will examine the record bound-by-bound and describe each of them using the names on today's Ordnance Survey maps.

Start Point – The jurors refer to 'a high hill' – note not 'the highest hill'. Cosdon, the third highest point on the moor, which looms over the northern quarter. Surely if the jurors had used this hill as a mete, they would have referred to it with more reverence. This seems to give an early indication that the later acceptance of the present day Cosdon as the 'Hoga de Costdonne' has been a mistake.

Bound 1 – The jurors' report here shows that by now they had started to regard tors as metes – something the 1240 perambulators did not do. They were clear that they approached Little Hound Tor from the west, not the north. This adds to the evidence that Cosdon was not the first mete. As Little Hound Tor (as named by the Ordnance Survey) was only erected in 1834 by a local farmer trying to increase his land holding!), they must have been referring to the ridgeline near today's Hound Tor.

Little Hound Tor and Whitemore Circle.

Bound 2 – Here is the first written mention that they considered Watern Tor to be a mete. As we shall see later, I regard this as an error.

Bound 3 – Having persuaded themselves that Watern Tor was a mete, they now sought the nearest stream confluence to fit the evidence – that of the tiny stream called Hugh Lake and the North Teign river near the 'rails'. They introduced the concept of naming the junctions between the four quarters of the moor here.

Bound 4 – 'Fernworthy Hedges' is not a feature on any of today's maps and so the Long Stone might well have been intended as the mete named the 'Hengestone'. It must have been in this area as the name Fernworthy is still attached to the reservoir and the forest.

Bound 5 – The orthostat near the entrance to Fernworthy Forest, Heath Stone, could well have been a mete but whether or not it was or has been moved, perhaps when the dam was constructed, is unknown.

Bound 6 – The name of this mete had changed by 1609 but it is clear that the jurors had to cross Chagford Common.

Bound 7 – No mention was made of following the line of the Walla

The Rails at Hugh Lake.

Bennett's Cross.

The ruins or burgh at Western Whittabarrow.

Plym Head.

Brook. Perhaps this was an oversight or perhaps Furnum Regis had gained stature and was now a thriving smelting house again. There was tin mining, as opposed to streaming, nearby on Bush Down (where there is an adit worth exploring).

Bound 8 – The exact location of 'Furnum Regis' is not at all clear as no real remains survive.

Bound 9 – They obviously climbed up the line of the North Walla Brook as they named its head as their next mete, or perhaps this relates to the head of the next Walla Brook! In either case, the most obvious route is up the North Walla Brook, over the road between Bennett's Cross and the Warren House Inn and down to the Walla Brook.

Bound 10 – Somehow they were not so clear about the fact that they must have crossed the ridgeline by Bennett's Cross having left one Wallabrook and found another. The one they did find they followed down to the East Dart river.

Bound 11 – This leads to Dartmeet.

Bound 12 – They went up the West Dart river to the O Brook.

Bound 13 – They followed the O Brook to the scar in the hillside, probably caused by tin streaming, called Dry Lake.

Bound 14 – They ascended Dry Lake to a ford – the name of which was uncertain. This mete is probably not a ford but is where their route crossed the Sandy Way.

Bound 15 – Ryder's Hill, the next mete, was called here by two names – Knattleborough or Gnattishill.

Bound 16 – This is a puzzle. One descends from Ryder's Hill to the head of Wellabrook Girt so perhaps the word 'ascending' was used in error.

Bound 17 – They followed the Western Wella Brook to the Avon.

Bound 18 – This bound is described very simply as going straight to a mete many have interpreted to be the present 'Eastern White Barrow', but if they went there and not Western White Barrow, the next bound is rather lacking in detail.

Bound 19 – This bound, if it had started at Eastern White Barrow would surely have included a reference to Western White Barrow when describing the passage to the confluence of the Red Lake and Erme. The site is prominent and the stones there cover a much wider area and are more likely to have been the site of hut circles, i.e. a 'burgh'.

Bound 20 – Here the jurors named Erme Head as the mete on the supposition that that is what the 1240 perambulators had meant as 'Grimes Grove'.

Bound 20a – Here they introduced a new mete – 'Plym Head'.

Bound 21 – The bound ended at Eylesbarrow.

Bound 22 – The reference to 'Sewards Cross' seems clearly enough to be indicating today's Siward's or Nun's Cross.

Bound 23 – 'Little Hisworthy' is probably South Hessary Tor.

Bound 24 – 'Another Hisworthy' is probably North Hessary Tor.

Bound 24a – They actually mentioned the mass of rocks that make up Great Mis Tor and one particular spot on the tor – 'Mistorpann'.

Bound 25 – They admitted uncertainty at this point and assumed that 'Mewborough' was the head of 'Due Lake'. Certainly Dry Lake is a good linear feature running in the direction of the boundary and does start near an ancient settlement so they could have been right.

Bound 26 – Here they assumed that 'Lullingsett' was now called 'Luntesborough' and if it were, then that would surely be where the remains of hut circles exist around Limsboro Cairn near Lynch Tor.

Bound 26a – They introduced a new bound as they clearly realised the wisdom of guiding riders to a good route to the Amicombe Brook, i.e. down 'Western Red Lake'.

Bound 27 – Rather puzzling is their idea that you go 'northward' to Rattlebrook Foot. As the crow flies, you would go northwest. It could be that they were indicating here that you should go northwards from the ford over the Amicombe Brook, skirt Watern Oke and its many rocks before heading for Rattlebrook Foot.

Bound 28 – They followed the Rattlebrook to its 'head'.

Bound 28a – Here the jurors introduced a new mete 'Steynchatorr' – or 'tor in a bog'. Quite what or where that was is open to doubt. Some have thought it meant Sourton Tors but that would be far-fetched as it is well off the natural line. Others think it might have been Stenga Tor.

Bound 29 – Rather than name the river they were to cross next, the jurors used the name of the ford – 'Sandiford'. On Dartmoor, 'sand' does not mean what one finds in a desert or on a beach. It means ground down granite. The ford on the West Okement river that the jurors surely crossed has such a base.

Bound 30 – The jurors missed out any mention of this rather large bound skirting what is now Okehampton Parish. So a rather large portion of the boundary in the north quarter is left in doubt.

Bound 31 – The mete at the end of this bound must surely be Cullever Steps.

Bound 32 – The jurors returned back to their start point.

Stenga Tor.

Three main points can be gleaned from this analysis. Firstly, there have obviously been incursions into the forest originally intended. Secondly, without maps and needing to call upon men with local knowledge for each section of the perambulation probably meant that the 1240 perambulation party was also much larger than just the twelve knights. Thirdly, if they were unsure in 1608 of the route taken in 1240 only four hundred years after the event, we too would be wise to be circumspect in our statements about it after eight hundred years.

Grimsgrave cist ('Grimes Grove'), as depicted by the antiquarian T.A. Falcon in 1900, stands on the banks of the Langcombe Brook, with Langcombe Ridge, on the horizon in the picture, standing between it and the Erme.

Chapter 5
Work of Previous Authors

Some Dartmoor enthusiasts boast not just about the number of books that they own but how many metres they fill on their shelves! True, there are a great many books about many of the facets of life on Dartmoor both now and in the past. Here is an introduction to some of the books that have been found useful in this study. They are listed in chronological order.

1598 – John Manwood – "Treatise and Discourse of the Lawes of the Forrest". In the medieval period, the practice of reserving areas of land for the sole use of the monarch and the aristocracy was common throughout Europe. There is no evidence of Anglo-Saxon monarchs creating forests. The Normans introduced this concept to England in the 11th century. At the height of the practice in the late 12th century and early 13th century, fully one-third of the land area of southern England was designated as 'Royal Forest' with its own set of laws. Forest Laws were laid down formally in 1217 and Manwood's Treatise has become perhaps the most-cited secondary source on Forest Law.[7] Forest Laws were designed to protect the 'venison and the vert', i.e. the animals of the chase and the greenery that sustained them. They prescribed harsh punishment for anyone who committed any of a range of offences within the forests. By the mid-17th century, enforcement of these laws had died out but many of England's woodlands still bear the title 'Royal Forest'.

1599 – John Hooker (or Volwell) – "Synopsis Chorographical or An Historical Record of the County of Devon". Descriptions of the perambulation writ and the return, written in Latin, later used by Rowe are contained in this handwritten book – of which two copies are known to exist. One is in the Devon Heritage Centre (DHC), Sowton, Exeter (folios 208-209) and another is in the Harleian Collection housed in the British Library (Harleian MS No. 5827, folio 58b). The work's aim in and around Dartmoor seems primarily to have been to describe the extents of the Parishes with ancient venville rights (i.e. an explanation for the Normans about the rights from Saxon times). The book was probably written before 1599 as Hooker was in poor health in later life and died in 1601. The text of the copy at Exeter is much clearer and easier to read than that in the British Library.

1630 – Tristram Risdon – "The Chorographical Description or Survey of the County of Devon" – commonly known as 'Risdon's Survey of Devon'. Risdon died in 1640. The survey was printed in 1714 but was probably written about 1630. No originals are known and the book was copied and printed, sometimes only in parts, with varying degrees of accuracy. A version from 1897 transcribed and edited by J Dallas and H Porter (MSN Digitized books) contains further details of Westcountry noblemen, their families and land holdings. An earlier version from 1811 printed for Rees and Curtis of Plymouth (Googlebooks) holds more details from Risdon's original work and a description of the return from the 1240 Perambulation.

John Hooker (c.1527–1601).

'This Parish, for largeness in lands and liberties, may compare with any in this kingdom, the whole forest of DARTMORE lying in the verge thereof, the charter for the limiting of whose bounds is as followeth: Perambulatio Richardi comitis Cornubia et Pictavia tenentis in com.

---

[7]The primary sources are e.g. Canute's Civil Dooms (ca. 1025) and the Charter of the Forest (1217)

*Devon. per praeceptum domini Regis Henrici filii, Johannis corona-
tionem dict. Hen. 240 in vigilia St. Jacobi per juramentum sacrusti
subscript scil Will. de la Bruer, Guidonis de Bretivile, Wil. de Widworthy, Hugonis de Bolhay, Rich. Giffard, Odonis de Treverby, Henricus
filius Henrici Wil. De Trenchard, Phil. Harrer, Nich. De Heamdon, Will.
de Northleigh, et Durat filii Boton, qui incipiunt perambulationem, ad
Hogam de Cosdowne, et inde linealiter usq ; ad parvam Hogam, que
vocatur Hounteret, inde usq ; ad Thurleston, et inde linealiter usq :
Wotesbroke, Lakefoot, que cadit in Teigne. et inde linealiter usq ; ad
Hangeston, et inde linealiter usq ; ad Gotestone, et inde linealiter usq ;
ad mediam Turbarium Aberhene, et sic in Longam Wallabroke, et inde
linealiter usq ; ad Walbroke-Head, usq; cadit in Darta et sic per Dartam,
usq; ad aliam Dart. ascendend. usq ; ad Abbot-Foot, et sic ascend.
Otbroke, usq ; ad Ledeereoke ; et ita ascendend. usq ; ad le Drifeildforde,
et inde linealiter usq ; at Batshill, et inde linealiter usq ; ad caput de
Westor Wellabroke, et sic per Wester Wellabroke usq ; cadit in Avon ; et
inde linealiter usq ; ad Easter-Wellabroke; et inde linealiter usq ; ad Redlake, que cadit in Erme, et inde ascend. usq ; ad Grimsgrove, et inde linealiter usque ad Ellisborough, et inde linealiter usque ad crucem Silward,
et inde usq ; ad Efforther ; et sic per aliam Efforther, et inde per medium
mistum usq ; ad Mewboron, et inde usq ; ad Willingsesse, et inde ad
Rahernbroke-Foot, et sic ad caput ejusdem quae et deinde usq ; ad Le
West Soll, et inde linealiter usq ; ad Grenestor, et inde linealiter usq ; ad
vadam proximum in orientali parte cappellae St. Mich. de Hallgestock,
et inde linealiter usq ; ad praedict. Hoentali paowne, in orientali parte.'*

Sir William Pole (1561–1635).

1610 – "Register of records of the manors of South Brent and Churchstow, co. Devon, formerly held by Buckfastleigh Abbey, co. Devon"
(British Library Add 37640). This record described the boundaries of
the moors of Brent and Buckfastleigh and of Dartmoor Forest, the latter
taken 24 July 1240 by Richard, Earl of Cornwall – folio 15. This gave
the familiar record in Latin of the 1240 perambulation return but
interestingly contained the words *'haga de Costdonne'* rather than the
normal *'hoga de Costdonne'*. Using *'haga'* meaning 'boundary of' rather
than *'hoga'* meaning 'hill' would thus have excluded the top of Cosdon
hill. However, on the next line the writer pens *'haga qui vocal parva
Houndetorre'*, i.e. the hill called Little Hound Tor. Thus the word written
'haga' is probably just the penman's style.

1635 – Sir William Pole – "Collections towards a Description of the
County of Devon" (Printed 1791). This book contained lists of the
Bishops of Exeter and Sheriffs of Devon and brief family notes of some
of the perambulators, e.g. Prouz and Giffard. He also referred to the
work of Risdon.

1671 – Sir Edward Coke – "Institutes of the Lawes of England Part 4"[8].
In the section entitled 'The Courts of the Forests', Coke expanded upon
and offered explanations of the laws of the Forest. These laws were
important as they had endured from Saxon times and been assumed
by the Norman conquerors. The punishments for transgressions of the
laws within any Forest were draconian. This portion of Coke's work
noted that a Forest (or Chase) should be enclosed by 'metes and
bounds' and without these could not truly be regarded as a Forest (or
Chase). Coke also explained how it was normal for rivers and highways
to form part of Forest boundaries. He also stated that where such rivers
or ways were used, the river or way itself was not necessarily to be
considered as within the Forest. These few lines give us the clue that it
was the practice for any perambulator to use rivers or ways as part of a
boundary. The boundary of the Forest of Dartmoor does follow rivers
or streams for much of its route and possibly an ancient track.

1793 – Richard Polwhele – "Historical Views of Devonshire in Five

Sir Edward Coke (1552–1664).

[8]Such is the importance of Coke's interpretations of the precedents that they are still
used today in, inter alia, England and the USA.

Volumes". Vol 3 of Polwhele's work included notes about the importance of tin mining on Dartmoor in the 13th century. Whilst we cannot know whether or not mining was being actively undertaken as the 1240 Perambulation was taking place, it is most probable that its effects could be noted in some places, such as the debris left lying as a result of tin streaming.

1822 – D and S Lysons – "Magna Britannia Vol VI Part II". The authors mentioned some of the family names of those associated with the 1240 perambulation, e.g. Briwere (or Brewer) and Giffard, and their land holdings but not in the context of the perambulation itself.

1826 – NT Carrington – "Dartmoor: A Descriptive Poem". This most important but largely overlooked book contained the work of two authors. The first is the named author, NT Carrington, who wrote the poem of the title – all ninety-one pages of it – *'Dartmoor! ...., A wild and wond'rous region.'* **W Burt** is the second named (Secretary of the Chamber of Commerce, Plymouth) who wrote a one hundred and five page 'preface' to the poem which indicated his extensive knowledge of the history of Dartmoor and a further one hundred and seven pages of most detailed notes about many topics relating to the Moor. It was referred to by Crossing in 1902 as containing a 'contemporary' understanding of the Forest boundary. Who would have guessed that from the title of the book? Burt truly hid his light under another's bushel! Where Samuel Rowe seems to get the primary recognition as the lead author when one researches this subject, Burt had actually done the legwork years beforehand and this is of most interest to us.

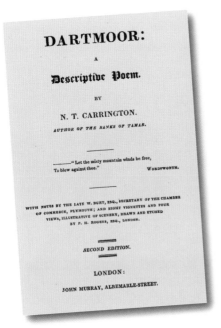

The title page to NT Carrington's Dartmoor: Descriptive Poem.

The preface and notes were full of details on numerous subjects and offered an excellent introduction to the history of the creation of Dartmoor Forest and the various perambulations for which records had been found. The book's stated aim was to encourage others to visit the moor – no easy excursion at that particular time. The book included details of, or references to, etymology, ancient records (including ancient manuscripts and the work of authorities such as Coke and Manwood), ancient tracks to, and on, the moor, tin-mining, flora, druids, some of the folk tales that abound on the moor etc. Whilst not including any details of the writs for the various known perambulations, Burt did offer details of what he considered to be the likely 1240 return and a record of the boundary accepted at the time of his writing:

'There have been various perambulations of Dartmoor, in order to define its metes or bounds, the parts lying outside those metes or bounds being disafforested by Charta de Foresta, and thenceforth considered as pourallees, or purlieus; a word derived by Coke from, pur, clear, exempt, entire, and lieu, a place; that is, places exempt from forest jurisdiction, and which purlieus now compose the commons surrounding the Moor, but in ancient times belonging to it.

The first perambulation on record, was in the 24th of King Henry III [1240], by command of Richard, earl of Cornwall and this traces the limits linealiter, viz. from tor to tor, and place to place, commencing with Hogam de Cosdonne, the high hill of Cosdon or Cosson, to Little Houndetorr, Thurlestone, Wotesbrokeslakesfote, Heighestone, Langstone, Alberyshede, Long Wallesbroke, the King's Oven, Wallesbrokeshede, the two Darts, Okebrokysfote, the Dryaworke, Dryfieldforde, Cattishille, Wester Wellesbrokeshede, Yester Whyteburghe, Redelake, Grymesgrove, Eleysburghe, Siward's Cross, the two Yffothers, Mystor, Mewyburghe, Lullingsfote, Rakernbrokesfote, Westsolle, Ernestorre, Chapel-ford of St Michael of Halstocks, and thence to Cosdonne aforesaid, where the perambulation began. On the back of a copy of this perambulation, amongst the Harleian papers, 5827, page 60, is a circular tracing of the forest, the middle part being intituled: 'This is the precincte about the foreste of dartmore;' and another circular line being taken, or drawn outside, for the surrounding commons …'

Burt mentioned various other perambulations either ordered and not completed, e.g. 1299, or ordered but the returns could not be found, e.g. 1387, 1556, 1602. Of further interest, he went on to quote the 'present bounds' on the authority of a Mr Shillibeer as follows:

'Commence in the north quarter, at Cosson Hill, and thence proceed by Little Houndtor, Wildtor Well, and Thurleston, otherwise Waterdown tor, to Wottesbrook lake foot, otherwise Woodlake, otherwise Rhode lake, which falls into the Teign, where the north quarter ends, and the east quarter begins. Thence by Stone tor, Kingstone, through Fernworthy Court, Heas or Heathstone, King's Oven, Wallabrook head, and down by that brook until it falls into the East Dart, then descending by the East Dart to the West Dart to Woobrook foot, where the east quarter ends, and the south quarter begins. Thence ascending by Woobrook to Drylake foot, thence ascending by the said lake to Creyfield ford, thence by Knattleborough, otherwise Gnatshill, to West Wallabrook head, and descending by the said brook until it falls into the Aun, otherwise Aven, at Huntingdon Cross, thence by Western Whittaborough to Redlake, otherwise Reedlake foot, where it falls into the Erme, then ascending by that river to Erme head, otherwise Grimsgrove, where the south quarter ends, and the west quarter begins. Thence ascending to a stone marked B B L B, thence descending to the Plym and ascending to Ellisborough, thence by Siward's Cross, otherwise Nuns cross, to South Hisworthy, and North Hisworthy tors, thence by Mistor Pan, Deadlake head, Huntsborough, otherwise Limsborough, to Western Redlake head, (the perambulation of 1786, says between the last two bounds, namely Huntsborough, and West Redlake head,) here the west quarter ends. Thence down by Redlake to the Tavy, then up by that river to Rattlebrook foot, thence by the said brook to the head of the same name, thence by Stenaker tor, otherwise Sourton, (the perambulation calls it Steynskatorr) Langsford, otherwise Sandiford, High Willows, and West Miltor, to Holstocke, otherwise Chapel ford, then across the West Okement to Belston tor, then descending to the Taw, where the boundaries of the forest terminate.'

Huntingdon Cross.

Burt's copy of the 1204 writ in Latin.

Burt's translation of the 1204 writ.

Burt must have been quite a scholar even though he was an amateur. He not only gained access to and read the Close Rolls, then held in the Tower of London, which contained much shorthand writing, but also provided his readers with both the expanded text and a translation. See this paragraph from the book showing the contents of the 1204 Close Roll with details of the disafforestation of Devon in Latin and then translated, and compare it (later) with that produced by Thomas Duffus Hardy (a professional archivist) in 1837.

1830 – Samuel Rowe – "Antiquarian Investigations in the Forest of Dartmoor, Devon". This article appears to be the first published work by Rowe and was contained in the Transactions of the Plymouth Institution. Primarily it started the process of enumerating the many supposed druidical relics to be found on Dartmoor – sacred circles, cromlechs, logan stones, rock basins, rock pillars (which he noted with scorn that *some regard as mere boundstones'*, e.g. near Gidleigh), barrows or cairns, huts and enclosures, trackways and tracklines (probably what we today call reaves) and of which Rowe described many that were explored later in more depth by Fleming. He referred to Burt's work in NT Carrington's book.

1832 – CP Cooper – "An Account of the Most Important Public Records of Great Britain". This book detailed the work that was to be undertaken to bring together and preserve and publish *'the Rolls of Parliament, accompanied by such other Records as may illustrate the Ancient Constitution and Policy of the Kingdom'*. One could regard this as the start of the creation of what is now the National Archive. Prior to this work, few would have had access to records in the likes of the Tower of London.

Close roll showing the writ for the perambulation in 1240.

1833 – Thoma Duffus Hardy – "Rotuli Litteratum Clausaram – In Turri Londinensi Vol I Ab Anno MCCIV ad Annum MCCXXIV". Sir Thoma Duffus Hardy, an English antiquary, has an interesting part to play in this story – see Wikipedia for more details of his personal life. His work was a continuation of that started by CP Cooper as described above and went a stage further. He made the Rolls previously held in the Record Office in the Tower of London and other locations more easily readable for other scholars – such as, we can suppose, those who subsequently wrote in the Transactions of the Devonshire Association or in books of their own. This first book in a series gave a useful introduction to the Close Rolls before printing their contents. With this, Hardy aimed to whet historians' appetites by calling up examples he had already found. Sadly, for us, this did not include any mention of the Dartmoor perambulations.

The work of Hardy in printing in book-form the contents of these Rolls in this and subsequent volumes at this time might well have been a spur to the Devonian historians. Previously, the Rolls were difficult to read.

1834 – HE Carrington – "The Collected Poems of the Late NT Carrington". Carrington's son collected and printed his late father's poems – one of which had earned him his freedom from the Royal Navy in 1804 and another, 'Dartmoor', fifty guineas from King George IV. Although not directly relevant to a study of the Forest Boundary, NT Carrington's work is remarkable for two reasons. Firstly, it is supposed to have ushered in the beginning of the interest in Dartmoor as an objective for tourists. Secondly, he is one of only three writers to have a permanent memorial on the Moor – on the higher rocks of the Dewerstone.

1837 – Thoma Duffus Hardy – "Rotuli Chartarum in Turri Londinensi Vol I Part I Ab Anno MCXCIX ad Annum MCCXVI". This volume, covering the period 1199 to 1216, included the text of the writ of 1204 disafforesting Devon apart from Dartmoor and Exmoor.

Compare the ease of reading this with that of reading the original document, seen above, which was written in a mix of shorthand Latin with Anglo-Saxon names and which is now in a secure vault at the National Archives, Kew.

Carta hõiu Devoñ de foresta. JoH's Di g͞ra ͠tc. Sciatis nos deafforestasse totā Devoniā de omib3 q̃ ad forestā ͠t ad forestarios p̃tinent, usq, ad metas antiquo3 regardo3 de Dertemora ͠t Exemora, que regarda fūnt tempe Reg͞ Hen͞r p'mi, ita qd̄ tota Devonia, ͠t hõies ĩ ea manentes, ͠t h̄edes eo3 sint deafforestati omĩo, ͠t q'eti ͠t soluti de nob ͠t h̄edib3 n̄ris, ĩ ppetuū, de omib3 q̃ ad forestā ͠t ad forestarios p̃tinent, exceptis duab3 moris p̃nõiatis, scl3, Dertemo3 ͠t Exemo3 p p̃d̄cas metas. Volum° & ͠t concedim° qd̄ p̃d̄ci hõies Devoñ ͠t h̄edes eo3 h̄ant çsuetudines infra regarda morā̆ illā̆, si͠c h̄re çsue͠vant t̄pe p̃d̄ci Regis Hen͞r, faciendo ĩ çsuetudines

Hardy shows the 1204 disafforestation order.

1845 – Thomas Westcote – "A View of Devonshire in MDCXXX". This book, written in 1630 but only published in 1845, contained mention of the disafforesting of Devon and the writs and returns for both the 1240 (in Latin) and 1609 (in Old English) Perambulations. The editor and publisher included extra details relating to the perambulation writs and returns probably unknown to Westcote himself. Also note the

THE PERAMBULATION – DARTMOOR'S ORIGINAL LONG DISTANCE WALK

We have formerly said that Devonshire was difforested by King John, Exmoor and Dartmoor excepted. The first intent thereof was (as I find,) begun by Henry I., third son to the Conqueror, and seconded by King John, but perfected by Henry III., yet without limitation or bounding the said moory wastes, until authority was granted by the last mentioned King to Richard Earl of Cornwall, his brother, to take survey thereof, and to limit and bound it; who, accompanied with twelve esquires and gentlemen of the country adjoining, did perambulate the said forest, and as they passed, did name certain rocks, rivers, rills, tors, &c. as bonds and meets thereof, as appeareth by the following documents :—

Left: *Westcote's note about the 1240 perambulation.*
Below left*: Westcote introduces the 1240 perambulation writ – note the publisher's footnote which gave clues about the whereabouts of the old records.*
Below: *Westcote's version of the 1240 perambulation return.*

COMMISSION TO THE SHERIFF OF DEVON TO CAUSE A PERAMBULATION TO BE MADE OF THE FOREST OF DARTMORE.*

Inter Recorda Curiæ Cancellariæ in Turri London asservata, scilicet Rot. Claus; de anno Regni Regis Henrici tertii vicesimo quarto, [1240] m. ii. sic continetur.

* For the satisfaction of the Reader, we supply a copy from the Tower of the original Commission for the Perambulation of the Forest of Dartmore, bearing date 13th June, 1240, and which was unknown to Mr. Westcote. The Return to this Writ is not to be found; but as Mr. Westcote's copy of the Perambulation in that year is very imperfect, we have endeavoured to offer one far more correct, by collating it with the copy in the Harleian Collection, No. 5827, fol. 58, b.;—with a manuscript copy of Serjeant Maynard's, at Lincoln's Inn;—and also with a copy in a book in the Treasury of the Court of Receipts, at the Chapter House, Westminster, indorsed "*Feoda in Capite*," p. 100. To these we add a copy of the Perambulation made in 1608, which is now acted upon in the Office of the Duchy of Cornwall —G. O.,—P. J.

* It will be observed that where the word "*linealiter*" is used in the Perambulation, the boundary is represented by a straight line, although a different construction may possibly be put upon the word. Nor should it be overlooked that, according to the Forest Laws, the object which forms the boundary (if it be a road, river, &c., and not a house or mill,) is wholly included within the franchise of the Forest. See 4. Coke's Institute, p. 318.—G. O.,—P. J.

Above: *Westcote's editor also added an additional thought.*

Editor's observation about the possible interpretation of the word *'linealiter'* and a reference to Coke's Institute.

1609 Court of Survey – Westcote's notes about this later perambulation quite rightly state that it occurred in 1608. However as it did not report to the Court of Survey until 1609 one finds it referred to in texts under either date.

PERAMBULATIO FORESTE DE DERTIMORE.

Inter Recorda in Thesaurario Curiæ receptæ Scaccarii asservata, videlicet in libro indorsato "Feoda in Capite," p. 100 continetur ut sequitur.

Hec est Perambulatio facta per commune consilium Ricardi, Comitis Cornubie et Pictavie in Comitatu Devonie, per preceptum Domini Regis Henrici, filii Johannis, anno coronacionis dicti Henrici vicesimo quarto, in vigilia Sancti Jacobi Apostoli, per sacramentum militum subscriptorum, scilicet, Willielmi de la Bruere, Guidonis de Brittevill, Willielmi de Widworthi, Hugonis de Bolley, Ricardi Gifford, Odonis de Feverbyn, Henrici filii Henrici, Willielmi Trenchard, Philippi Perer, Nicholai de Heaunton, Willielmi de Morelegh, et Durant Filii Botour, qui incipiunt Perambulationem ad Hoga de Cossdonne, et inde linealiter* usque ad parvam Hoga que vocatur parva Houndtorre, et inde usque ad Theurleston, et inde linealiter usque ad Wotesbrokesfote que cadit in Tenge, et inde linealiter usque ad Hengston, et inde linealiter usque ad Yesceton, et inde linealiter usque ad mediam Turbariam de Alberesheved et sic in longum Walebroke, et inde linealiter usque ad Furnum Regis, et inde linealiter usque ad Walebrokesheved, et sic in longum Walebroke usque cadit in Derta, et sic per Dertam usque per aliam Dertam ascendendo usque ad Okebrokfote, et sic ascendendo Okebrok usque ad la Drylake, et ita ascendendo usque ad la Drydellford, et inde linealiter usque ad Cattishill, et inde linealiter usque ad Caput de Westere Walebroke et sic per Westere Walebroke usque cadit in Avona, et inde linealiter usque ad Ester Wightburgh, et inde linealiter ubi Redelake cadit in Erme, et inde ascendendo usque ad Grymesgrove, et inde linealiter usque ad Elesburgh, et inde linealiter usque ad Crucem Syward, et inde usque ad Estfothere et sic ad aliam Estfothere, et inde per mediam Mistmore usque ad Mueburgh, et inde usque ad Lullingesfote, et inde usque ad Rakernebrokesfote et sic ad caput ejusdem aque et inde usque ad Westsoll, et inde linealiter usque ad Ernestorre, et inde linealiter usque ad vadum proximum in orientali parte Capelle Sancti Michaelis de Halgestok, et inde linealiter usque ad predictam Hoga de Cossdonne in orientali parte.

Westcote's version of the perambulation return presented to the Court of Survey in 1609.

PERAMBULATION OF DARTMOOR. 6 JAMES I., 1608.

On the sixteenth day of August, in the sixth year of King James the First, a Court of Survey was held at Okehampton, before Sir William Strode, knight; Richard Connock, esquire; Robert Moore, esquire; and Robert Paddon, gentleman; Auditors of the duchy of Cornwall, and Commissioners appointed for that purpose: when the Jury, Edward Skirnett, Walter Hole, Roger Cole, Henry Burges, Richard Edmond, Gregory Grey, John Bickford, Hugh Elford, John Massey, Roger Drake, Walter Lillicrap, John Chubb, Stephen Taverner, Andrew Heywood, Roger Wicket, Robert Hannaford, John Wills, John Hele, Walter Tuckerman, William Mudge, William Ilbert, Thomas Sturges, and Elias Harris, inter alia, found the bounds of the Forest of Dartmoor to be as underneath, viz.:—Beginning at a high hill lying in the north quarter of the Forest, called at this day Cosdon, alias Cosson, and in the old records Hoga de Costdown; and from thence lineally eastward, by estimation one mile or more, unto Little Houndetorr, which in the said record is called Hoga de parva Houndetorr; and from thence lineally to a place named in the same record Thurleston, now, as we suppose, called Water Donter, being about three-quarters of a mile from Houndetorr aforesaid, and from thence near a mile to Wates Brook head, (foot, as corrected in the margin,) which falleth into Teigne, and which lake they now think to be the same which is now called Hood Lake, at which place they account the north quarter ends. And from thence near one mile to Hengeston, alias, Heighstone, in the east quarter, lying near Fernworthy Hedges; and from thence lineally near one mile to Yelston, alias, Gesstone, now commonly called Hethstone; and from thence lineally through a fenny place now called Turshill, but named in the records per mediam Turbariam de Alberesheved, to a place called King's Oven, and in the said records named Furnum Regis; and from thence to Wallbrook head,

and so along by Wallbrook until it fall into the East Dart, and so downwards by the said East Dart to another Dart called West Dart; and from thence ascending by the said West Dart to Wobrook foot, where the east quarter endeth. And from thence lineally ascending to Drye Lake, alias, Drywork; and from thence ascending by Dry Lake to Creyselford, or Drydelford; and from thence to Knattleborough, which they take to be the same which, in the old records, is called Gnattishill; and from thence ascending lineally to Wester Wellbrook head, and so by the same Wester Wellbrook until it falleth into Owen, or Avon; and from thence lineally to East Whitaborough; and from thence lineally to Red Lake foot, where it falleth into Erme; and from thence lineally ascending unto Erme head, which they take to be the place in the same record named Grimes Grove; and from thence to Plym head, where the south quarter endeth. And from thence lineally to Ellisborough; and from thence lineally to Sewards Cross; and from thence lineally to Little Hisworthy; and so from thence to another Hisworthy; and so from thence through the midst of Mistermoor to a rock called Mister Pan; and from thence lineally to Due Lake head, which they think to be the next bound, and which is called in the said records Mewborough; and from thence lineally northwards to a place called Luntesborough, which they think to be the same that is called in the records Lullingsett; and from thence lineally to the Wester Red Lake, between which two bounds the west quarter endeth. And from thence northward to Rattlebrook foot, and so from thence to the head of the same Rattlebrook; and from thence lineally unto Steynchatorr; and from thence lineally unto Langford, alias, Sandiford; and so from thence lineally to the Ford which lieth in the east side of Saint Michael's Chapel of Holstock; and so from thence lineally to the said hill called Cossdon, alias, Cosston, where they began.

53

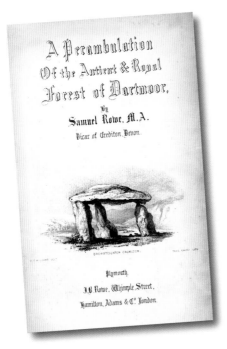

Ttile pages to Samuel Rowe's 1848 'Perambulation'.

King's notes on Forest Law.

As well as these documents, Westcote mentioned (rather like Risdon before him) the genealogy of 'leading' Devon families including the continuing existence (in 1630) of the families of Sir Robert de Hellion and Sir William de Proux (two knights named in the 1240 writ as having a dispute over the boundary) and of Richard Gyffard one of the perambulators. Unfortunately, Westcote did not include any dates and so determining which of the many Williams in the Prouz family was the knight with the grievance that partly led to the 1240 perambulation is not at all straightforward.

1848 – Samuel Rowe – "A Perambulation of the Antient and Royal Forest of Dartmoor and the Venville Precincts" (First Edition). Almost all those who study the perambulation will be attracted to this book purely by its title. It is considered by many to be the most important work about the subject and is still being reprinted today. This just goes to illustrate that picking a title is very important. As we have seen, others had described the Forest boundary beforehand and so Rowe should not be regarded as the leading authority but rather as just one of many. His book does not add to the sum of our knowledge about the boundary but uses the possible boundary route as a framework for describing walks around and on the moor. Crossing followed rather the same idea later by describing walks in the various 'Districts' of the moor. Rowe included almost the same descriptions of the Perambulation writs and returns word for word as published earlier by Westcote.

1856 – Richard John King – "The Forest of Dartmoor and Its Borders A Historical Sketch". King started by using the term 'Forest' to describe the whole of Dartmoor rather than the forest at its core. He described the disafforestation of Devon as something the local inhabitants would have welcomed as they loathed the Forest Laws. King described the route of the 1240 perambulation using few bounds and added the titbit that at King's Oven *'according to the tradition of the forest, the commissioners rested during the first night of their perambulation'*. This is the only note found in any of the literature about possible stopping places. He further conjectured that the word *'oven'* had been derived from the Saxon *'hof'*, meaning a dwelling. Of further interest is his exclusion of the names of Watern Tor and Eastern Whittabarrow as markers but inclusion of Huntingdon Cross and Peter's Cross (meaning the cross on Western Whittabarrow).

1866 – Richard John King – "The Forest of Dartmoor". In this article in 'The Fortnightly Review Vol VI August 15 to December 1, 1866' p. 300, King again waxed lyrical about Dartmoor. He noted that the tin of Devon was surely worked in pre-Roman times and would have been a major source of income in the early 13th century. In 1238, when Dartmoor was granted to Richard, Earl of Cornwall by his brother, Henry III, substantial Royalties also passed. He merely described the Forest in round terms as extending *'over all the hill country of Dartmoor'*. Whilst noting that the red deer had been extinct on Dartmoor for *'nearly a century'*, he reminded us that the deer would have liked most the *'lying'* in the *'long deep hollows, lined with fern and heather, and by the river sides among beds of tall rushes and bog myrtle'*. This was a timely reminder to scholars of what the earliest perambulators must surely have known, namely in the creation of a forest for hunting, be sure to include the ground where the foremost prey, deer, is most likely to graze. He also mentioned the possible etymology of some of the names on the Moor.

1869 – T L Pridham – "Devonshire Celebrities". This work dealt mainly with famous Devon men from Elizabethan times onwards. It mentioned some earlier ones but none that could be identified as amongst the party that undertook the Perambulation in 1240. It mentioned some of their possible peers and ancestors, e.g. William Brewer, Bishop of Exeter in the time of Henry III and a Gifford born in 1779 who became a Master of the Rolls.

1878 – J Brooking Rowe – "Contributions to a History of the Cistercian Houses of Devon". The cistercian order started in France in the 11th century. There were Benedictine monks at Buckfastleigh in Buckfast Abbey, endorsed by King Canute in 1018, before it became a Cistercian house 40 years later. Another Cistercian house was Buckland Abbey, near Tavistock, that was founded in 1280. This author's look at the records of these establishments, which being supported by farming had a direct interest in the rights and use of the Forest, showed the continuing bickering over the rights of use of the moor. He quoted examples of inquiries into trespass in 1291, 1463 and 1478. In 1538, Buckland was given up to the King (Henry VIII) at the time of the dissolution. It subsequently passed to Sir Francis Drake. Brooking Rowe mentioned the map now at DHC, Sowton only so far as to point out that it could not have been drawn in 1240 as Buckland Church, which is shown on the map, had not yet been built.

Buckland Abbey.

1884 – The Publications of the Pipe Roll Society Vol. III – "Introduction to the Study of the Pipe Rolls". In this volume, the Society aimed to acquaint beginners with the text, arrangement, form and general nature of early Pipe Rolls. It also included a most useful guide to the abbreviations used by the early scribes, some of which were reproduced in the work by Hardy mentioned above.

1885 – Stuart A Moore – "A Short History of the Rights of Common Upon the Forest of Dartmoor and the Commons of Dartmoor". This paper was read at the Athenaeum, Plymouth on 26th October 1885 at the 'request' of the Dartmoor Preservation Association. Moore investigated his subject with the view of attaining the 'objects' of the association – here it was seeking to stop further enclosure of parts of the Forest. He had access to the Pipe Rolls, knowledge of the Forest Laws and knew the history of the disafforestation and several perambulations. He tried to trace the boundary but eventually adopted the line 'laid down' by Samuel Rowe. He deduced that the first perambulation established three key facts: one, that the moor was originally part of a Royal Forest; two, that the Commons of Devon and surrounding parishes were once part of the forest; and three, that the moor was not a Waste of a Manor.[9] His conclusions were that the commoners rights had existed from antiquity and as they represented the valuable *'right to liberty over these wild regions'* that they should continue to be preserved. He noted that since the early laying out of the boundary, there had been many attempts at encroachment. He also called for a central body to represent the ancient rights – perhaps an early plea for something like the DNPA! What we may conclude from this is that Moore supposed that in an ideal world the creation of a forest with a boundary would have little – indeed almost no – effect upon the owners of the lands immediately surrounding the Forest with regard to grazing rights or the extraction of peat. The subsequent boundary disputes obviously show that we do not live in an ideal world!

1891 – William Crossing – "The Land of Stream and Tor". In this rather lyrical book imbued with the enthusiasm normally found in a tourist guide, Crossing mentioned the disafforestation in 1204 and described the probable route taken in 1240 in very lengthy but general terms and opined the uncertainty of describing it accurately. He was specific though in suggesting that the route was from Cosdon direct to King's Oven; went via Western and not Eastern Whittaburrow; and stayed to the south of 'High Willes'. He made the point that the holding of the Forest by the Earl of Cornwall did not 'dispossess the commoners of the rights which they had upon it previously ... for the charter of John expressly states that the men of Devon and their heirs were to have the customs with regards of those moors which they were wont to have in the time of King Henry I'. He clearly knew Spence Bate as he described

William Crossing 1847–1928.

[9]Thus dispelling any idea that local lords might have had rights, including that of exclusivity – all the rights belonged to the Crown.

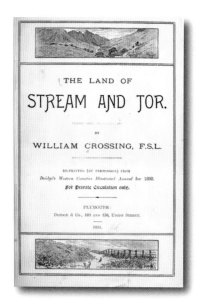

The title page of William Crossing's The Land of Stream and Tor *published in 1891.*

a trip they made together to open a cairn. (The 1994 reprint by Forest Publishing of this book included a map of the 'Perambulation of 1240' which showed little regard to what Crossing actually said and in two places at least contradicted him.) He described the bounds as follows:

[Present] – *'On what particular part of Cosdon the Perambulators set forth on their journey around the ancient forest we cannot now with certainty determine, and indeed the bounds as specified by them vary considerably in many parts of the moor from those generally recognised at the present day. Some of the spots mentioned in this Perambulation can now be scarcely identified,[10] and the boundary line of the duchy does not always agree with that which the commoners of certain of the parishes surrounding the forest consider to be the correct one.*

From Cosdon the line the Perambulators took led them to Little Hound Tor, whence, pursuing a southerly direction, they reached the Teign, and passed onwards to King's Oven, which is not very far from the present high road that crosses the moor from Princetown to Moretonhampstead. Thence down the Wellabrook until that stream falls into the East Dart, when the latter became the boundary as far as Dartmeet. The Perambulators then ascended the West Dart to a point where that river receives the waters of the Wobrook, which stream becomes in turn the boundary. Just above a spot now known as Horse Ford the Perambulators left the stream, and proceeding over the hill in due time reached the source of another. This was the Western Wellabrook, and their course lay along it to its confluence with the Avon. The Perambulation says that the line then goes to Ester Whyteburgh (Eastern Whitaburrow) but this, which is a fine cairn, twelve yards high and ninety yards in circumference, is now looked upon as standing some distance without the bounds, and it is probable that Western Whitaburrow was meant. This is also a cairn, but not as large as the former, and on it formerly stood a granite cross, erected to serve as a boundary mark to Brent Moor, which here abuts the Forest. This cross is mentioned in an inquisition which was held on these bounds dated 1557, at which time Sir William Petre, who owned the manor of Brent, possessed certain rights on the moor.

From Western Whittaburrow the line proceeds to Red Lake and the Erme, and crossing the Plym runs on to Siward's Cross, and from thence to South Hisworthy, or, as it is now more often called, Look-Out Tor, and so on to North Hisworthy Tor. This is the commanding eminence which overlooks Princetown on the west, and the visitor to that place will do well to follow the example of the old perambulators and climb to its breezy summit, for he will be rewarded by a view of such extent and of such varied character as is not often to be obtained. The line proceeds from Hisworthy to Great Mis Tor, a truly magnificent pile of granite rocks, which the sojourner at Princetown should also endeavour to visit. Across the Walkham the Perambulators made their way, and so on to Lynch Tor, and Western Red Lake which they followed to the Tavy, and then proceeding to Rattlebrook foot they ascended that stream, and passing over the ridge descended to Sandy Ford on the West Ockment. Across the heathery sweep that stretches from the summit of High Willes southerly, to a tributary of the stream just named, they pursued their course to the upper waters of the Black-a-vain Brook, which they followed to the East Ockment. Thence over the hill on which is the fine range of tors near Belstone, and down to the Taw, at the foot of the hill of Cosdon, whence they set out.'

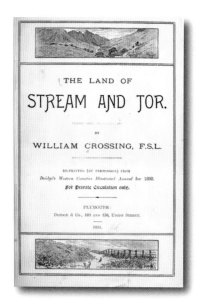

The title page of John Page's An Exploration of Dartmoor and its Antiquities.

1892 – John Lloyd Warren Page – "An Exploration of Dartmoor and Its Antiquities". Page's aim in producing this book, which followed the layout chosen by S Rowe before and that has been copied by Crossing and Hemery since (namely a historical introduction followed by the

---

[10]A frank admission on the part of one of Dartmoor's pre-eminent writers that might have been taken hard by previous writers, especially members of the TDA, who had worked hard to transcribe what they found sometimes using their knowledge of etymology as a guide.

description of excursions on a district by district basis), was to 'arouse in the public mind a greater interest'… of the Moor. It added nothing new to our understanding of the history of the people and artefacts of the Moor but did describe them in clear simple terms. He included mention of the need for delineating the bounds of the Forest and reprinted the descriptions of the 1240 (Latin) and 1609 (Old English) Perambulation writs and returns contained in Rowe's book. He also repeated the venville rights explained by Moore and introduced the likelihood that tin was extracted and traded well before Roman occupation, possibly with the Phoenicians.

1896 – J Brooking Rowe – Third Edition of "A Perambulation of the Antient and Royal Forest of Dartmoor and the Venville Precincts". This edition included the same route perambulation descriptions as his uncle had in the 1848 edition.

1896 – S Baring-Gould – "Dartmoor Idylls". Baring-Gould gathered together eleven of the old folk tales associated with places on Dartmoor such as the 'Snaily House' near Bellever, 'Jolly Lane Cot' above Hexworthy and 'John and Joan' which conjured up a vivid picture of the Tavy Cleave in mid-winter.

1900 – S Baring-Gould – "A Book of Dartmoor". Baring-Gould noted that probably no other tract of land of the same extent in England contained such numerous and well-preserved remains of prehistoric antiquity as Dartmoor. The curious feature about them was that they all belonged to one period, that of the early-Bronze Age (in Britain 2700 – 700 BC). Not a trace had been found so far of the peoples who intervened between these primitive occupants and the medieval tin-miners. Iron had been introduced a couple of centuries before the Christian era but no marks of its use could be found on the moor. This could only be accounted for by the fact that Dartmoor was a virtually depopulated area between the Bronze Age and medieval times. It was not even mentioned in the Domesday Book, nor mined for tin by the Romans (no Roman coins – except two brought by French prisoners during the Napoleonic wars – or pottery had ever been found) and there were no traces of Saxon cattle driving over the moors.

1901 – William Crossing – "One Hundred Years on Dartmoor". Crossing printed the summonses for the 1240 and 1609 Perambulations (as per Rowe) and then added a list of boundmarks for the boundary as 'recognised' but not published by the Duchy 'today'. In some places, that list varied somewhat from the routes of 1240 and 1609 as interpreted by other authorities. Indeed he used names, such as 'Stone Tor' and 'King-de-Stone' that are not seen anywhere else. Note that he excluded the top of Cosdon as a mete. He quotes as his authorities a Mr W. Burt and a Mr Shillibeer and noted that NT Carrington had included the bound marks in the introduction to his book about Dartmoor.

F J Widgery's painting of the menhir at Merivale illustrated the jacket of the 1985 reprint of Rowe's Perambulation, edited by J Brooking Rowe. We should be grateful to this author in that he persuaded the well renowned West Country artist, F J Widgery, to paint some two dozen lovely watercolour pictures to illustrate his 1896 edition. The originals are now held by the Royal Albert Museum, Exeter and are occasionally exhibited.

'From a place called Chapel End, on the East Ockment, adjoining Halstock manor, in the parish of Okehampton, to Belston Tors, Cosdon (the foot of the hill), Hound Tor, straight line to Thurston, or Stone Tor, Woodlake Head, or Wottes Brook, across Little Teign (or South Teign) to King-de-Stone, Heath Stone, King's Oven, on by the Wallabrook, to the east Dart. On to Dartmeet, thence by West Dart to Wobrook Foot. Wobrook, Drylake Foot, Corfield Ford, Knattleborough, Western Wellabrook Head, Western Wellabrook, Huntingdon Cross, Eastern Whitaburrow, Western Whitaburrow, Red Lake Foot, Hux lake, Erme Head, Plym Head, straight to Eylesbarrow, Nuns' Cross, South Hisworthy Tor, Prince Town Enclosures west side, Miss. Tor, cross Walkham to Dead Lake Head, Limsboro' Western Red Lake Head, to Rattle Brook Foot, Rattle Brook Head to Steng-a-tor, or Sourton Tor, Lang-a-Ford, High Willes, Rough Tor to Halstock Manor and Chapel End.'

William Crossing's One Hundred Years on Dartmoor.

Crossing mentioned that where the forest boundary line differed now from the earlier perambulations it

'will invariably be found that it has been thrust back – that the bounds of the Venville commons have in fact, been extended, and an encroachment has taken place. But the fact of the Venville commoners choosing to regard the forest boundary line as being placed otherwise than where the ancient records say it should be, of course gives them no title to the parts of the Forest which they claim, boundary-stones notwithstanding. The Duchy authorities maintain their rights by driving every year the whole of the Forest and Commons to which they lay claim'.

1902 – William Crossing – "The Ancient Stone Crosses of Dartmoor". Here Crossing again mentioned the perambulations of 1240 and 1609 but did not define the routes. He did note that Siward's Cross had been named as a boundary mark for the perambulation. He also reported that the cross, the tallest on the moor, was thrown down and broken in 1846 but was repaired and re-erected before 1848. He referred to an 'ancient map', most likely the one now held at Sowton, and stated that it cannot date to 1240 – it shows the Abbey Church of Buckland which was not founded until 1278 – but to the middle or latter part of the 15th century because of the handwriting.

1905 – William Crossing – "Gems in a Granite Setting". In this book, Crossing constantly referred to Dartmoor as the 'Forest' and described it beauties within its four *'Quarters'*. When a *'gem'* he described was a boundmark of the forest, he made mention of this fact. It seems that he might have regarded the list of boundmarks from the 1609 Perambulation as the more authoritative as he noted that Sandy Ford (in the W Okement valley below Kitty Tor and Fordsland Ledge) was a *'point marking the boundary'*. This had not been mentioned in 1240. Crossing described Gidleigh Chase in some detail having personal acquaintance with its owner. It is noticeable that he stated that he thought that the upper limit of this chase was the confluence of the N Teign and Wallabrook near the holed stone – i.e. did not include the Galaven Mire.

1905 – John Charles Cox – "The Royal Forests of England". Amongst other forests, Cox described the Forest of Dartmoor using data from Rowe's books and added other references of the outcome of examinations of the forest use in later times.

1906 – Dom Adam Hamilton – "History of St Mary's Abbey of Buckfast". The author added information gained from the Abbey's records to that of other Devonshire Association members. He named several of the knights on the 1240 Perambulation and provided some other interesting details about their holdings and lives.

1912 – William Crossing – "Crossing's Guide to Dartmoor". This book, regarded by many as the 'Bible' for moor walkers, followed the outline adopted by earlier authors, namely a general introduction of facets of moorland history followed by descriptions of interesting points in various parts of the moor. He shortened the descriptions of both the 1240 and 1609 perambulations to just named key points. He also included a description of the bounds accepted by the Duchy at that time. The bounds he printed are as follows:

[1240] *'Hogam de Cossdonne – Parva Hundetorre – Thurlestone – Wotesbrokelakesfote – Heighestone – Langestone – Turbarium de Alberysheved – Wallebroke – Furnum Regis – Wallebrokeshede – Wallebroke usque cadit in Dertam – per Dertam usque ad aliam Dertam – per aliam Dertam ascendendo usque – Okebrokysfote – ascendendo Okebroke usque ad – la Dryeworks – Dryfeld Ford – Battyshull – Caput de Wester Wellabrook – Wester Wellabroke usque cadit in Avenam –*

William Crossing's Gems in a Granite Setting.

Ester Whyteburghe – Redelake – Grymsgrove – Elysburghe – Crucem Sywardi – Ysfother – aliam Ysfother – Mystor – Mewyburghe – Lullingesfote – Rakernesbrokysfote – la Westsolle – Ernestorre – vadum proximum in orientali parte capelle Sancti Michaelis de Halgestoke – Hogam de Cossdonne.'

[1609] *'Casdon – Little Houndetore – Thurlestone or Waterdonntorr – Wotesbrooklakefoote (at that time called Whoodelake) – Hingeston or Highstone – Yeston, or Geston (at that time called Hethstone) – Turfehill – Kinge's Oven – Wallebrookeheade – by Wallebrooke to Easter Dart – thence to Wester Dart – thence to Wobroovefoote – Drylake – Crefeildf-ford or Dryefeild ford – Knattleburroughe – Wester Wellebrooke headd – thence by Wester Wellebrooke to Owne, or Aven – Easter Whitaburrowe – Redlake foote whir it falleth into Erme – Arme headd – Plimheadd – Elisboroughe – Seaward's Crosse – Little Hisworthie – another Hisworthie – Mistorrpan – Dedlakeheadd – Luntesborowe – Wester Redlake – Rattlebrooke foote – thence to the headd of the same Rattlebrooke – Steinegtorr – Langaford, or Sandyford – thence to the ford wch lyeth in the east side of the chapple of Halstocke – Cosdon.'*

[Present Day] *'Foot of Cosdon, where Small Brook falls into the Taw the line runs over Metheral Hill to White Moor Stone and thence to Little Hound Tor – Wild Tor Well – Thurlestone, or Watern Tor – Hew Thorn Clitter – Manga Rock – across the North Teign – Stonetor Hill – Longstone – Woodlake Head, across the South Teign – along Hurston Ridge to King's Oven – Walla Brook Head (near the Warren House Inn) – down the Walla Brook to the East Dart – down the Dart to Dartmeet – up the West Dart to Wo Brook Foot – up the Wo Brook to Dry Lakes – up Dry Lakes and across the hill to Corfield Ford – Knattleborough on Ryder's Hill – West Walla Brook Head – down the West Wella Brook to the Avon – a short distance up the Avon, thence up the hill to Western Whitaburrow – thence to Red Lake Mires – and down Red Lake to the Erme – up the Erme to Erme Head – Boundary Stone – Broad Rock –Plym Head – a short distance down the Plym, and thence to the cairn on Eylesbarrow – Siward's or Nuns' Cross – South Hisworthy Tor – North Hisworthy Tor – Rundle Stone – Great Mis Tor – across the Walkham under Greena Ball – Dead Lake Head – White Barrow – Higher Pile of Lynch Tor – Homer, or Wester Red Lake, a short distance below its source – down Red Lake to the Tavy – down the Tavy to Rattle Brook Foot – up the Rattle Brook to its source – Stinka Tor – Sandy Ford – across Dinger Plain to Curtory Clitters – across the Blackaven under Row Tor then down by the right bank of that stream to Crovenor Steps – up the hill to the summit of the Belstone ridge, to a point just north of Winter Tor, down the further side, and across the Taw Plain to the starting point at the confluence of the Taw and Small Brook.'*

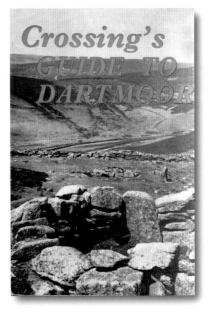

Crossing's Guide to Dartmoor – the 1965 edition with an introduction by Brian Le Messurier.

Crossing added the following comments:

'That the bounds recognised by the Duchy are the true ones, or at all events are much nearer to the true ones, than those that the commoners contend are correct, there cannot be a doubt. The perambulation of 1240, and the surveys of the forest made since that date, show this to be the case. Nothing can be clearer, for instance, that the line drawn from Eastern Whitaburrow to the Erme by the jurors of 1609. They name the boundary as running from the Avon to Eastern Whitaburrow 'and from thence lineallie to Redlake Foote whir it falleth into Erme.' Now the boundary line, as contended for by the commoners, leaves Eastern Whitaburrow outside the forest altogether, and running to Western Whitaburrow goes thence to Red Lake – not, however, to its foot as the jurors say, but nearly to its head. By this very convenient arrangement a considerable portion of the forest has been claimed by the commoners

as belonging to Brent, Ugborough and Harford Moors. The fact that they do so does not, however, make this tract less a part of the forest, and the Duchy maintain their rights over it, and over all other disputed tracts, by annually driving them for estrays.'

R Hansford Worth.

Dartmoor: A New Study *edited by Crispin Gill.*

1921 – Cecil Torr – "Small Talk at Wreyland". In this book Torr gave a charming example of his need to pay the Duchy half a crown per annum for his Venvill right of owning Hurston.

1953 – R Hansford Worth – "Dartmoor". In the chapter called 'The Tenants and Commoners of Devon', Worth presumed that the forest was perambulated earlier in 1224 following the issue of a statute by Henry III but noted that no evidence has been found of this. He expanded on the rights of those: in the Forest; on the Commons of Devon; the venville men[11]; and in the *'Rest of Devon'*. He went on to explain how the men of Devon would have regarded the holding of land private to the King, a forest, as *'burdensome'* but, in mitigation, there were some *'public rights'*. One charter clause allowed that cattle could be driven onto the forest by day but there would be a charge made for any that stayed overnight. Thus this public right was limited to the advantage of the King. Records show that by 1627 there were thirty-five *'Ancient Tenements'* within the Forest itself, the holders having the right of *'customary freehold'*. They had rights but also obligations to the King and generally were better placed than those outside the Forest. They enjoyed one particular right – *'newtake'* – whereby an heir to an ancient tenement could enclose eight acres of the forest for his sole use. This would always have been an irritant to the commoners and by the 17th century resulted in many enquiries as the limit of eight acres was often flouted – one such being the enclosure of one hundred and seventy-five acres! The Commons of Devon stretched from the forest boundary to cornditches and leap/lid gates and the rights of those living therein were often the cause of friction if not violence from at least 15th century. The jury of 1609 made mention of the difficulties as they had to respect what had become accepted as *'rights'* by those in the many parishes and manors in contact with the forest boundaries.

1958 – EW Martin – "Dartmoor". In Chapter VI, 'Dartmoor Forest and the Commons of Devon', Martin restated much of what Hansford-Worth had said earlier, about the rights and responsibilities of those in, around and using the forest. He, too, pointed out the centuries of bickering that had gone on about where exactly the boundary lay.

1970 – Crispin Gill – "Dartmoor: A New Study". Gill's stated aim in bringing together articles from colleagues was to present a 'survey of modern knowledge of Dartmoor'. John Somers Cocks wrote an appendix to this book that made a *'fresh'* attempt to identify the 1240 route but he seemed to err towards a description of the likely 1609 route. Prior to the printing of this book, Somers Cocks wrote two articles printed in 'Devon and Cornwall Notes and Queries – 1965–1967' in which he sought to explain why the civil and ecclesiastical boundaries of the forest differed, especially in the area of the Gallaven Mire. He described what he supposed was the route in 1240 but we should note that his ideas about the boundary, especially in the area of Gidleigh, altered between his first article in 1965 and this book printed in 1970. This short appendix dismissed the work of many previous researchers without giving reasons or alternatives and has only been included here for the sake of completeness as it is the most recent attempt at a new interpretation found.

[11] The rights of the venville men were probably first described clearly as part of an inquisition of 1382. In short, they were allowed to graze animals on the forest freely by day but only on payment of an annual fee if allowed to stay overnight and could take certain other items such as peat, turf and stones. Where venville areas did not abut the forest boundary, corridors of up to four miles in length were used across the commons to reach the forest. And, by building pounds for their animals to occupy at night on the commons but outside the forest, they could avoid payment to the Duchy. As well as rights, they also had responsibilities such as attending court, possibly in Lydford, as often as three times a year.

'Cosdon – Hound Tor – Watern Tor – Woodlake – Longstone – Heath-stone – Metherall Marsh – King's Oven. From the (genuine) Walla Brook down to the East Dart – Dartmeet – up the West Dart to the O Brook. Left the O Brook at Drywork – ran up to Dryfield, alias Crefield Ford – Ryder's Hill – down the Western Wellabrook to the Avon – Eastern Whitaburrow – Redlake Foot – the now vanished Grymsgrove was in the hollow by Erme Head – Eylesbarrow – Syward's or Nuns' Cross – South Hessary Tor – North Hessary Tor – Great Mis Tor – White Barrow – Lynch Tor – Rattlebrook foot – Rattlebrook head – Stenga Tor – Yes Tor – Cullever Steps – summit of Cosdon.'

Somers Cocks asserted that the Duchy line was *'very nearly correct'*.
1983 - Eric Hemery – "High Dartmoor Land and People". In this tome, Hemery described the probable route undertaken in 1240 and the newer interpretations that described possible encroachments in the areas of the Gallaven Mire, Eastern Whitaburrow, Broad Rock and Bagga Tor.
1986 – Helen Harris – (Ed ERR Green) "The Industrial Archaeology of the British Isles". This book included a useful map of the peat passes of northern Dartmoor. The existence of the passes shows us today that it is possible to access most of the area of the forest but that some portions deserve extra care.
1986 – RA Skelton and PDA Harvey – "Local Maps and Plans from Medieval England". The authors, with assistance from J Somers Cocks, provided a history, description, photographs and a detailed description of the map referred to by Rowe and now at DHC, Sowton. They listed the boundmarks shown on the map (using spellings not seen else-where) as follows:

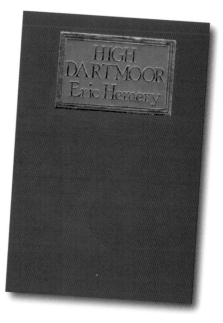

Eric Hemery's High Dartmoor.

'Howndetorre, Therlestone, Wotesbrokeslake, Tenge, Heghstone, Lange-stone, Alberyshede, Wellebroke, Furnum regis, Capud wallebroke, East Derte, Wester Derte, Okysbroke, Dryworke, Dryfeldforde, Catteshille, Westerwelbrokishede, Auena, Esterwhiteburgh, Rodelake, Erme, Grymes-greue, … (erased), Elysburgh, Crux Sywardy, hysfoder, … (erased), … hysfoder, … (erased), Mystorre[pan], Caput de walkham, Mewyburgh, Lullyngyssete, Caout de Tauy, Rakernebrokeshede, Westsolle, Ernestorre, Hoga de Cosdonne.'

They drew the conclusion that the map should best be considered to be in three parts. Firstly, the basic purpose of the map was to show the southern portion of the Moor, the commons near Harford and Ugbor-ough parishes. Both these parishes were shown in some detail and most noticeably had 'extraordinary' shapes in order to provide an actual boundary with the forest itself. The second portion is the country to the south and west of Dartmoor where less detail was shown. Thirdly, the circular rendering of the Forest itself was almost cartoon-like - being distorted to maintain the circle. It did show the rivers quite plainly. They noted that on the dorse of the map is a recital of the forest bounds of 1240 and statements about the rights of the Commons of Devon from 1199 and 1252. They estimated that the map came into existence around 1500 - possibly created by copying details from an earlier doc-ument or documents.
1987 – Bill Ransom – "Dartmoor's Greatest Walk". Ransom's pocket sized walkers' guidebook used Rowe's description of the boundary but also mentioned other possible interpretations of the route.
1988 - Andrew Fleming – "The Dartmoor Reaves". Fleming's most valuable research showed the probable extent of settlement and farm-ing in the Bronze Age. This might well provide clues as to why the per-ambulators stayed so deep within the area of Dartmoor, e.g. they did not take in Hamel Down. If one considers the evidence that by 1240

Andrew Fleming's The Dartmoor Reaves.

climatic changes had already made areas originally cultivated in the Bronze Age suitable for farming again, the perambulators probably sought to avoid including such areas within the forest. [Comment – we will see they were largely but not completely successful].

1988 – Grenville Astill and Anne Grant – (Editors) "The Countryside of Medieval England" Blackwell. This work with its combination of archaeological survey and documentary evidence showed that some areas of what are now regarded as high moor were probably populated and cultivated in the 11th and 12th century. Indeed, in the period 1150 to 1250 climatologists had identified a 'warm epoch' when winters were milder and wetter and summers drier and warmer. Such climatic conditions would have moved the cultivation level up the slopes of the moor's fringes and of sheltered valleys. There was evidence of crop rotation in moorland fields and heavy use of trackways giving access to adjacent moorland from this time. However, this usage and increased surface drainage probably contributed to the decline in fertility of the soil and subsequent abandonment of these areas for all except grazing. [Comment – from this evidence, it is possible to postulate that in 1240, at the time of the first perambulation, the land areas previously earmarked by the Bronze Age reaves might well have been fertile enough to have been in use once again.] We are also reminded that at this time, the average life expectancy even for noblemen was only 22-28 years. So, memories were never long!

1992 - Helen Harris – "The Industrial Archaeology of Dartmoor". Harris's work did not concern itself with the perambulations but did describe the impact of changes after them and so aids any understanding of what the perambulators would have seen – such as the fact that the peat passes on the northern moor were only built between 1895 and 1905 at the behest of Frank Philpotts.

2002 - Mary R Ravenhill and Margery M Rowe – "Devon Maps and Map Makers Before 1840". This catalogue of known maps had brief notes about nine maps relating to Dartmoor. It described and attempted to date the map now held in the DHC, Sowton.

2002 – Dave Brewer – "Dartmoor Boundary Markers". Brewer's work is probably the best modern précis of the history relating to the various boundaries I have read. Brewer described the bounds taking as a start point Rowe's description of the 1240 and 1609 events. He referred to the map held at DHC, Sowton, described by C Spence Bate and added to it a detailed knowledge of the stones now delineating the present parish boundaries. He also gained access to various Ordnance Survey (OS) Boundary Report Books and maps predating the OS. He collated a wealth of information about the boundary markers that abound on Dartmoor. His 1986 'classic' work "Boundary Markers On and Around Dartmoor" went out of print in the 1990s and he continued to research the subject up until his death in 1998. His final notes were put in order and published by his widow in 2002. Whilst most of the book concentrated on the boundaries of parishes around the Moor, one chapter was devoted to the Forest boundary itself and neatly summarised most, but not all, previous studies. His examination of the bounds showed how they have *'changed over the centuries'*. He firmly believed that, in general, the surrounding parishes have encroached upon the ancient bounds. Strangely, in a case where such an encroachment might seem most likely, that of the Gallaven Mire, he did not hold this view. His description of the route probably taken in 1240 used few boundmarks, as follows:

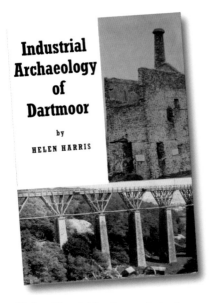

Helen Harris' Industrial Archaeology of Dartmoor.

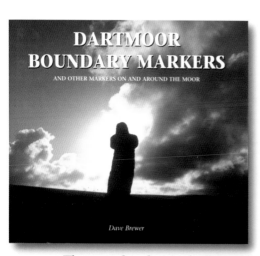

The second and revised edition of Dartmoor Boundary Markers *by Dave Brewer.*

> *'Summit of Cosdon - Hound Tor - Watern Tor – Longstone - Heath Stone – Turfhill - Cairn at King's Oven - Down the Wallabrook into the East Dart – Dartmeet - O Brook Foot - Yonder Drylake - Dryfeild ford - Ryder's Hill - Down the Wella Brook to the Avon - Eastern Whittabarrow? -*

Western Whittabarrow - Grimsgrove/Erme Head (being one and the same) – Eylesbarrow - Nun's Cross - South Hessary Tor - follow the reaves to North Hessary Tor - Great Mis Tor - across Greena Ball and Walkham to Dead Lake foot - Dead Lake head - White Barrow - Limsborough cairn near Lynch Tor - Ascend the Rattlebrook – Stengator - Ernestorre - Chapel Ford – Cosdon.'

2004 – Michael Hedges – "Walking the Forest Bounds of Dartmoor". This was another straightforward black and white pocket sized walking guide laid out in twelve stages retracing the probable 1609 route as described by Samuel Rowe. Hedges made no mention of any possible variations of the route.

2006 – Sam Turner – "Medieval Devon and Cornwall – Shaping an Ancient Countryside". Turner gave us a history of the likely human impacts upon Devon and Cornwall before and during the medieval period. Of interest to us are five of his main topics:

Firstly, he mentioned that Aveton Giffard was probably a community of small, scattered farmsteads unlike nearby Bigbury that was a nucleated village. It was entirely possible therefore that one of the perambulating knights, Richard Giffard, may have had a direct interest as one of 'his' community's farms would most likely have used land on Dartmoor. Secondly, he concluded that most of the two counties would have been affected by human activity at some point, even the high ground, and thus boundaries (such as reaves) would have been present from the 7th century. Thirdly he noted that most of the medieval parish churches were founded during the early Middle Ages (AD500 to AD1000) starting as burial grounds or small manorial chapels for instance. Of course, the existence of a church did not signify that a parish, with its associated roles and responsibilities, was a fact of everyday life at this time. Fourthly, he described the castles of the region and whilst noting that some may have disappeared altogether, offered a map of the known sites. These could be significant for us where they are close to the forest boundary. The perambulators most likely started from Okehampton Castle and others could have been used as stops en route. The castles were of many forms from stone built, e.g. Okehampton and Lydford, to motte and bailey such as at Hembury.

Finally, he discussed tin-working from 1150 onwards. He noted that the stannaries operated from 1201 and that tin production in Devon was greater than in Cornwall in the second half of the 12th century. Thus the perambulators probably passed tinners in the streamworks on Soussons Down after passing King's Oven; above the Oke Brook below Ryder's Hill; and in the upper reaches of the Erme and Plym.

2006 – Patricia Milton – "The Discovery of Dartmoor". Milton offered a succinct history of the moor in the 13th century. Two areas covered are of interest to us. The first was the inclusion of an early map of the moor produced by Donn in 1765. This was remarkable in that it showed little of the detail on the present OS maps and the names of major features shown often differ from today's names, e.g. 'Limsborrow' for Lynch Tor, 'Hampster Tor' for High Willhays and Peter Cross Tor for Western White Barrow. The other was the description of the rights and duties or costs of those living on or adjacent to the forest and those in 'venville'.

2009 – Ian Mercer – "Dartmoor". As a past Chief Officer of the Dartmoor National Park Authority, Mercer wrote about the natural history of the moor in great depth. He also conjectured what might happen to the flora and fauna if farming practices alter (i.e. if financial pressures bring the need for changes) and what parts of the moor might have looked like in the past. He also brought us right up to date about the acceptance by the Duchy in 1967 to accept the registration of the 'Forest' as common under the Commons Registration Act of 1965.

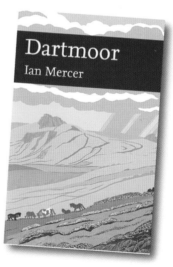

Ian Mercers' Dartmoor.

Chapter 6

Transactions of the Devonshire Association

The Devonshire Association is a learned society formed in 1862. It is still active and its members are dedicated to the study of subjects linked to Devon in the fields of science, literature and the arts. The members meet once a year and present papers that are then recorded in an annual record – the "Transactions of the Devonshire Association". These are available in many libraries and recently have been scanned and now appear on-line. For the purposes of this study, work undertaken in the 19th century with relation to Dartmoor has been used mainly.

There is much interleaving of the work recorded in the transactions and books written in the same period. Presented here in chronological order is a quick digest of the articles most relevant to this study. The views expressed in some of these articles seem sound whilst some seem far-fetched. It is left to the reader to decide which views to support and which might now be challenged.

1871 – C Spence Bate "On the Prehistoric Antiquities of Dartmoor" – TDA Vol 4 pp 491-502. In this article Spence Bate referred to Samuel Rowe's book of 1848 and the latter's description of Grimspound. He also mentioned in passing that a perambulation occurred in 1240; and that the word 'Forest' here did not indicate a region of trees.

1872 – C Spence Bate "On the Original Map of the Royal Forest of Dartmoor", Illustrating the Perambulation of Henry III, 1240" – TDA Vol 5 pp 510-548. Whilst earlier descriptions of the 1240 Perambulation (such as by Samuel Rowe in 1848) referred to writs and returns, this article was the first major recorded attempt at describing and deciphering a fascinating map of Dartmoor found by Spence Bate which showed the Forest boundary. It was subsequently referred to by Samuel Rowe's nephew, J Brooking Rowe, in a reprint (1896) of his uncle's book as being held in the Albert (now Royal Albert Memorial) Museum. The map is now archived at the Devon Heritage Centre (DHC), Sowton, Exeter. The article included an excellent tracing from the original. As well as describing the map and the text on its obverse, Spence Bate attempted to interpret both the words and the map to divine the metes and bounds. He guessed that the map was dated 1240 but this is unlikely as has been described by later writers.

Spence Bate's depiction of the map now held at the Devon Heritage Centre, Exeter.

1876 – J B Davidson "Some Anglo Saxon Boundaries" – TDA Vol 8 pp 396-406. Davidson mentioned a Latin record printed by Hooker that was the same one as described by C Spence Bate above (for the 1240 Perambulation) and described the rights and privileges of bordering parishes associated with their use of the Forest land.

1879 – Robert Dymond "Historical Documents Relating to Dartmoor (Thirteenth and Fourteenth Century)" – TDA Vol 11 pp 371-382. Dymond provided a list of the ancient documents relating to perambulations owned or known to him, some, but not all, of which had been used by Samuel Rowe. He mentioned that the map described by Spence Bate had been dated by the Albert (now Royal Albert Memorial) Museum, Exeter, as of the 14th century but it could be 15th century. He also included notes about possible interpretations of the names of places and people mentioned in the documents and possible alternative spellings or modern equivalents. This included the view that if *'Hoga de Cosdonne'* was meant to be read as *'Haga de Cosdonne'*, it would have meant the boundary of rather than the top of Cosdon and that the word *'haga'* had been used in several old perambulation returns. Also mentioned was a letter from Rev. J H Mason noting that *'no man on horseback could get from Ermehead to Plymhead. I imagine, and I speak from local knowledge, that the forest bounds were fixed that they should be approachable on horseback'*.

1887 – W F Collier "Venville Rights on Dartmoor" – TDA Vol 19 pp 377-385. Collier explained that a *'chace'* [sic] was an area for hunting that the King had bestowed upon a subject – in 1239 this was Henry's brother, Richard, Earl of Cornwall and since 1336 has been the Duke of Cornwall, the Prince of Wales. He supposed that the preservation of such an area by the Normans for red deer for themselves would have been seen as *'cruel and arbitrary'* and Devonshiremen would have been against this. He imagined the moor in *'English'* times, i.e. pre-Norman, and explained the probable origination of the use of the word *'vil'*, meaning a community with rights – such as the *'rights of common'*. In noting that *'…the vils were granted to lords of manors by the Conqueror and his successors … and the parishes were in course of time formed'* Collier opined two important observations. One was that the manor boundaries did not lie flush with the perambulated forest boundary, the land in-between with its *'valuable pasturage'* being known as the *'Devonshire Commons'*. The other was that parishes were not yet formed in 1240. He also mentioned that since 1240, the church with its parishes had taken on the responsibility for much of the communal work previously the remit of the Manor and had extended the parish holdings up to the boundaries of the forest. He also described the present duties and rights of the Duchy of Cornwall. His tone was very much one of someone with a grievance at that time, as he noted that the Duchy exercised the right of drift at arbitrary times, not only on the forest but also on the Devonshire Commons. This attitude was indicative of the ongoing tussle over the rights arising from 'ownership' of the Devonshire Commons and he urged the men of Devonshire to join the Dartmoor Preservation Society to *'protect their own rights'*.

1889 – Robert Burnard "The Great Central Trackway on Dartmoor" – TDA Vol 21 pp 431-436. Burnard noted that the line of the ancient track of the title had been traced running east-west from *'Hamildon'* to *'Cocks Tor'* and was supposed to be a continuation of the Roman Fosse Way. However, as it did not appear on the ancient map (now in the DHC) and is not mentioned in any record of a perambulation, it was supposed to have fallen into disuse after the end of the Roman occupation. This would give an indication that Dartmoor at that time was a mostly uninhabited place of little value, i.e. there was no trade necessitating the use of a road.

1889 – W F Collier "The Duchy of Cornwall on Dartmoor" – TDA Vol 21 pp 289-299. It can be deduced from Collier's rather wordy article that there were three main parties with a direct interest in the position of the Forest boundary. Firstly, the Lords of the Manors – who lived in the vils or manors adjacent to the forest or commons surrounding the forest and who paid a fixed annual rent or fine to the Crown – *'fines villarum'*. They would have benefited by any alteration of the boundary such that their manor (later the parish) expanded. Secondly, the Men

Robert Burnard.

65

of Devonshire – who would have paid for pasturing animals within the forest on a per head basis for horses and bullocks and by the score for sheep. They would not have had to pay such a rent for use of common land and thus would not want such land engulfed by the forest. Thirdly, the Duchy – which itself benefited from the use of the forest. These useful notes were not the main agenda pursued in the article. Collier expressed despair that the Duchy had allowed so much of the forest and common land to be enclosed with *'no profitable purpose'* and, in so doing denied that land to venvil and the Devonshire men's useful purposes. Despite stating in his introduction that he wanted to explain the Duchy's rights, once again he took the stance that he hoped the Duchy would change its attitude and act more responsibly for both the good of the public as well as its own self-interest.

1890 – Arthur B Prowse "The Neighbourhood of Taw Marsh, North Dartmoor" – TDA Vol 22 pp 185-199. Prowse in this article and another two years later made a real effort to explain possible alternatives to the boundary as it was accepted at that time. In this first article, he quoted the boundmarks given by Rowe for both the 1240 and 1609 perambulations in the *'Northern Quarter'* and, using his *'knowledge of etymology'*, made a different interpretation of the likely boundary at several points. Some of his article is repeated here:

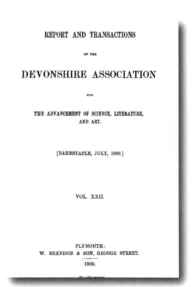

REPORT AND TRANSACTIONS

OF THE

DEVONSHIRE ASSOCIATION

FOR

THE ADVANCEMENT OF SCIENCE, LITERATURE, AND ART.

[BARNSTAPLE, JULY, 1890.]

VOL. XXII.

PLYMOUTH:
W. BRENDON & SON, GEORGE STREET.
1890.

Title page of Vol 22 of the 1890 Transactions.

"I will now consider briefly the Forest boundary in the "North Quarter" of the Moor, which is as a rule held to meet the West Quarter not far from the point where the Rattlebrook joins the Tavy at the south end of Amicombe Hill. The limits as set down in the Perambulations of 1240 and 1609, will first be quoted from Rowe's (1848) edition:
1240
'Ad Rakernesbrokysfote, et sic ad caput ejusdem aque, et deinde linealiter usque ad la Westsolle, et inde linealiter usque ad Ernestorre, et inde linealiter usque ad vadum proximum in orientali parte capelle Sancti Michaelis de Halgestoke, et inde linealiter usque ad predictam hogam de Cossdonne in orientali parte.'

'The officials began the round "ad Hogam de Cossdonne et inde linealiter usque ad parvam hogam que vocatur parva Hundetorre, et inde linealiter usque ad Thurlestone et inde linealiter usque ad Wotesbroke-lakesfote que cadit in Tyng.'
1609
'Northward to Rattlebroke foote and soe from thence to the headd of the same Rattlebrooke, and soe from thence linyallie unto Steinegtorr, and so from thence linyallie to the ford which lyeth in the east side of the chapple of Halstocke and so from thence linyallie unto the said hill called Cosdon al's Cosson, wher they did begin.'

'Beginning at the high hill lying in the north quarter of the said fforest, called at this day Cosdon, al's Cosson, and in the old records written Hoga de Costdonne, and from thence lineally eastward by esti-macion one mile or more unto little houndetorre which in the said records is called 'hoga de parva houndetorr,' and from thence lineallia to a place named in the said records Thurlestone, now as they suppose called Waterdontorr, being about three quarters of a myle from the Houndtorr aforesaid, and from thence near a myle to Wotesbrookelake-foote which falleth into Teynge, and which lake they thincke to be the same which is now called Whoodelake.'

'From the confluence of the Tavy with the Rattlebrook the boundary runs nearly three miles due north along the latter stream as far as its source near Hunt Tor. From this point to the nearest of the fords on the east side of the land owned or pertaining to the chapel of Saint Michael of Halstock, the forest bounds mentioned differ in the two accounts.'

'The earlier one gives "La Westsolle" and "Ernestorre" as intervening

points while the latter gives "Steinegtorr" and "Langaford" alias "Sandy-ford." The derivation of these words may help us to fix upon the places they refer to: for these old names almost always describe faithfully some marked physical feature of the object to which they are given.'

'The first, "La Westsolle", is plainly a Keltic name in a Norman dress, and means "the west head," from slol. I identify it with what is now called "Forstand Ledge", the abrupt rocky south-west end of the towering mass which rises into Yestor and High Willis. It is about 1930 feet above sea level.'

'Ernestorre" may, I think, be traced to the Keltic yr ynys twr, 'the island tor'. Possibly this word is an early form of Yestor; Ernestorre becoming Estor by the accentuation of the penultimate syllable, and the slurring-over followed by the elision of the first one in accordance with the well-known Keltic tendency to the suppression of unaccented sylla-bles. The final result, Yestor, being due to the West Country tendency to prefix a y to words beginning with vowel or aspirate, as in the case of yarth for earth, yether for heather. I am the more inclined to this deri-vation of Yestor because it certainly describes the idea of its insulation, suggested by the appearance of the tor from the border lowlands to the north and west. From other points of view it would have been relatively rarely seen.'

'The third name, 'Steinegtorr', may be from the Saxon Stan – stone, and ig or eg – island; and, if so, it is probably but an alternative form for Ernestorre. Rowe, on page 198, mentions Stengator alias Steincator, as being at the north end of Amicombe Hill. These names are plainly forms of Steinegtor, for the transposition of letters in a word is a very common thing in rustic speech (and typing!!). On the new six-inch Ordnance map also is marked "Stinkator" (evidently a further corruption of the name); it is on the verge of the deep gorge of the West Okement River, just opposite to Forstand Ledge. I do not believe that this tor is the original "Steinegtor", for its physical features do not agree with those suggested by what seems to me a reasonable derivation. It is also an insignificant landmark compared with the other points not far off, and is very near the preceding forest-bound, in point of fact little over half a mile from it.'

'The names "Sandyford" and "Langaford" (i.e. the long ford), seem to define fairly well the characters of the next boundary (though one may remark that all fords in a granite district are likely to be sandy), and after careful consideration I have come to the conclusion that a ford over the Blackaven Brook is meant, rather more than half a mile below the old bridge at the foot of East Miltor.'

'In accordance with the views just put forward, the forest boundary would have formerly passed from the head of the Rattlebrook north-east across the West Ockment to Forstand Ledge; then to Yestor, and the ford over the Blackaven; and so on to Cullever Steps.'

'From this point it is said in the Perambulations to go to Cosdon; and if in a direct course it must have passed over the Belstone Tor ridge near the line now marked by the so-called Irishman's wall.'

'The question now arises "What part of Cosdon was taken by the officials as the forest-limit, the summit or some point at the foot?" I think it most probable that in 1240 the summit was the starting point; but as will be seen further on, in 1609, the evidence points to the western foot of the hill, just where the Taw River leaves its marshy valley – i.e. the horseshoe bend in the river.'

'From Cosdon to the "foot" or end of "Wotesbrokelake" (or "Whood-elake"?) the boundary line is uncertain; and the account of 1609 is very inaccurate if the line followed were at all like that now marked on the Ordnance map, which is a point of fact nowhere touches Cosdon.'

'In the first place we read that the boundary goes "lineallie eastward

by estimacion one mile or more unto little Houndetorre". What is now known as Hound Tor is more than one and a half miles in a bee-line south by west of the top of Cosdon; but if the western foot of Cosdon were the starting-point, the 1609 account would seem rather more accurate for Hound Tor lies S/S/E of the most likely starting-point, i.e. just where there are two good fords over the Taw. ***What effect has the new reservoir had on the river and fords? The 1240 document speaks of "the little hill which is called little Hundetorre", so it would seem that there must have been a great Hundetorre also. A hill between the present Hound Tor and Cosdon, crowned by the tumulus mentioned previously seems best to answer the description of the "little hill". It is distant from the fords one and a quarter miles in a S.E. direction.'

'The next point mentioned in the 1240 document is "Thurlestone" which the 1609 jurors thought must mean "Waterdontorr"; and modern writers seem to have fallen in with this idea because of the appearance of a part of the rocky crest of Watern Tor as it is now called. Two of the granite piles incline towards each other in somewhat different planes; and so, from a distance, there seems to be a hole through the rocky mass. Now the Anglo-Saxon for hole was thyrel; and this word appears in such compounds as Nosthyrl (Anglo Saxon) or Nosethirle (Medieval English); modern, Nostril. In using the phrase, "to drill a hole" the same root is employed as a verb. Now, since holes usually have an outline that is more or less circular, I see no incongruity in the application of then same word to denote a circle; and the "Thurlestone" of 1240 may surely have meant "circle of stones" or "stone circle". The name Thurlestone appears nowhere on the old one-inch Ordnance maps (1809) of Dartmoor; but in the new six-inch map the Watern Tor rocks are marked "Thirlestone" probably in deference to the suggestion of the 1609 jurors, which has since become the popular belief.'

'There are three stone circles in this area – White Moor in good condition, Scorhill in good condition and one on the side of Buttern Hill – thrown down – why is this one down unless by man's efforts and, if so, why?'

'On the one-inch Geological Survey Map, corrected to 1866, I find the name Thurlestone upon the rising ground called "Kennon Hill" on the new six-inch map; and one would think the geological surveyors must have had the guidance of local usage when they inserted the name on this particular hill, which is three-quarters of a mile ESE. from the tumulus-hill, just now mentioned as possibly being 'little Hundetorre.'

'I am inclined to think that a "sacred circle," or rather its remains (about 25 yards in diameter) which is upon the slope of Buttern Hill, and one and a quarter miles west of Gidleigh Castle, is the "Thurlestone" of the 1240 Perambulation.'

'The next forest-bound mentioned is the "foot", or ending, of a stream called "Wotesbrokelake", which joins the river Teign. This name seems to have been lost locally before 1609, and the jurors thought it might mean a stream then known as "Whoodelake". This name, in its turn, has now vanished; and its derivation and that of the first part of the older name – Wotesbrokelake – is not apparent; so this help to localization is denied us. If, however, I have been right in defining the position of the two preceding bounds, then this Wotesbrokelake would almost certainly be the stream now called Wallabrook, which joins the Teign a short distance south of Gidleigh Circle [now called Scorhill Circle]; or possibly the large affluent of the Wallabrook coming from below Hound Tor.'

'The Forest boundary thus sketched, from the western base of Cosdon to the union of the Wallabrook and Teign deviates widely in its latter part from that now accepted and recorded in the new map; but this cannot be considered strange, for a pushing back of the old bounds has *occurred in comparatively modern times in other parts of the Moor; as I have good reason last year for believing has been the case in the Neighbourhood of White Tor and Great Mistor. The line I have suggested has the recommendation that it avoids sharp angular bends, and by a gradual turning follows the direction of the moorland towards the next landmark in the "East Quarter".'*

1892 – Arthur B Prowse "The Bounds of the Forest of Dartmoor" – TDA Vol 24 pp 418-430. Prowse continued his previous work by producing a table starting with Rowe's lists of the boundmarks (from both 1240 and 1609) to which he added lists of the many variations of the names used by historians which came from other documents and from the recollections of local people (remembering that they had been first transcribed and then later translated). He also added any intervening points mentioned in subsequent inquiries. It is notable that some of the variations between what was accepted as the boundary in 1609 and what it might have been in 1240 are quite significant – the exclusion of the Gallaven Mire and an area between the two Whittaburrows, a deviation down to Bagga Tor rather than staying on the high ground near Lynch Tor and that Stenga Tor was not a boundmark. [Rather than include the whole transaction (even though it is well worth reading) included here is a copy of a map showing possible alternatives.]

1893 – Rev. T W Whale "Some Remarks on The Bounds of the Forest of Dartmoor, with Special Reference to the Parishes of Throwleigh, Chagford and Gidleigh" – TDA Vol 25 pp 510-534. Whale used his knowledge of etymology [the study of the derivation of words] to decipher the possible meanings of words in documents from 1221 onwards relating to land holdings of the owners or parishes adjoining the Forest. His work covered that part of the Forest boundary from Lynch Tor to Furnum Regis. Most notably for us, he suggests that the Gallaven Mire would have been within the forest in 1240.

1893 – Robert Burnard and Arthur B Prowse "Place Names in Vol 1 of the Publications of the Dartmoor Preservation Association" – TDA Vol 25 pp 482-509. The authors created this record of the many variations of spelling of Dartmoor names for *'fear that they would be lost in obscurity'*. Many of the names included are the boundmarks of various perambulation records.

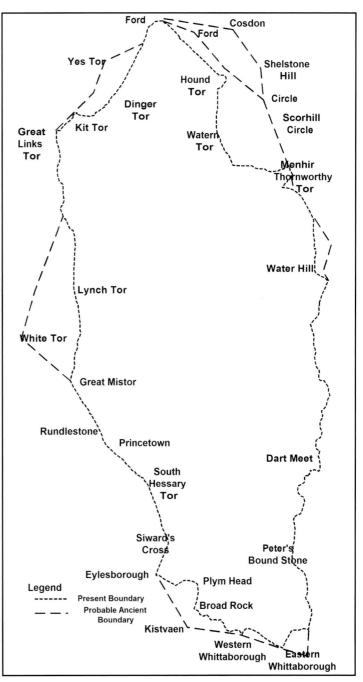

The 'Bounds of the Forest of Dartmoor' as described by Arthur B Prowse

1895 – W F Collier "Sport on Dartmoor" – TDA Vol 27 pp 113-123. Collier waxed lyrical about hunting on Dartmoor throughout the ages. Of interest to this study were his reminders that when the whole of Devon was afforested, Dartmoor would not have been a primary source of sport but only a last refuge for any animal being hunted; chases of thirty or so miles were common and whilst the peripheral lands of the moor were firm, its interior contained many treacherous bogs.

1905 – Arthur B Prowse "An Index to Articles on Dartmoor and its Borders Contained in TDA Vols I to xxx" – TDA Vol 39 pp 482-502. This index was intended as an aid in earlier times before the advent of the Devonshire Association's growing web page and access to both summaries and the articles themselves. Of note is that Prowse indicated (p 483) that the Duchy at that time accepted that the ancient boundary (i.e. 1240) was the same as the one he had proposed in 1892 and which he redrew in simpler form, as shown on the previous page.

1906 – Arthur B Prowse "The Forest Bounds Near Princetown" – TDA Vol 38 pp 411-415. Prowse started his article with a paragraph describing how *'defining the boundary by natural or artificial features, situated at considerable distances from each other along the forty-two miles circuit, was not sufficiently definite for practical purposes'*. This could lead us to four natural conclusions: Firstly, the acknowledgement that natural features would have formed the best means of defining the boundary, e.g. the use of streams. Secondly, that when the boundary was first set it must have been thought to be too much in the Duchy's favour as so many have since transgressed in pursuit of their supposed 'rights'. Thirdly, the boundary had to be a practical one. Can one imagine any sort of sensible outcome arising over a dispute about whether or not animals were inside the forest or not where the boundary was an imaginary line between two points hidden from each other by terrain or weather! Fourthly, the route taken on foot or horseback would not necessarily be along any straight line between two points on the boundary itself, that often being impractical. He then described the later efforts, especially in the Princetown area, to define the boundary better with marker stones where the ground on both sides was good and firm and offered good grazing. He shared the opinions of other writers that the Rundlestone mentioned as a marker had since probably been taken down and re-used and the boundary between North Hessary Tor and Great Mis Tor today taken as a straight line was now further to the east than the original. Prowse stated that he intended to continue investigations in detail of other sections of the boundary to see if any other variations might have ensued. I can find no records of any such work.

1907 – Robert Burnard "The Ancient Population of Dartmoor" – TDA Vol 39 pp 198-207. Burnard explained that no evidence of Roman interest in the tin of Dartmoor had been found. He did note that artefacts from old tin workings possibly dated them to the 10th century. From examining ancient records he noted that the population of Dartmoor in 1240 would have varied greatly in number between summer and winter and at most would probably have amounted to no more than a few hundred and that the number did not greatly increase for many centuries.

1914 – R Hansford Worth "Stray Notes on Dartmoor Tin Working" – TDA Vol 46 pp 286-294. The notes here are of interest to anyone studying the likely boundary as it can be deduced that some of the tin workings to be seen today might not have been there in 1240 but could have been there in 1609. In particular there are the open workings in the area now called Erme Pits. It seems likely that these were not present in 1240 when the firm ground we now find beside the river approaching Erme Pits would have been a peat bog with the tin bearing ore deposited beneath it. This could lead one to believe that the route the 1240 Perambulators took would have been along the hillside south of the Erme and thence over the hill and into the Langcombe Brook valley to what is now called Grim's Grave. Following the efforts of the tin miners after 1240, the way would have been open by 1609 for subsequent perambulators to travel up through the excavated Erme Pits area and over the ridge beyond via Erme (or Arme) Head and Broad Rock.

1915 – William J Blake "Hooker's Synopsis Chorographical of Devonshire" – TDA Vol 47 pp 334-348. In this paper, Blake transcribed eleven pages of Hooker's book (produced in the 16th century) that mentioned that *'the Forest of Dartmoor was confirmed as disafforested by King John* *along with the rest of Devon and Cornwall but subsequently re-afforested by his son Henry III after his father had previously agreed to this but failed to do so'*, i.e. by the carrying out of a perambulation.

1918 – Hugh R Watkin "A Great Devonian William Briwer" – Presidential Address TDA Vol 50 pp 69-169. Unravelling the genealogy of the family "Brewer" is complicated by the similarity of the recorded names of four of the main members. Indeed, it is possible to think that some authors have attributed actions from two different family members to just one. It would be too easy to assume that the perambulator named 'Willielmi de la Bruere (Brewer)' in the 1240 return was the one who became Bishop of Exeter (remembering that all Bishops were knights). However, that is unlikely to have been the case. Watkin diligently traced the family tree of the family 'Brueria' and identified whom he thought had taken part in the perambulation of 1240. This 'poor relation' is exactly the sort of person who would have been seen in the company of other knights at, for instance Okehampton Castle, the sheriff's abode.

1926 – Frances Rose-Troupe "Report on Place Names in Devonshire" - TDA Vol 58 pp 163-166. The author noted that the late Arthur B Prowse was a Colonel and that his *'painstaking … remarkable collection'* (of Devon place names) had been donated to the English Place Name Society.

1926 – R Hansford Worth "A Note on Dartmoor Place Names" – TDA Vol 58 pp 359-372. Worth gave a practical and scholarly guide to anyone trying to understand the etymology of place names on Dartmoor.

1941 – R Hansford Worth "Dartmoor 1788–1808" – TDA Vol 73 pp 214-215. Worth offered evidence that the map referred to by Samuel Rowe and Spence Bate now held at the DHC, was probably prepared for a hearing held in 1478 of a suit about boundaries *'involving the Abbot of Buckfast'* (Buckfast Abbey is in Buckfastleigh to the south of the moor) and the *'men of Devonshire'* , i.e. it probably dates from the late 15th century.

1962 – I G Simmons "An Outline of The Vegetation History of Dartmoor" – TDA Vol 94 pp 555-572. Research presented here showed that there seemed to have been little natural change in the vegetation cover of Dartmoor except through man's interference, such as by the cutting of peat, in Saxon or Norman times and that in earlier times the moor could well have supported more agriculture than today. Simmons also postulated that the disappearance of the alders from about 1000BC was probably because of man's interference – alder made excellent charcoal that would have been prized by tinners needing to smelt their ore.

1965 – Brian Le Messurier "The Philpott Peat Passes" – TDA Vol 97 pp 161-170. This paper with its accompanying photographs illustrated well the difficulties of walking/riding over large parts of the North Moor. The Philpott peat passes (cut in the period 1895–1905) were, and still are, excellent routes through the worst of the remaining areas of deep peat once one is well inside the forest (see map overleaf).

1968 – E Gawne and J V Somers-Cocks "Parallel Reaves on Dartmoor" –TDA Vol 100 pp 277-291. The authors dated the creation of the reaves (long, parallel generally straight low banks) on Dartmoor to the late Bronze, early Iron Age, i.e. well before the first perambulation and recommended that further archaeological work be conducted to determine further details about them. (Most notable amongst the follow-up work is that of Andrew Fleming – described later). They postulated that the reaves were probably ancient land boundaries and that subsequently many medieval boundaries could have been based upon them.

1985 – D G Price "Changing Perceptions of Prehistoric Tinning on Dartmoor" – TDA Vol 117 pp 129-138. Price proposed the hypothesis that the locations of early (Bronze Age) settlements on Dartmoor, such as along the banks of the moorland Plym, would have resulted from

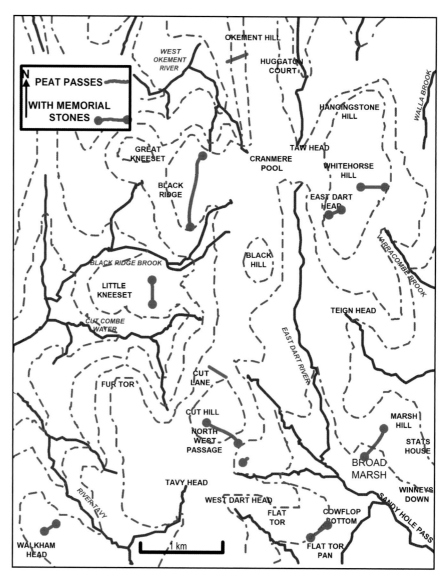

Philpott peat passes.

both agricultural pressures as well as the needs of tinners. Thus there appeared to have been a great likelihood that the upper Plym was a busy area at the time of the first perambulation.

1987 – Andrew Fleming "Prehistoric Tin Extraction on Dartmoor: A Cautionary Note" – TDA Vol 119 pp 117-122. Fleming explained the need for caution in postulating any direct link between Bronze Age settlement density and sites of tin extraction. He did not demur from the evidence that tin was extracted from Dartmoor in the Bronze Age, only that there was no direct correlation between the settlements in the upper Plym valley and tin mining at that time. He did note the documentary and archaeological evidence that there was extensive tin extraction on Dartmoor during the 12th century.

1988 – D G Price "Prehistoric Tin Extraction on Dartmoor: A Reply to Andrew Fleming" – TDA Vol 120 pp 91-95. Whilst this academic exchange adds little to our research, it is worth bearing in mind that the perambulators must have passed four areas where Bronze Age tin workings and settlements would have been evident – below King's Oven and Soussons Common; the O Brook/Dry Lake area; the Upper Plym; and at Watern Oke above the Tavy/Rattlebrook junction.

PART TWO

Chapter 7

A New Interpretation of the Forest Boundary

So far, we have examined copies of the perambulation return and looked at various translations of the text and the shorthand. We have also studied various different interpretations of the route that the original perambulators might have taken. Now a new interpretation involving both theoretical and practical work will be explained.

Before we start, let us consider the overall form of the return. It was stated in the writ that the perambulators were to identify clearly the 'metes' (identifiable objects or places) and 'bounds' (the line of the boundary between the metes). Now this would have been necessary as it is often difficult on the Moor to travel in a straight line between two points – i.e. directly in a straight line from mete to mete. The bound therefore would also need to be described and often was – along the Okebroke for example. The bound would be the practical boundary that the Quartermen would use to see if animals were in the Forest or still outside on the Commons. Whilst it would be expected that the perambulators would follow the bound itself, that would not always be practical. For instance, one cannot imagine taking a horse along the river in the valley of the young River Tavy below Watern Oke. Therefore, the perambulators actual route would often be beside the boundary but not actually on it.

We will now examine the text of the return itself. Both the names of objects used as metes and the way in which the bounds themselves were described will be reviewed. Something as simple as the variations in the shorter words used – the prepositions and the conjunctions – could be revealing. Then we will look again at the named metes and features followed or passed whilst on the bounds and try to relate them to the modern names recorded by the Ordnance Survey. Finally sixteen excursions will be suggested whereby one can test the validity of what is being proposed here from a practical point of view.

As we have seen, reorganising the wording on the copies of the return to a more logical form reveals that there appear to have been thirty-two metes and bounds. That there were so few when the whole route is over forty-three miles long could be argued to show that, in the most part, the ground was open. It could also suggest that many of the metes should have been inter-visible. However, this was not always the case. When you walk Dartmoor, you soon realise that many of the hills are convex in shape and hilltop features such as standing stones or even tors are often out of sight for much of the climb up to them – the ascent to the top of Ryder's Hill is a very good example of this. This could be taken to mean that the metes themselves were not that important and should not necessarily be taken as points on the boundary but rather as generally descriptive of the features passed. They might not even have been visited or indeed might not have lain on the line of the intended boundary at all. The perambulators certainly used line-features such as streams quite often and, I believe, would have sought good going for their horses.

It would appear that the two hundred or so tors listed in various publications today were either not named in 1240 or that they were not regarded as important by the perambulators at that time. The fact that the perambulators only referred to what we now call a tor three times

– Houndetorre, Ysfothere and aliam Ysfothere (there is, I believe and will try to persuade you, another explanation for the use of the name 'Ernestorre') – shows that they probably followed established paths rather than marched on a line-of-sight hilltop to hilltop route as we might do with a compass today (a tool which of course they would not have had). Indeed, I consider that the boundary probably passed some hundreds of meters from Hound Tor (below today's Cosdon) on a natural path rather than on a cross-country route taking in the tor as a mete. Such an understanding can be bolstered if one considers the task of the overseers of the four quarters of the moor. They were responsible for gathering *'villes fine'* (payment) for animals grazing within the forest. That task would be much more practical if the boundary were a path or river rather than a compass bearing across rock strewn ground.

It is generally recognised that at the time of the first perambulation, the highest parts of Dartmoor were all but deserted. Bronze Age settlements had dispersed leaving behind just some relics. What is remarkable is that although the boundary passed several ancient stone monuments that are prominent today, for example the stone circle on White Moor Hill and stone rows on Scorhill Down (pronounced 'scurel' by the locals), Shovel Down and Red Lake, they were not mentioned in the perambulation return. It could well be, of course, that at the time they were recumbent and hence unremarkable as we know that many of the stones were raised again to their present positions in the Victorian era. Indeed, one recumbent stone row has just (2015) been revealed on the hillside above Grey Wethers.

Only in three places are Bronze Age remains mentioned as metes – namely 'EstereWhyteburgh', 'Elesburghe' and 'Menweburghe'. Today we take these metes to be cairns. However, the Latin word 'burgh' was normally used in reference to a built up area (today a borough), which in 1240 might have meant an area where the remains of Bronze Age settlements could be seen. Of course, such settlements might have contained a cairn and after despoliation of the area, the pile of stones that made up the cairn could have been the only prominent feature left.

THE PREPOSITIONS AND CONJUNCTIONS USED

As we can see, the first five columns on the tables showing the copies of the perambulation returns (see Appendices 1–9) contain eleven different forms of introduction to the respective bounds as follows:

1. Fourteen times – *'et inde linealiter usque ad'* – translates as 'and then in a straight line to'
2. Once – *'et inde linealiter usque per'* – translates as 'and then in a straight line until by'
3. Once – *'et inde linealiter ubi'* – translates as 'and so on that line to where the'
4. Four times – *'et inde usque ad'* – translates as 'and from there to'
5. Twice – *'et sic in longem .... usque ad'* – translates as 'and so along .... up to'
6. Four times – *'et sic per .... usque ad'* – translates as 'and thus by/through .... up to'
7. Twice – *'et sic ad'* – translates as 'and thus to'
8. Once – *'et sic ascendo .... usque ad'* – translates as 'and so by climbing the .... up to'
9. Once – *'et ita ascendendo usque ad'* – translates as 'and so by climbing up to'
10. Once – *'et inde ascendendo usque ad'* – translates as 'and then by climbing up to'
11. Once – *'et deinde usque ad'* – translates as 'and next to the'

Now Latin is known to be a very precise language and so we should take due account of the reasons why these many different forms were used.

THE PERAMBULATION – DARTMOOR'S ORIGINAL LONG DISTANCE WALK

PROPER NOUNS – THE NAMES USED

Transcribing the names given to the perambulators by their local guides would have been challenging. The recorder would write down phonetically what he was hearing. How the names originally written in the return were related years later to the features known to the locals before maps became commonplace led to several known requests for further perambulations – one such was held in 1609. Such controversy was obviously fuelled by greed. It was easy to claim that the metes and bounds noted in the return should be interpreted differently. These claims, nearly always at a cost to the Crown, could be explained as being the result of simple misunderstandings of the object or feature supposedly named in the transcription. This was exacerbated of course by simple spelling differences. One only has to look at the various renderings of the family name of the knights from Gidleigh in the Close Rolls and Fine Rolls as an example – Sir William Prouz, Pruz or Prous. They all sound the same but when entered into most simple modern word search tools, bring different results. The possibilities for misunderstanding make it worth challenging whether or not the metes named by the 1240 perambulators are always the features mapped by the Ordnance Survey.

Today, nearly every tor or rock pile on Dartmoor has been named whether significant or not. The perambulators passed close by many of them and we can but wonder why they were not chosen as markers. Perhaps they had not been named at that time. This may not have been unsurprising as Dartmoor after the Bronze Age settlements had fallen into disuse, was pretty much unpopulated.

As the perambulators only used three of the tors that have now been named as a mete we can deduce that: a. they were not concerned with just going from hilltop to hilltop but rather more probably concentrated on following existing paths or streams; and b. if a hill was chosen, the mete itself was easily identified on that hill.

Many of the rivers emerging from the moor had names as indicated on early maps. Some streams might have been named but it is disconcerting today to note that the old Devon word for a stream was 'Walla'. Therefore the 'Walla Brook', of which there are many on the moor, is the 'brook, brook'! Also two of the largest hills and some ancient artefacts had names. In some places, it appears as though the perambulators used a description of an object rather than a proper noun to describe the mete.

The challenge the scribe faced was to write down in characters what he was hearing – that is phonetically. A simple example occurs right at the start in the written word 'Hogam'. If the perambulators and their guides were asking him to write down the Latin word for ridge, which is 'Iogum', then 'hogam' was a pretty good approximation. Say it out loud and you will soon appreciate this. Of course since then others have taken it literally and ascribed it to mean 'edge of' or the 'hedge' but I think it was much simpler than that. They were on the ridge, not at a point with a tor or other artefact but on a path over the ridge where horses could pass easily.

THE CHALLENGE FOR THE PERAMBULATORS

When King John ordered that Devon was to be disafforested less Dartmoor (and Exmoor), it was to be *'up to the metes of the ancient regardes of Dertemore..'.* Quite what he expected to retain as Forest is difficult to determine exactly as there was no written record of such *'ancient regardes'*. Although his father, King Henry II, had established a means to record decisions, payments and holdings (with the creation of a bureaucracy that was later to become the Civil Service), it would take time to record everything that had gone before. Also, what John was actually doing was retaining for his personal benefit land that many

75

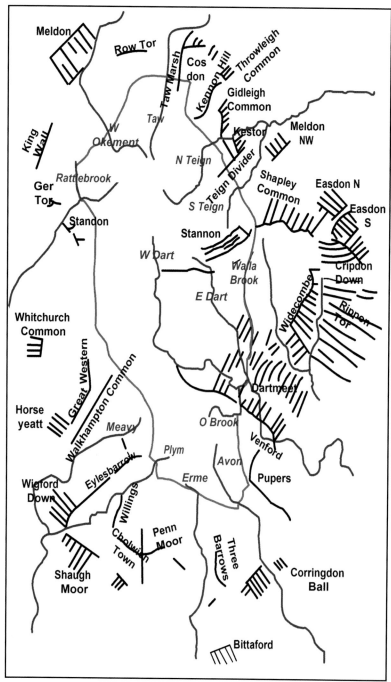

Reaves, rivers and the Duchy boundary.

might have considered previously to be common. Thus there would have been a tussle between adjacent landowners and the Crown right from the start.

It would seem sensible for the perambulators to have chosen for themselves a few guidelines. Assuming the vegetation such as tree cover was then much as it is now, these may have included:

1.   Not circumnavigating all the common land but rather just a smaller area within the Commons of Devon.

2.   Having a boundary along which, as far as possible, a horseman could ride easily.

3.   Using streams/rivers as the boundary wherever possible.

4.   Staying above the areas previously marked out with ancient reaves (low boundary walls/hedges). These reaves are obvious even now, 600 years later, and were boundary markers of land that, from evidence gathered, was farmed in the Bronze Age. It might have been considered that such areas might still be suitable for cultivation again. As can be seen from the map, they were fairly successful in following this guideline except at Stannon and near the O Brook.

5.   Not using the obvious high tors as metes. They might well not have been named at that time.

6.   Being prepared to compromise where necessary, e.g. including the land on which stand the Stannon reaves so as to be able to follow the Walla Brook.

7.   Completing the task within two days. It is not that they would have been unwilling to stay longer but down to sheer practicalities. Although in modern times one couple have reportedly followed the whole boundary in some 15 hours, the knights' journey would not have been that quick. Retainers and servants on foot would have accompanied them. They would have met and greeted local guides for different sections on route, each occasion taking time. They would have had to take notes. We should remember that at that time the King's Messengers were only expected to cover up to thirty-five miles per day and they were hardened to covering such distances. Most Moor walkers can only achieve two miles in the hour and so they must have expected to stay out for at least one night.

These guidelines would not preclude going in straight lines between hilltop features but rarely on Dartmoor can you walk in a straight line for too long. To find the easiest path underfoot, one is wise to allow oneself to deviate from the direct route to bypass obstacles such as mires or areas of clitter (fallen smaller rocks). Riders tend to stick to easier paths, paths likely to have been created by animals heading for areas of good grazing or beside streams, and around areas of difficult ground. We must also remember that this boundary had to be clear and easily identifiable by the quartermen when actually rounding up stray animals on the moor, sometimes on hillsides in deep valleys, and more often than not in bad visibility.

THE METES AND BOUNDS – A NEW INTERPRETATION

BEFORE starting to describe what I consider to have been the most likely route that the perambulators took and the boundary so defined, it is worth restating a couple of general principles followed in my reasoning. The first derives from the writings of Sir Arthur Conan Doyle and is simply put as follows – 'When you have eliminated the impossible, whatever remains, however improbable, must be the truth.' This is particularly apposite when deciding exactly which hill might have been called 'Costdonne'. The second is not to over complicate the task. Occam's Razor[12] is a law of parsimony: the principle gives precedence to simplicity – of two competing theories, the simplest explanation is to be preferred. Thus when you are standing at Huntingdon Cross about to ford the Avon, ask yourself which is the easiest way to the White Barrows ridgeline and then westwards. You soon eliminate any notion of visiting Eastern White Barrow.

Throughout this exercise we should remember that we are making deductions from just a few key facts.

	1335 RETURN FROM FEODARY	1609 RETURN	COMMENT	GRID REFERENCE
1	*Hogam de Costdonne*	*Cosdon alias Cosson*	We start this interpretation by stating that I do not think that today's Cosdon Hill was the hill named in the return. This is for five reasons. Firstly, Cosdon is a truly convex hill, the third highest on Dartmoor topped by only a few, now ruined, cairns and stands somewhat apart from the main depth of the moor. It is not on any walker's easy route to or from anywhere on the moor. Paths by-pass it at lower levels. Access to it from Okehampton Castle, where the perambulators surely started, via Belstone is not easy. True Belstone village was mentioned in Domesday and so would have had a track leading to it but by the time you have reached there from Okehampton, you have already travelled round a major portion of the north moor. Then, the access from Belstone over the rock-strewn bed of the Taw is treacherous right upstream to today's Horseshoe Ford. Then one has to double back to reach the actual summit. At the end of the perambulation, if one finished on Cosdon, one would have a long trek back to Okehampton. Secondly, the ridge ('iogum') on which stand Belstone, Higher and Winter Tors would appear not to have been mentioned at all. The return indicates no major distance, climb or difficulty getting from the ford beside Halstock to Costdonne. This then would be the only major ridgeline excluded from the return. Thirdly, the 1609 jurors were rather dismissive of this mete naming it but '<u>a</u> high hill', not the highest hill. Fourthly, the route onwards would most naturally be due south towards Hound Tor, but once again this is after a ninety-degree turn in the route. Fifthly, in 1609 the perambulators went *'linealie eastward by estimacon one mile or more unto little houndetorr'*. They could only do this from Belstone Ridge. I believe that the Belstone Ridge was the perambulators' *'Hogam de Costdonne'*. They would have approached it from Okehampton up the East Okement valley, climbed slant-wise to the ridge top between Higher Tor and Winter Tor. From there the route to the next mete is open and obvious.	SX611913

[12] Occam's Razor – Entia non sunt multiplicanda praeter necessitatem or entities should not be multiplied more than necessary or all things being equal, the simplest solution is the best.

2	*parvam hogam que vocatur parva Houndetorre*	*Little Houndetorr*	Today's Hound Tor is almost non-descript when looking from Higher Tor but the dip in the ridgeline to the north of the tor is much more obvious. Whitemore Circle, which sits in the col, was most probably prone in 1240 and possibly even buried. (This was the case of the recently discovered prehistoric stone circle found near Sittaford Tor in 2015.) The circle was raised again in Victorian times. Thus the perambulators would not have seen it and hence would not have mentioned it.	SX632895
3	*Theurlestone*	*Thurleston, or Water Donter being about three-quarters of a mile from Houndetorr aforesaid*	White Moor Stone is an obvious marker on the route from the Whitmoor Circle towards Gidleigh. It stands high out of the ground and so probably has a major portion below ground and has probably has stood for centuries. The perambulators did not travel to it as along fourteen other bounds *'et inde linealiter usque ad'* but rather passed by it – *'et inde usque ad'*. The idea that a Thurleston is a stone with a hole might be a mis-conception. The rock stack at Thurlston in South Devon does lean against another thus forming a gap but I believe it is the leaning that is significant. White Moor Stone can be seen from a range of anything up to a mile+ in any direction and always seems to lean! It is, I believe, the *'Theurlestone'* of the perambulators.	SX633894
4	*Wotysbrokelakys-fote que cadit in Teng*	*Wates Brook head which falleth into Teigne, or Hood Lake*	The area around the confluence of the Walla Brook and North Teign River has been somewhat complicated since 1240 by the building of a leat, two clapper bridges and the re-erection of Scorhill Circle. The rivers do meet and little can have been done to alter that. This point would have been clear in 1240 and the idea that the confluence of Hugh Lake (which is paltry) and the North Teign River was the mete is, in my opinion, nonsense.	SX654870
5	*Hengheston*	*Hengeston alias Heighstone*	Long Stone on Shovel Down is once again an artefact that is likely to have stood the test of time. There is however one reason for doubting that this was the perambulators' mete. Namely that it cannot be seen until one is almost upon it. If it were not the mete, it might well have been possible that one of the fallen stones in the double stone row on Shovel Down was used. In which case the Long Stone was only a few yards further on.	SX659860
6	*Yestetone*	*Yelston alias or Gesstone now commonly called Hethstone*	Quite where or what this mete might have been has truly been clouded by the building of Fernworthy dam and reservoir. The perambulators would have had to cross the South Teign river and probably did so upstream of the dam's location where the going would have been easier. The present Heath Stone, that is supposed to be the *'yestetone'*, lies between the Long Stone and the next mete and so will be accepted as the mete intended.	SX671837
7	*mediam turbarium de Alberesheved*	*mediam Turbarium de Alberesheved*	Crossing Chagford Common due south of the Heath Stone towards Water Hill is sure to bring you wet feet. Many initially stick close to the wall surrounding Fernworthy Forest before heading for the cairn on Water Hill. This whole hill could well have been where local people came to cut peat. The perambulators needed to establish a boundary and so probably headed southwest into the valley of the North Walla Brook.	SX6783

8	*Walebrokum*	*Not Mentioned*	They would then have followed the line of the brook upstream, passing...	SX678824
9	*Furnem Regum*	*King's Oven*	...the area of Furnem Regis of which little remains today.	SX675812
10	*Walebrokehenyd*	*Wallbrook head*	Having continued up the North Walla Brook to its head, the perambulators would then have crossed the line of the present road and descended to the head of another stream – the Walla Brook. (Quite why this tautology persists is unknown. 'Walla' is the old Devonian word for 'Brook'!) The location of the head of this brook has probably been altered slightly since by the tinners working in the nearby Birch Tor and Vitifer Mining complex, but not too much.	SX678808
11	*cadit in Derta*	*the East Dart*	The Walla Brook would have been easy to follow all the way down to the East Dart but modern enclosures mean that today's perambulators have to take diversions around the enclosed fields of Runnage and Pizwell Farms and over Riddon Ridge to Babeny.	SX672747
12	*aliam Dertam*	*another Dart called West Dart*	Dartmeet is an obvious point on the boundary but where exactly the perambulators forded the rivers is difficult to see today as there is so much modern building.	SX671731
13	*Okbrokysfote*	*Wobrook foot*	Walking close to the river from the last mete to the confluence of the O Brook and the West Dart river is difficult on the south bank because of soft ground and rocks. This could be another area where the perambulators intended that the watercourses were the boundary but actually rode on the hillside above the river.	SX661724
14	*linea Dryeworke*	*Drye Lake, alias, Drywork*	The perambulators were destined to reach the top of Ryder's Hill and taking the route up the Dry Lake wide gully away from the O Brook points you directly at the summit. Quite when the tin was extracted from here is difficult to determine but as it was extracted by streaming, it could well have been before 1240.	SX660710
15	*linea Dryefeldford*	*Creyselford or Drydelford*	Quite why a so-called 'ford' appears on this bound is strange. Although the perambulators actually forded several rivers/named streams, this is the only time the word 'ford' is used. Rather than a water crossing, this is actually where the perambulators' route crossed the line of the Sandy Way track. Monks probably used this track when traversing the moor from Buckfastleigh to Buckland or Tavistock. They might have decided to introduce this seemingly superfluous mete here as a guide as Ryder's Hill is so smoothly convex that the summit seems further away each time you look up.	SX659696
16	*Cattyshill*	*Knattleborough*	This is now taken to mean Ryder's Hill on which stands a cairn, a Trig Point and Petre's Bound Stone. This is one example of where today's name does not relate in anyway known to what was written in 1240 or 1609 but is surely the way into this part of the south moor.	SX659690
17	*capud de West-erewelebrok*	*Wester Wellbrook head*	Having left the top of Ryder's Hill, the perambulators headed not immediately south through soft, boggy and difficult ground but diverted to the head of the Wellabrook Girt. They then followed it south until it joins the Avon.	SX664686

18	*cadit in Avena*	*falleth into Owen or Avon*	The confluence of the Western Wella Brook and Avon is above the upper stretch of the Avon reservoir. There is now a cross here, Huntingdon Cross, but that was added later. At this point, a puzzle emerges. The river is actually rock strewn upstream from here for some three or four hundred meters and hence difficult to ford. It becomes easier to cross just before the clapper bridge that was probably not there in 1240. Having got that far, the route would bend back on itself if Eastern White Barrow is taken as the next bound.	SX664661
19	*Estere Whyteburgh*	*East Whitaborough*	Many take this mete to be the Eastern White Barrow but the language just does not fit. *'East'* is *'orientali'* in Latin. *'Whyte'* does not translate. *'Burgh'* is not a barrow but probably refers to some form of settlement – today's 'borough' derives from that source. Thus the perambulators were making for a collection of stone hut circles on what is now the ridge between the Eastern and Western White Barrows. In fact, they were probably making for what is now known as Western White Barrow (Petre's Cross did not appear for centuries after 1240). This would have given them the easiest way across the Avon and the easiest climb up and over the ridge as they made for the Red Lake river.	SX659654
20	*linea Rode Lake cadit in Erm*	*Red Lake foot, where it falleth into Erme*	Having gained the head of the Red Lake river, now somewhat altered by the mining activities that have occurred since 1240, they followed it downstream to the Erme (or Arme) river.	SX635661
21	*Grymesgrove*	*Erme Head*	Quite where or what 'Grymesgrove' might have been has been argued over many times. We know that the perambulators 'ascended' to it and you certainly do that to get to Erme Head but let us consider the conditions underfoot here in 1240. The tin streaming and mining operations had probably not started hereabouts as this was too distant from any known tracks. Thus the ground around the present Erme Pits would have been a deep peat quagmire and very unpleasant to traverse. South of the river Erme, the ground is more stable and the stream leading up into Hortonsford Bottom is a clear route to the top of Langcombe Hill and its cairn. Beyond the top of the hill lies another stream, Langcombe Brook, and on its banks is a pre-historic tomb or cist – Grim's Grave. Surely the coincidence of such a similar name cannot be ignored. Perhaps we should also stop at this point to consider how the perambulators were faring at this point. The King's Messengers were only expected to travel thirty-five miles a day. Here we have knights and followers, perhaps not all on horses or ponies, carrying kit for an overnight stop and at this point they were twenty miles into their journey and roughly halfway round the boundary. Also they were not moving at speed and, no doubt, had to keep slowing as new guides met them and were introduced. Thus it would have been getting late. What an ideal place for a camping ground. I have surprised cattle and moorland ponies several times in this quiet valley and although some tin streaming and earth movement has occurred, that might have been since the perambulation and does not appear to have gone to any great depth. Thus the valley would not have looked that different in 1240.	SX612664

21a		*Plym Head*	The 1609 jury probably introduced this mete having accepted Erme Head as the previous one. Even so, they were somewhat woolly here. The best route from Erme Head to Plym Head is actually to take a detour onto the Abbot's Way via Broad Rock. The direct route has been judged too hard for riders by experts before now.	SX620682
22	*Elesburghe*	*Ellisborough*	Having ridden down the Langcombe Brook, the perambulators would have had to cross the Plym river. There are many crossing points but also some treacherous boggy patches on both sides of the river to avoid. Then they would have made directly for Eylesbarrow. Again it was not the cairn they were heading for but the ruins of the burgh thereabouts.	SX599685
23	*crucem Syward*	*Sewards Cross*	This is the only example of a named man-made object being used as a mete on the perambulation. It is on the direct line from Eylesbarrow to South Hessary Tor and might therefore seem redundant. Perhaps they were just paying due respect to this ancient cross.	SX604699
24	*Ysfothere*	*Little Hisworthy*	South Hessary Tor stands alone and obvious and needs no further mention.	SX597723
25	*aliam Ysfothere*	*Another Hisworthy*	North Hessary Tor stands above Princetown which, of course, did not exist in 1240. Come to that neither did any of the roads that the route now crosses.	SX578742
25a		*Mistorpann*	We now come to a part of the boundary where once again the 1240 perambulators did not name the most obvious and huge natural feature, Great Mis Tor, as a mete. It was included by the 1609 jury but was probably passed to the east where the ground is most open.	SX563768
26	*Menweburghe*	*Due Lake head*	There is no immediate way to identify where *'Menweburghe'* might have been. If we assume it referred to a collection of ruined stone huts, there are several on the slopes above the river Walkham on Langstone Moor. These are those most directly in line of where we believe the perambulators were going – from North Hessary Tor to the foot of the Rattlebrook. In 1609, the jury decided that the perambulators had probably intended the stream called Dead Lake to be used as a pointer to the north. Following Dead Lake up we come to White Barrow and this should therefore be our next mete.	SX568793
27	*Lullyngessete*	*Luntesborough*	Again, whatever the perambulators meant by *'Lullyngessete'* is not an obvious feature on today's maps. In 1609 the jury referred again to a 'borough' and perhaps the cast down stones in the vicinity of Lynch Tor were what they meant. I am convinced that the notion that the stone hut circles on White Tor might have been on the boundary as one of these 'burghs' is false. That route would have taken the perambulators off the high moor while the final approach to the Rattlebrook foot after crossing Standon Hill is treacherous.	SX565805
27a		*Wester Red Lake*	The 1609 jury obviously thought like me and decided that the best approach to the Rattlebrook Foot was down the line of Western Red Lake, across the easy ford (now stepping stones) and then probably over the top of Watern Oke. The route down the valley of the Amicombe Brook is too difficult to ride and so whilst it might have been the boundary it would not have been ridden by the perambulators.	SX566832

28	*Rakernebrokefote*	*Rattlebrook Foot*	Rattlebrook Foot is an obvious mete where there are numerous crossing points to the west bank.	SX560837
29	*capud ejusdem aque*	*head of the same Rattlebrook*	The line of the Rattlebrook is obvious and easily followed. It is most easily walked today on its west side. Its head is in a rather wet area of mire but if one stays west of this until reaching Hunt Tor (now is that name a coincidence or what?) and then turn to the east, the going is easier. At this point Stenga Tor is out of sight but the col beside Kitty Tor is obvious.	SX556874
29a		*Steynchatorr*	This mete was not referred to in 1240 but added later. It has been taken to mean Stenga Tor that does indeed sit in its own bog as the name suggests! However, the route eastwards from the tor is steeply down over rocks and would be an impossible ride. It is, in fact, a very uncomfortable walk, steep and rocky. Travelling to the tor and then back along the ridgeline toward Kitty Tor is a diversion from the most direct route down into the West Okement valley. Therefore I do not consider that the perambulators would have gone near it.	SX567880
30	*linea Westfolle*	*Langford, alias, Sandiford*	Quite what the scribe meant by the line of the 'Westsolle' is difficult to decide. The 1609 jury decided that it was the Sandy Ford across the West Okement River and that seems most likely. This is the only place in the return that the scribe uses the shorter form of words – *'et deinde usque ad'*. He seems to be being rather dismissive, as if it were obvious where they were to go – straight down and across! Thereafter, I believe they rode up the easiest path to the col near Dinger Tor.	SX574879
31	*Ernestorre*	*No mention*	The word *'Ernestorre'* has been taken to mean the ridgeline along which lie Fordsland Ledge, High Willays and Yes Tor. The men of Okehampton when later siting their parish boundary stones took a rather different view. If one starts northeast from Dinger Tor, the ground is open and easily rideable as one heads in the direction of East Mill Tor. Soon one reaches the upper stretches of the Black-a-Ven Brook that runs via New Bridge all the way to Cullever Steps. This area is still marshy and home to a summer growth of reeds suitable for bedding, thatch or animal feed. Here then is a clue as to what the perambulators meant. They were to pass through the area where summer matting *'aestas storea'* was gathered. (If you sound out the words you will note how much like 'Ernestorre' they sound). That would make the boundary the brook itself.	SX596903
32	*vadum proximum in orientali parte Capelle Sancti Michaelis De Halghestoke*	*Ford which lieth in the east side of Saint Michael's Chapel of Holstock*	Although no physical remains of a chapel or its accompanying buildings survive, two farms, Lower and Higher Halstock, still bear the name in the valley of the East Okement river. The nearest ford *'vadum proximum'* is at Cullever Steps near the confluence of the Black-a-Ven brook and East Okement.	SX606921
33	*predictam Hogam de Costodone in orientali parte*	*hill called Cossdon*	The first 600 or so meters down the East Okement towards Okehampton from the ford at Cullever Steps are difficult to walk, let alone ride. Therefore we can surmise that the perambulators crossed at Cullever Steps but stayed on the higher ground leading towards Scarey Tor. From there they could pick their way easily over the open hillside and back down to Okehampton. Quite why the scribe needed to repeat the words *'in orientali parte'* is not clear. Certainly many of those who copied the return over the centuries made errors.	

THE PERAMBULATION – DARTMOOR'S ORIGINAL LONG DISTANCE WALK

Arriving at a definitive statement of where the 1240 perambulators went is clearly not going to be easy. However certain factors should enable us to make a good attempt. We have the advantages of being able to reach parts of the moor easily that before the turnpike roads were built would have been quite difficult to reach. We also have detailed maps and navigational devices so that we know (or should know) where we are at any time on the moor and can thus explore more freely.

There are simple walking guides to the whole boundary – whatever you take that to be. What can be more informative in forming views of the perambulators' likely route is to visit key points. In the following chapters, sixteen such excursions are described.

Map showing the start points for the sixteen excursions described in the following chapters.

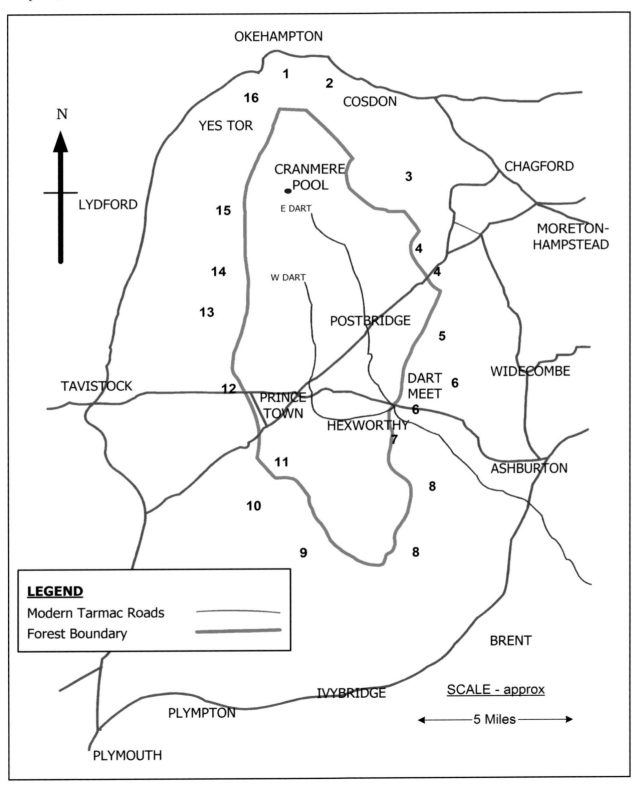

Chapter 8

Excursion 1 – Start and Finish of the Perambulation – from Okehampton to the Belstone Ridge

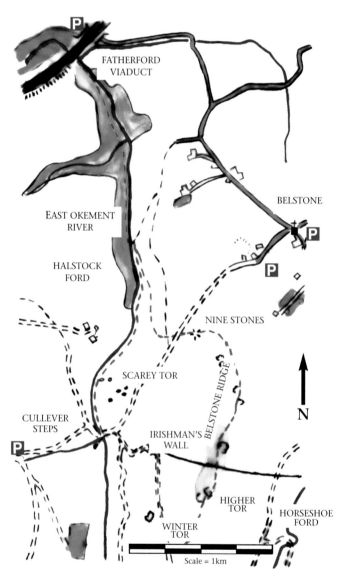

Here we will be exploring that part of the perambulation route that we might suppose the knights took in order to get to and from the moor having started at Okehampton Castle, the home of the Sheriff – namely via the banks of the East Okement river. In addition, whilst walking along the Belstone Ridge, the possible routes the perambulators might have taken onwards to the Hound Tor ridge can also be assessed.

Start – *'Qui incipiunt perambulationem ad Hogam de Costdonne et inde linealiter usque ad parvam hogam que vocatur parva Houndetorre*

Finish – *'ad Vadum proximum in orientali parte Capelle Sancti Michaelis de Halghestoke; Et inde linealiter usque ad predictam Hogam de Costodone in orientali parte.'*

This walk of about 9km starts under the Fatherford Viaduct carrying the railway line to Meldon quarry over the East Okement river. It also passes under the new dual carriageway that bypasses Okehampton. Ignoring the noises from overhead, we soon enjoy the peacefulness on the riverbank.

Why, we might ask, would the knights have come this way? Three reasons may be suggested.

Firstly, ease of passage. Rivers were important to travellers both as navigational aids and as obstacles to be overcome. Whilst crossing rivers was a challenge, there would have been tracks alongside them made by animals and travellers. If, as we might suppose, the populace (including farmers) at the Chapel at Halstock travelled to market or were often visited by those trading or seeking advice, travellers could well have used the track beside the nearest river, the East Okement.

An ongoing indication of the importance of rivers is that even in later centuries, old maps of the region show little detail except major towns, villages, hills and rivers and their bridges. The map (shown below left) from 1676 is an example and clearly shows the East and West Okement rivers (*'flu' being* the Latin short form of 'flumen' or 'fluvius' meaning river).

Secondly, travellers in 1240 were faced with land covered by extensive tree cover. Whilst today we can drive directly up the hill from the town easily on a road in our cars, imagine how steep and overgrown the slope would have appeared on riding out of the castle. Trees would certainly have lined the immediate hillside in 1240 – as they do now in the valley we will walk.

Thirdly, what other 'easy' route might there have been in 1240. To the west, the knights would not have wanted to start up over Prewley Moor. Access to the moor proper means climbing from there up the steep rock strewn face leading up to Branscombe's Loaf and then over Corn Ridge and its bog. If they diverted from Prewley into the West Okement river valley, the entry and exits are also very steep. Directly southwards, the climb up and over Black Down would certainly get the

The 1676 map showing East and West Okement rivers.

heart pumping followed by a further climb up and over the ridge between West Mill Tor and High Willhays. Farther to the west is Belstone which today is reached easily. Now it might be thought that as Belstone existed in 1240 (it was mentioned in the Domesday book as '*Bellestam*'), it might have had a good track, perhaps along the route of the present road. However, the place must have been very small as it does not even appear on 17th century maps at all whilst Gidleigh and Throwleigh do – and they are not exactly large themselves even today.

So we will suppose that the perambulators used the banks of the East Okement to reach their start point.

Before describing the route of the proposed walk, let us address a puzzle in the wording of the return. Why does it state that the boundary started *on* the ridge (Latin – 'iogum' which when spoken sounds like hogam if written phonetically) – '*ad hogam de Costdonne*' but ends supposedly in the area of '*ad predictam Hogam de Costodone in orientali parte*'? This surely is just style. The perambulators would have wanted to make the first point one of significance – the ridgeline itself. After two days on the moor and having covered nearly fifty miles, getting close to the top of the ridge would have been quite enough!

Okehampton castle seen from the south.

Start – Park at the Fatherford Viaduct site (SX603948). At the end of the road just before the house is enough room for about six to eight cars.

Walk down past the house and across the river using the newly built wooden bridge whilst under the road and rail bridges above. Turn left and follow the signed footpath/bridleway upstream. En route we can climb a steep ramp beside the waterfall, staying close to the river, or take the easier bridleway deeper into the woods. Observe how thick the natural vegetation is on the valley sides. Most of the edge of Dartmoor was probably like this in 1240. It is supposed that whatever chapel

Start of the valley trail.

Ancient stone slabs, looking back downstream.

Steep and narrow climb beside the river.

Waterfall.

Tree cover on the valley sides.

Arriving at Chapel/Halstock Ford.

East Okement rising to Cullever Steps through Halstock Cleave.

existed here, in what is now called Halstock Wood, it might have been in the trees just before the ford. However, no immediate signs of a building can be found – so it could have been anywhere hereabouts. William Crossing noted that the settlement of Halstock was reputedly of a considerable size. So, as the farms above this valley are named Lower and Higher Halstock, any chapel buildings might well have been above on the hillside.

On emerging from the wood and crossing the river at Chapel/Halstock Ford (where there is now a footbridge) we are on a grassy area where it might be nice for a picnic on a sunny day. Now comes another decision about the immediate route to take. There is a signed footpath rising diagonally left as we face away from the river, leading to Old Rectory Farm. This joins a track that then leads back right towards the moor contouring at a higher level below Watchet Hill Cottage. We might want to return this way. Or, we can turn half right and start to rise slowly up across the face of the valley wall as if trying to get just above Scarey Tor. Or we can follow the stream all the way to Cullever Steps through Halstock Cleave (with its lovely swimming holes). The latter is hard walking, with some rock hopping involved, and would be even harder if on horseback.

Cullever Steps and beyond to Yes Tor from Scarey Tor.

Route up from Halstock Ford from Scarey Tor.

Higher Tor (centre) and Winter Tor (right) from Scarey Tor.

Whichever way we proceed, I would recommend a visit to Scarey Tor at some point for the views it affords. From here we can see Cullever Steps which most suppose to be the ford mentioned in the perambulation return as that at the eastern part of the Chapel of St Michael. If we considered that the whole cultivated hillside around what are now called Lower and Upper Halstock Farms probably 'belonged' to the chapel (where they would have raised crops and livestock for their own sustenance) then Cullever Steps is indeed to the East. We can also see the route a rider would probably choose to come up from Halstock Ford. Lastly, looking towards the moor, we can view the Belstone Ridge and note the route to Winter Tor.

Whilst at Cullever Steps, we will notice two boundary markers. On one side they are both clearly marked 'OP' 'B' – Okehampton Parish Boundary. The stones would not have been here in 1240 as parishes as such did not yet exist. Even when they did come into existence, in the early years parishioners tended to use existing rocks on which to carve their symbols – there is a good example on Hound Tor where the letters 'TP', indicating Throwleigh Parish, are carved. The smaller rock at Cullever Steps bears feather and tare marks and was thus probably made and placed in the 19th century. The larger one was probably raised even later.

Standing by the marker stones and looking eastwards, we get a clear view of the Belstone Ridge and the clitter (rocks) that cover much of its side. Through this clitter passes Irishman's Wall (built and struck down

Boundary stones.

sometime before 1811). The perambulators' route is supposed to follow the line of the wall. If we do choose to walk up it, we will discover how hard it is on foot and can appreciate how very difficult it would be if on a horse. Unless using the wall as a navigational 'handrail', there is no possible reason for taking such a route

The route probably taken by the perambulators from Cullever Steps would be along the line of what is now a well-defined track passing Winter Tor – now regularly used when placing the military range warning flags on Oke Tor and Steeperton Tor. As we walk it, note the rocks strewn on both sides of the track. Or, possibly the perambulators might well have continued up the riverbank until rising to Winter Tor itself but it is unlikely as the hillside is very rock strewn.

Belstone Ridge and Irishman's Wall.

Having climbed up the track above Winter Tor, on reaching the crest we will turn back left and ascend the Belstone Ridge via Higher Tor and Belstone Tor. The reason for climbing this ridge is to afford good views of the next leg that would have been taken by the perambulators to Hound Tor. Today, the large whale backed hill rising to the east is called Cosdon Hill. It was called Cawsand Beacon when I was a boy. Most presume that this was the '*Costdonne*' or '*Costodone*' referred to in the perambulation return. Let us suppose something rather different. The word '*hogam*' used in the perambulation return has been taken to mean either 'hedge' (hence edge) or 'hill'. What if it was a transcription error and the word actually spoken was '*iugum*' which sounds like '*hogam*' when heard. '*Iugum*' translates as 'ridge'. Now the return starts to make sense if we considered the Belstone Ridge to be the '*hogam de Costdonne*' and the next ridge to be the '*hogam que vocatur parva Houndetorre*'. Looking eastwards, a well-beaten track has been made over many centuries from the Horseshoe Ford on the river Taw to the ridgeline near the Whitestone Circle by walkers and riders seeking the easiest passage. Also, in 1609 another perambulation was conducted. The return from that later perambulation states that Hound Tor was 'eastward, one mile or more' from Cosdon. It is from this ridge!

Obviously, changes have occurred since 1240. The Small Brook has seen much activity by medieval tinners and the Taw Marsh is now drier as over two million gallons of water are extracted from it daily. This latter point is mentioned as perhaps the perambulators might have considered avoiding the marsh by continuing on from Winter Tor

Towards Hound Tor from Belstone Ridge.

Chapel Ford.

The Nine Maidens.

towards Oke Tor before descending and crossing the Taw below Steeperton Tor and climbing Metheral Hill to Hound Tor. However, if we try this, we will realise that it is not at all easy on foot and, once again, would have been treacherous on horseback.

Another reason for supposing that the boundary does not go to the top of Cosdon Hill is that the perambulators had been exhorted by the King to define clear metes and bounds. Cosdon has an extensive summit plateau with many large cairns. But the perambulators did not name cairns as metes but they surely would have chosen and mentioned any stone hut circles or 'burgh'. They did so later in the return on three similarly geographically featureless areas – 'EstereWhyteburgh', 'Elesburghe', and 'Menweburghe'. These perambulators did as they were charged and chose metes that could be clearly identified: stones; 'burghs' (hut circles); named places or objects, for example 'Grymesgrove' and 'crucem Sywardi'; or used bounds that followed rivers. Never once were they so woolly as to leave difficulty in understanding the boundary as would have arisen by just going to the top of a large flat topped hill such as Cosdon without mentioning a stone or cairn.

Having enjoyed the view and pondered the possible routes the perambulators might have taken onwards from the Belstone Ridge, we continue along the ridge towards Belstone (possibly as far as the flag pole to avoid the clitter) and descend to Nine Stones (or Nine Maidens) – an ancient stone circle. Supposedly, several young ladies gathered here to dance on a Sunday and were punished by being turned to stone. Of course, the ancient word for stone is 'maen' and so when corrupted it might have become the modern 'maiden'.

If Scarey Tor was not visited on the way up to Cullever Steps, now might be a good time to do so. Otherwise it is probably easiest to follow the track until above Halstock or Chapel Ford and then descend and return along the river in the woods.

Chapter 9

Excursion 2 – Route Over the Taw and Past the Taw Marsh – from Belstone

Here we will be exploring that part of the perambulation route described as follows: *'ad Hogam de Costdonne et inde linealiter usque ad parvam hogam que vocatur parva Houndetorre'*. This exploration of some 9km should only be undertaken when river levels are low enough to allow safe fording of the River Taw that will be crossed at least twice. If we undertake it on a fine sunny day, we might like to include climbing up to some of the vantage points around the marsh in order to see more clearly the route the perambulators probably took.

We can park at many places in Belstone village but the villagers will appreciate us using the car park at the northern entrance to the village (SX618936).

To get to the moor itself, walk carefully along the narrow road between the houses into the village centre, passing en route the stocks and the cross on the village green that celebrates several Royal jubilees (granite recycling!).

Probably the easiest access to the moor is via the track that leaves the small muddy car park under the trees as we reach the southern end of the green overlooking the river valley (SX620930).

The reason for using this track is immediately clear if we just look at the clitter (rocks) on either side. In the photo (below right), a rider is on the track but just look at the jumble of rocks to the side of it. It is like this for the first few hundred metres of the route.

Soon we should come across a stone shaped like half a bell – it can be hard to find in summer – as the local ferns grow almost as high as the stone.

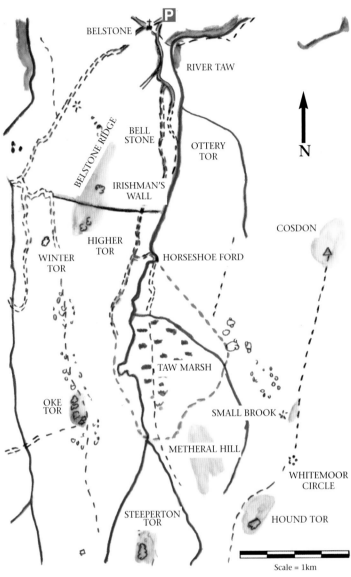

Left: *Jubilee stone and stocks.*
Below: *Rider leaving Belstone.*

The River Taw.

The 'Bell Stone', Ladybrook or Ottery Tor beyond.

Eastwards, above and beyond the stone, (by the distant tree in the photo left) we can see a small unnamed tor – but known locally as either Ladybrook Tor or Ottery Tor. As a side trip, if we clamber down from the bell shaped stone and it is safe to cross the river (it can be seen from the photo of the river that a bit of rock hopping might be required) we can ascend to the tor. The views from there of the Belstone Ridge reveal just how rocky that is.

If we ascend even further, perhaps to the top of Cosdon, the whole of the Belstone ridge is revealed as very rocky as far south as was explored in Excursion 1 – clearly visible in the photo below where drifting snow highlights the presence of the many rocks.

As a reminder, we are heading for the track leading from the Horseshoe Ford (which is not named by the Ordnance Survey but is known as such because of its shape) to the slight col on the ridge where we find White Moor Circle close by Hound Tor – which we last saw from the top of the Belstone Ridge.

Below: *Ottery Tor to Belstone Ridge.*

Right: *Belstone Ridge from Cosdon Hill.*

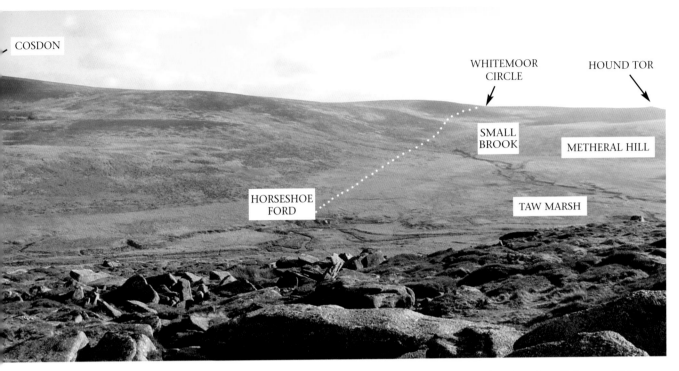

The view from Belstone Ridge.

If we do not divert to Ottery Tor and hence over White Hill to Small Brook, but continue along the track Horseshoe Ford is soon reached. The area of the ford is a favourite spot for picnicking and cooling off in the river on a hot day. The ford should be easy to cross. I have known of people putting carrier bags over their boots to keep dry but I recommend either stripping off or getting good boots.

Having crossed the river, turning south soon brings us into the marsh – which is not impossible to cross but not pleasant either. Imagine how much wetter it would be if the water authority did not extract up to two and a half million gallons a day. The famous Exeter based artist F J Widgery created a series of paintings on the moor that were included in the 1896 re-printing of Samuel Rowe's book (the originals are now owned by the Royal Albert Memorial Museum in Exeter and occasionally go on display). If we look around, we might well find the exact spot where he must have set up his easel here in the marsh area.

Whilst much has changed on Dartmoor over the centuries, the shape of the hills – here it is Steeperton Tor in the distance – remains the same. We can note the very wet ground ahead of the artist. Much of this is far drier now.

Turning to the east, now we are seeking the path that leads to the next ridgeline. It was easy to see from the Belstone Ridge but might be a little indistinct closer up until we are well on the way. The amount of traffic along it has worn the ground down to the rocks beneath.

Horseshoe Ford.

Steeperton Tor (below left) with Widgery's painting of the same scene.

Track to Whitemoor Circle.

Small Brook valley seen from White Hill.

Hound Tor.

If we persevere and continue to the ridgeline ahead, Hound Tor will appear to our right as a rather indistinct mound. The tor's rocky face is only revealed from the east. In the photo to the left, it is clearly identifiable as four people are kindly standing on top of it.

If you choose not to walk all the way up the hill, I recommend that we climb up about half way before diverting south (and down) into the old tin workings in the course of what is called 'Small Brook' (south of White Hill from whence the picture above was taken). This brings us to another pleasant picnic area. In this picture the spot recommended is just below the tree in the Small Brook

To continue the circumnavigation of the Taw Marsh, we must now contour around Metheral Hill, which, in summer, is waist high in ferns and can be a little tricky underfoot.

En route, looking back northwards from Metheral Hill, we can again clearly see the rocks strewn on the eastern flank of the Belstone Ridge.

Steeperton Tor from Metheral Hill.

Having carefully re-crossed the Taw somewhere below Steeperton Tor, the track back to Belstone is fairly obvious and firm underfoot. If we are lucky, we might well see enthusiasts hang gliding in the updraft over Oke Tor above us. To get a better appreciation of why the perambulators probably did not continue along the ridge to Oke Tor before descending to the Taw Marsh and Metheral Hill, climbing a little way up the ridge on a well defined sheep trail/track towards Higher Tor reveals the almost scarp face from Oke Tor down into the Taw Marsh. Looking back towards Steeperton Tor reveals just how steep and rocky a descent that would have been from Oke Tor.

Belstone Ridge from Metheral Hill.

Taw Marsh and Steeperton Tor from Belstone Ridge.

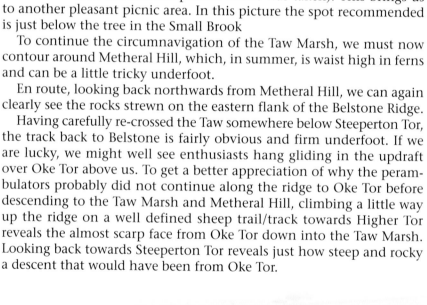

Chapter 10

Excursion 3 – Two Possible Routes from Hound Tor to the Long Stone – from Berrydown

Here we will be exploring a part of the peram-bulation route that has been disputed over the years. The boundary accepted since the perambulation of 1609 describes a route west of the Galaven Mire taking in Watern Tor en route to the Long Stone. I believe that the 1240 perambulators travelled east of the mire via the site of the Teign-e-Ver clapper bridge: *'Et inde usque ad Theurlestone et inde linealiter usque ad Wotysbrokelakysfote que cadit in Teng. Et inde linealiter usque ad Hengheston'*

This walk of at least 13km starts from a small car parking area at Berrydown (SX661877) that has room for half a dozen cars. If full, there may be room instead at Batworthy Corner. During the walk, it might be necessary to wade at least one river. Only do so if safe. We enter the moor via the gate and climb until Cosdon appears to our right. The track to be followed can now be seen climbing the flank of Butter Hill. Heading for it, there are plenty of well-defined sheep trails. The track once joined is obvious, and, I consider, was part of the 1240 route.

As we climb, Rippator will be to our left. It is a nice place to stop for a drink and offers a good view of the Gallaven Mire itself. It can be reached by any of several sheep trails (choose a short direct one as the vegetation can be fierce). In the photo on the following page, the tor is rather indistinct in the foreground compared to Watern Tor on the horizon.

As we keep climbing we will pass a scar in the hillside left by me-dieval tin miners, Ru-elake Pit, and can note the track at its foot heading toward Wild Tor Well. Soon, Hound Tor will ap-pear on the horizon to our left.

Looking ahead and slightly to the west of the looming whale-back shaped Cosdon hill, a leaning stone soon appears on the horizon – White Moor Stone. This stone has a very dis-tinctive shape and

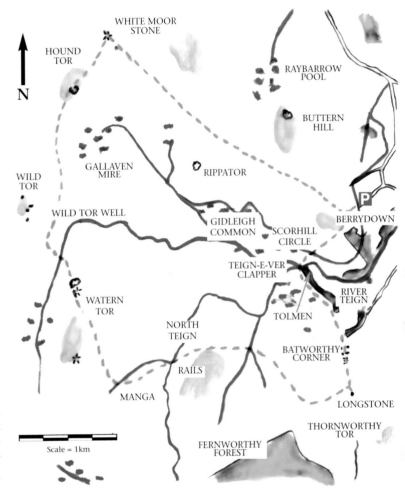

Scale = 1km

Track on the side of Butter Hill.

TRACK

BUTTER HILL

COSDON

Above: *Walkers near Rippon Tor.*
Above right: *Hound Tor. A check-point set up as part of the annual Ten Tors expedition is about to be re-supplied by helicopter.*
Below: *Medieval miners' track.*

posture and is visible and easily identifiable for miles from many directions. I believe it to be the *'Theurlestone'* named by the perambulators and we will examine its setting in more detail as we pass.

The form of the track we have been following is worthy of further attention. It is not of any great stature and has been formed by the simple passage of men and animals over the centuries. I have often seen the cattle and sheep heading for the farms in Gidleigh and Throwleigh following this route as the easiest way home. Nearby, on the eastern flank of Cosdon is a more distinctive track formed by medieval miners that led off the moor from the Knack Mine below Steeperton Tor. The passage of many heavily laden pack animals has scoured out a track several feet deep.

Almost straight ahead is the obvious White Moor Stone. To the south is the rather indistinct hummock that is Hound Tor.

To the north is Cosdon and if we wish to climb it, this is actually a good place to start. The track rises past Little Hound Tor (which is not actually a true tor as it was made by a local man in about 1834) and is easily followed on a clear day. I say 'clear' as I was badly 'pixie led' here one day in low cloud and had to get my GPS out to get to the top! On the summit of Cosdon are several cairns, in ruins, of which the one by the Trig Point is the largest. From the top, as we gather our breath and admire the view all the way to the Bristol Channel if we are lucky, we might have time to consider whether or not the perambulators came to the top of this hill. They didn't mention a cairn, or *'burgh'* as they called stone hut circles and so the mete itself would have been indistinct. They were much more careful to identify a specific point on three other large featureless hills – *'Ester Whyteburgh'*, *'Elysburghe'* and *'Menweburghe'*. I consider that this point adds to my belief that the perambulators did not come this way. Still, the climb brings us to a good viewpoint.

White Moor Stone on the horizon.

White Moor Stone from the stone circle.

White Moor Stone and track – looking south.

Hound Tor from the stone circle.

Cosdon Cairn and trig point.

The route up from Horseshoe Ford.

Returning from Cosdon, our route from the ridge near the stone circle now takes us to what has been supposed to be a mete since at least 1609 – Hound Tor. There is a clear path along the ridge to Hound Tor as we see in the photograph on the right as youngsters on the annual Ten Tors expedition approach the tor checkpoint having come up from Horseshoe Ford via Whitemoor Circle. The tor now has etched upon it a boundary marker for Throwleigh Parish – 'TP'.

Watern Tor, the next point on our route and supposedly reckoned by some to be the *'Theurlestone'* can be seen clearly from here and the easiest route there takes us down and through Wild Tor Well.

If instead, we stay on the higher ground and brave the difficult vegetation protecting Wild Tor, we will be rewarded with another view of the route the perambulators probably took into and out of the Taw valley from the Belstone Ridge to the Hound Tor ridge.

Using the obvious path from Hound Tor to Watern Tor takes us past the Gallaven Mire and into Wild Tor Well. If we are lucky, we might see

Approaching Hound Tor.

View from Wild Tor.

Above: *Watern Tor from the TP boundary stone at Wild Well Tor.* Above right: *Cosdon from the Wallabrook.*

Watern Tor on a snowy day.

The Thurlestone, near Salcombe.

the resident buzzard. It often perches on the rock in the foreground that is actually another marker for the boundary of Throwleigh Parish.

The stream to be crossed at the foot of Watern Tor is normally simple to hop across – but take care. The only fatality of anyone taking part in or practising for Ten Tors occurred by drowning in this stream when it was swollen.

Watern Tor (here seen on a snowy day) has a gap between its stacks wide enough to allow a rider on horseback through. Later, this is what the Gidleigh parishioners wanted the world to believe was the *'Theurlestone'* named in the 1240 perambulation return. That is, they wanted us to believe that it indicated a gap between stones. The exact meaning of the word has been argued over many times. Of note is that the village of Thurlestone in South Devon takes its name from the rock formation in the bay (seen left). Clearly, there is a hole but surely equally clearly is that it has been formed by one stone stack leaning against another. Therefore, I think we should take the 1240 'Theurlestone' to be a leaning stone not a holed stone. As we have seen, the Whit Moor Stone leans in a way that is very noticeable from many directions. I believe that we should take that as the perambulators' *'Theurlestone'*.

Leaving Watern Tor, we head for Manga Rock. In order to get there, the best route is down to the New Take wall and over the stile near the upper northern corner. Once inside the New Take, Hawthorn Clitter is below us and is best passed by staying high and contouring around following the line of the wall until the stream is crossed. Then we can more easily head down to the rock itself.

From the rock, we can see most of the rest of the route for today and an alternative – a short cut along the river. The easiest place to cross the North Teign River near here is below using the fence rails. Then following the New Take wall will bring us to Shovel Down. Alternatively, having crossed the North Teign using the 'Rails', we can then take the shortcut back to the car park by following the river's course to the Teign-e-Ver clapper bridge.

Beside the Rails is where a brook, called 'Hugh Lake' by the Ordnance Survey, joins the North Teign. This has been taken by later generations

View from Manga Rock.

SCORHILL CIRCLE

TEIGN-E-VER CLAPPER BRIDGE

KESTOR ROCK

SHOVEL DOW

NEW TAKE WALL

RAILS

MANGA ROCK

Above: *'Two Stones'*.
Above left: *The crossing point called 'Rails'*.

to be what the 1240 perambulators meant by *'Wotysbrokelakysfote'*. On passing it is obvious what a feeble brook it is, especially when compared later with the Walla Brook flowing from Wild Tor Well into the river by the Teign-e-Ver bridge. I consider that this latter river junction is much more likely to have been the mete in 1240.

Having left the New Take wall, we will find two prominent stones in the mire before the ascent of Shovel Down. They are now taken as boundary stones between the Forest and Gidleigh Parish.

The ascent of Shovel Down is most easily taken by using the wide smooth track that exists – avoiding the tussocks on the direct line. At the top but short of Kestor Rock there is a 'cross tracks'. Turning right and down towards Thornworthy Tor brings us to the Long Stone – *'Henghestone'*. Two things may strike us about this stone. The first is its sheer size – it is very tall. The second is that although large, it cannot be seen from directions other than marked by Kestor Rock and Thornworthy Tor.

Whilst here, possibly gathering breath, it might be worth noting that here is an example of where the perambulators did not always choose metes that could be seen one from another. We must recall that their aim was to create a boundary that could be policed. Rather than relying on using intervisible points, which would have required a lot of metes over forty-three miles, and knowing that it had to be policed in all weathers including days of poor visibility, I consider that they concentrated more on following easily identifiable bounds. The metes chosen would only have been intended to indicate the general route to the local population. If you walk Dartmoor in the dark (with great care of course) perhaps you too will note, as I have, that certain routes not so obvious by day just open up under your feet. This is just such a place. The route to here follow wide animal tracks and from here southwards naturally takes us around Thornworthy Tor. Today of course, the ground throws us towards the middle of Fernworthy Reservoir and so the route of 1240 is impossible to follow now except by boat! But we

If we take a short cut along the river, we must be prepared to wade – but it is often easier than fighting through the morass on the southern bank.

Above: *Long Stone and Kestor Rock*.
Left: *The edge of Fernworthy forest and a rare sight of deer in the open.*

97

From left above: Shovel Down stone row. Scorhill circle. Tolmen in the North Teign.

know that under the water is an ancient bridge and bridges were generally built beside fords over which I consider the perambulators would have gone in 1240.

Turning back now towards the car park, we re-climb the ridge and descend towards Batworthy Corner. Here is an ancient double stone row with a large recumbent and broken stone at its head. At least one earlier scholar has suggested that this was the perambulators' *'Henghestone'*. If we consider the use of the word 'henge' in 'Stonehenge', perhaps it could refer to a stone monument such as this double stone row. In my opinion, it is not that important as the probable line of the boundary passes both this and the Long Stone, both of which lie on the path that is most easily followed on this part of the perambulation.

Now we head back alongside the wall and tree line bounding Batworthy. To the west, the mire leading all the way to the foot of Watern Tor is still farmed.

Before heading back to our cars it is well worth exploring the area around the junction of the Walla Brook and North Teign river. There are two clapper bridges, a large tolmen (holed stone) in the river bed downstream from the two span clapper bridge and of course Scorhill Circle itself. The perambulators of 1240 did not mention this large prehistoric monument and we might wonder if it was re-erected to its present state perhaps in Victorian times. We can but wonder how much wetter the Galaven Mire might have been before the leat just below Scorhill Circle was built.

After leaving the car park a visit the centre of Gidleigh can be informative. There we will discover the ruins of what must have been the home of the Pruz family and a fine church with a board proudly recording the list of rectors and patrons from 1259 onwards (see page 25), including the names of William Prous and later Sir William le Pruz.

Wallabrook clapper bridge today (above) and as depicted by the artist F J Widgery in his watercolour c.1890.

Chapter 11

Excursion 4 – Yestetone, Turbaries de Alberesheved, Walebrokum, King's Oven and Walebrokehenyd – from Fernworthy Reservoir and Bennett's Cross

This part of the perambulation route is difficult to fathom today and so we will explore it from both ends. The building of the dam across the South Teign river to create Fernworthy Reservoir has had a major impact on the local topography. Whether or not what is shown on modern maps as the 'Heath Stone' is the one noted as *'Yestetone'* by the perambulators is uncertain. If this is the *'Yestestone'*, the question also remains about whether or not it might have been moved – they had the equipment to build the dam and thus would certainly have the ability to lift this relatively small stone. Continuing along Hurston Ridge, part of Chagford Common, the going is quite smooth as although we know the locals cut turf here, they left no clear evidence of this - unlike the trenches left by later industrial turf cutters above the Rattle Brook near Bleak House. The one feature that does remain is the North Walla Brook. However, any traces of the activity that we might assume would take place around an industrial site such as *'Furnum Regis'*, the King's Oven, have become obscure. Finally in this excursion, whether or not *'Wale-brokehenyd'* is a feature on the North Walla Brook or perhaps is the start or head of the Walla Brook south below the Warren House Inn is also open to debate. The route is described in the 1240 return as follows: *'Et inde linealiter usque ad Yestetone. Et inde linealiter usque per mediam turbarium de Alberesheved. Et sic in longum Wale-brokum. Et inde linealiter usque ad furnem Regis: Et inde linealiter usque ad Walebrokehenyd.'*

Firstly we will visit Fernworthy dam and reservoir. There is a public car park (where a small charge is made) and a picnic area (with facilities) at the entrance to the forest (SX668839). From this viewpoint we can look across the lake to Thornworthy Tor. The perambulators might well have come *'linealiter'* to here but now of course we have to go via the bridge across the stream just below the dam or use a boat.

Rhododendrons now line the valley sides below the dam. They would not have been here in 1240 as they were only introduced to England in 1763. We will note the steep sides of the valley that, I am sure, the perambulators would have avoided by crossing the South Teign river higher up, i.e. under the surface of today's reservoir. The perambulators next mete was the *'Yestetone'*, a

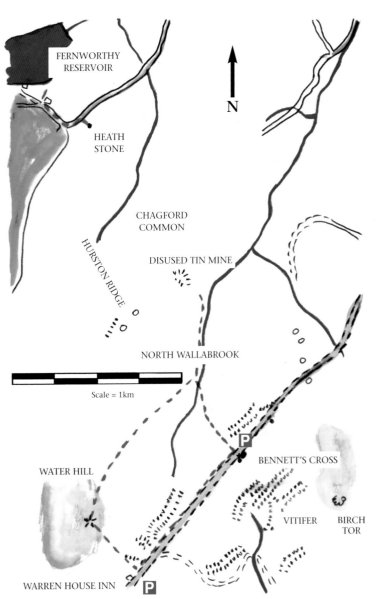

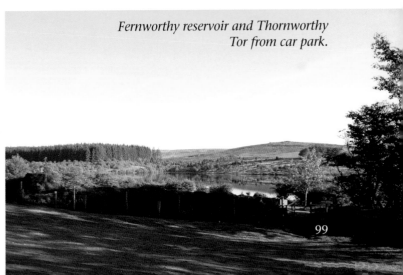

Fernworthy reservoir and Thornworthy Tor from car park.

A beautiful start to the day.
Inset: *The Heath Stone.*

Rhododedrons on the valley sides.

Towards Cosdon from below Bennett's Cross.

word which when spoken could easily be likened to 'Jurston' or 'Hurston'. In this area are farms and a ridge with those names so we must be in roughly the right place.

There is an orthostat (a large stone set upright) beside the road short of the entrance to the forest called on modern maps the Heath Stone. It is neither tall nor very large but it is taken by many to be the 'Yestetone' mentioned in the return. Whether it is or is not the mete, or whether it might have been moved when the dam was built, will probably never be known. These days, its main feature is some lines from the Bible crudely carved in 1979.

I believe that the perambulators came this way as, once again, the lie of the land hereabouts leads us from the area at the exit from the forest, which of course did not exist in 1240, upwards onto Hurston Ridge and towards the first of the four linear features mentioned in the return. This is a stream called 'Wallebrokum' in the return but is now marked as the North Walla Brook and is known by others as Bovey Combe Head or Hurston Water.

Instead of walking directly southwards across the rather boggy Chagford Common or SSW and into the valley, most modern walkers choose to hug the forest wall for about 500m to avoid the marsh before heading up and over the crest to the cairn on Water Hill. The perambulators would, in my opinion, have headed slightly east of south, crossed the Metherall Brook and dropped into the valley of the North Walla Brook. Rather than follow them, let us take our car to the car park near either Bennett's Cross (SX675811) or the Warren House Inn.

North Wallabrook Bottom looking southwards.

Leaving the car park beside Bennett's Cross and heading westwards, we start to drop into the valley of the North Walla Brook. To the north in the far distance are Cosdon and closer Kestor Rock. The scar on the hillside is the remains of a track to a disused mine in the valley floor. The perambulators probably came into the valley near this and then rode up the stream to its head. Once in the valley bottom, look southwards. The col ahead is probably where the perambulators left the valley to continue southwards. Today, of course, the ground by the stream is criss-crossed with the tracks and excavations made by miners who came later than 1240 and there is old adit to explore here if you can find it.

After crossing the modern road, the perambulators would have dropped down the other side to another Wallabrook heading south. Now of course that whole area is littered with the waste from the much later Vitifer mine (see photograph on following page).

Coming back out of the valley directly, Bennett's Cross appears on the horizon. This ancient marker was not mentioned by the perambulators so may well have been re-erected since their passage.

Bennett's Cross as we emerge from the valley.

Water Hill cairn with Cosdon in the distance.

Mine working is much in evidence in this view over Vitifer mine c.1910.

If we take the time to climb to the cairn on Water Hill, on a fine day we will have a long view towards Cosdon. The ruins of buildings purported to be *'Furnem Regis'* are marked on the map as being between here and the North Walla Brook. Whether these indistinct ruins truly were here in 1240 will probably remain unknown as there has been so much industrial activity here since.

Chapter 12

Excursion 5 – Pizwell, Cator Common Bridge and Riddon Ridge

This part of the perambulation route is clear – it is along the banks of the Walla Brook as far as the East Dart river. However, the route cannot be followed exactly today as private land has been enclosed and impassable walls and fences built. The Duchy of Cornwall owns the two farms along this part of the route (Runnage and Pizwell). The route of the perambulators is described simply in the 1240 return as follows: *'Et sic in longem Walebrokum usque cadit in Derta.'*

First, we will be visiting the area at the entrance to Pizwell Farm owned by the Duchy of Cornwall (SX668789). This is a pleasant spot to sit and have a picnic on a sunny day. Here the stream runs clear and is a spawning ground for trout and possibly salmon. The perambulators would have approached this spot from the north using the brook as a 'handrail', along the edge of what is now Soussons Down plantation. If we choose to re-trace their route northwards from here, the right of way is only a couple of metres wide – defined by the wall of Runnage Farm to the west and the plantation fence to the east. Beware – it can be boggy.

Another pleasant place to sit in the sun by this same stream is by the bridge to the south of Cator Common (SX669776). We could also use this as a start point for a walk up onto Riddon Ridge. Most modern followers of the Forest Boundary climb up onto this ridge. This is because it avoids the bogs beside the stream and anyway the perambulators' route onwards enters what is now the private farmland of Babeny and Sherwell.

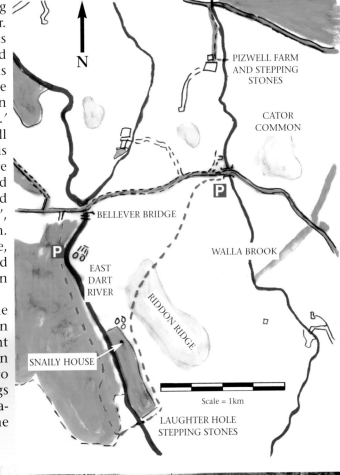

N

PIZWELL FARM AND STEPPING STONES

CATOR COMMON

BELLEVER BRIDGE

WALLA BROOK

EAST DART RIVER

RIDDON RIDGE

SNAILY HOUSE

Scale = 1km

LAUGHTER HOLE STEPPING STONES

Pizwell Farm stepping stones.

Cator Common bridge.

Alternatively, we could park (for a small fee) in the Bellever Forest (SX655771) where there are lovely picnic areas by the East Dart river. The walk up over Riddon Ridge offers excellent views of Bellever Tor and towards Yar Tor (part of another excursion). If we are lucky, we might well see a local hunt out exercising the hounds. The overgrown enclosure between here and the East Dart River is the site of Snaily House. Following outside the wall and down to the river brings us to the stepping-stones at Laughter Hole. We cross these and follow the forest tracks back to the Bellever car park.

Bellever picnic site.

A huntsman below Bellever Tor.

Hounds at full stretch.

Snaily House.

Laughter Hole stepping stones.

Yar Tor beyond the horses at Babeny.

Chapter 13
Excursion 6 – Dartmeet and the O Brook

Here we will be exploring that part of the perambulation route described by Westcote/Rowe as follows: *'Wallebroke usque cadit in Dertam et sic per Dertam usque ad Aliam Dertam [Dartmeet], et sic per aliam Dertam ascendendo usque Okebrokysfote [Week Ford], et sic ascendendo Okebroke [O Brook] usque ad la Dryeworke' [Dry Lake].*

Yar Tor (SX678740): Drive to Yar Tor – to the north and above Dartmeet. Park beside the road (SX682739) and walk across the firm ground to Yar Tor itself. On a clear day, we will be rewarded with views of the perambulators' route along the Wallebroke from Cator Common and today's route over Riddon Ridge to the northwest (i.e. skirting the now enclosed land on the banks of the Wallebroke above Babeny) to Dryeworke on the slope leading to Ryder's Hill in the south.

From Yar Tor, the perambulator's route down the Wallebroke can be seen as well as the route modern perambulators must take over Riddon Ridge.

EAST DART

YAR TOR

PENNEY CROSS

N

P

DARTMEET

COFFIN STONE

WEST DART

Scale = 1km

RIDDON RIDGE

LAUGHTER HOLE

WALLEBROKE...
CADIT IN DERTA

WALLEBROKE

Looking southwards – showing the perambulators' route from Dartmeet along the West Dart ('Alium Dertam') to and up the 'Okebroke' to 'Dryework' and on to Ryder's Hill.

RYDER'S HILL

DRYWORKS

OKEBROKE

OKEBROKYSFOTE

ALIUM DERTAM

DARTMEET

Dartmeet (SX672732): Now drive down to Dartmeet itself where there is a large car park, public toilets, a café/ restaurant and, possibly, a lot of tourists. We are here to see the stepping-stones across the West Dart (SX670731). To reach these, leave the car park, cross the river on the road bridge towards Princetown and follow the signs that lead us behind the private house(s) on the south side of the road just above the bridge. En route, we can take in both the old Dartmeet bridge and the new one – neither of which were mentioned by the perambulators.

Above: *Dartmeet clapper bridge.*

Above right: *Dartmeet 'new' road bridge.*

From left to right above: *West Dart stepping stones, passable with care. Impassable – in flood. Even when partially covered, take great care. I crossed here after taking this picture and almost had a swim!*

Hexworthy (SX655726): Having driven towards Princetown and turned off left for Hexworthy (where swimming under the bridge is popular in warm weather) we pass the Forest Inn, climb the hill and take the sharp turn right to the road leading to Sherberton and Swincombe.

Access by Car: Part of the route is on the road from Holne to Hexworthy and car parking can be found either at Saddle Bridge (SX664719) or beside the lesser road to the south of Hexworthy (SX654725).

Going: A short 5km walk will take us along a part of the perambulators' route along the upper 'Okebroke' (now called the 'O Brook' on the OS 1:50,000 map) and then ascending Down Ridge opposite *Dryeworke* will reveal panoramic views of the perambulation route. Whilst we start on tarmac, later we will encounter the need to avoid or wade through boggy patches, scramble over some rocks and jump streams.

Route: Leave the road east of Saddle Bridge and walk parallel to and upstream beside the O Brook. This was the 'Okebroke' of the perambulators. We will encounter the Holne Moor Leat that continues past Combestone Tor to the Holy Brook above Buckfastleigh and will pass the paddle gates by which the rate of water flow can be adjusted. If we are stealthy, we might also see the fish that inhabit the leat.

Continuing past the base of the old tin workings known as Dryeworke (there is a nice picnic spot under the tree), follow the stream to the substantial granite slab bridge carrying the track to Hooten Wheals. There is a sheep trail but we may need to scramble over some rocks as we progress as well as minding our heads on some low hanging branches of the occasional hawthorn tree. Thereafter, follow the well-used trail back to the car.

Viewpoint: As we walk the track from the Hooton Wheals bridge to Hexworthy, in the region of the Horse Ford Cross, which is not far off the track to our right, we should look south towards Ryder's Hill. The scar that is 'Dryeworke' is clearly visible.

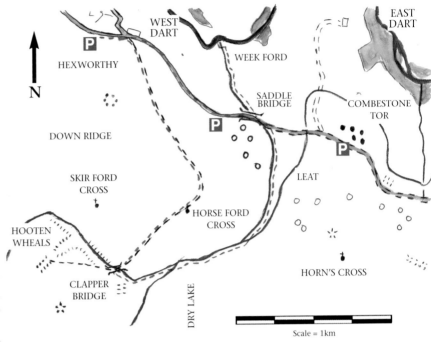

'Dryework' on the hill behind Horse Ford cross.

FURTHER DIVERSIONS (SEE MAP ABOVE FOR SUITABLE START POINTS)

D1: At Hexworthy:

The bridge at Hexworthy attracts swimmers and fishermen. In 2013, my son was fly-fishing for trout upstream from this bridge towards the junction with the Swincombe when he was startled as eight full grown migrating salmon passed him going upstream, one slapping his waders. Up the steep hill heading south is an inn, The Forest Inn, reputed to be one of William Crossing's favourites. Opposite the inn is a relatively young stone cross – erected to commemorate Queen Victoria's Diamond Jubilee, 1897.

Hexworthy bridge.

107

Queen Victoria's cross.

D2: **From the Saddle Bridge:** The O Brook north of the road can be followed by a well marked track, rocky and wet in places and with stiles, to the point where it joins the East Dart at Week Ford (SX661724). There is a pleasant picnic spot here by the river as well as the stepping-stones for enjoyment – as long as the river is not too high.

Start of the path from Saddle Bridge to Week Ford.

The path beside the O Brook is narrow, muddy and rocky.

Stepping stones at Week Ford.

D3: **From the Saddle Bridge:** The old mine workings of Hooten Wheals (SX655708) are just south of an old clapper bridge (probably built in the 19th century to serve the mines) and the Hensroost to the west (SX651710). These workings probably date back to the 18th century and continued under the joint name of Hexworthy Mines into the 20th century. Exploring these can take time and, if we do, we can discern ruined buildings, wheel pits, buddles (for washing the ore), dressing floors and blocked adits and shafts.

Hooten Wheals.

Old ruins.

Dressing floors.

Chapter 14

Excursion 7 – Ryder's Hill or *'Catteshill'* –
from Combestone Tor

This walk of about 6km does not actually follow the perambulators' route but does offer an easier route to the top of Ryder's Hill and views from above of the route up the *'Okebroke'* and *'Dryeworke'*. Beyond the summit of Ryder's Hill we will see the head of the *'Westerewelebroke'* and as far as the White Barrows.

There is easy parking for the planned walk at Combestone Tor (SX670717). This can be approached from either Hexworthy (see Excursion 6) or from the Holne direction.

As a side trip, if we park by the Venford Reservoir and walk the one kilometre or so to Bench Tor (SX690719) we can gain an appreciation of just what an obstacle the Dart Valley would be to perambulators. They really needed to cross this river at no lower than Dartmeet.

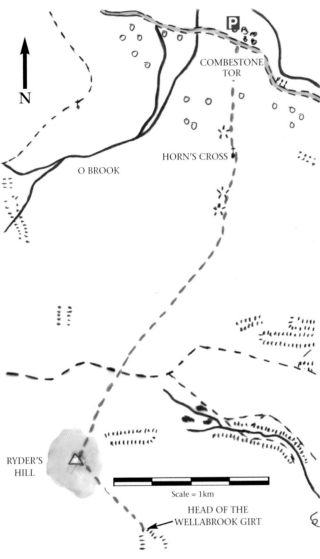

Dart Valley from Bench Tor.

Having parked at Combestone Tor, we can take in the views northwards towards Dartmeet and Yar Tor – sites that might have been visited on a previous excursion.

Dartmeet and Yar Tor from Combestone Tor.

TO RYDER'S HILL

DRYEWORKE

OKEBROKE

Towards Ryder's Hill.

Heading south we start to climb. To our right we will see the course of the O Brook ('*Okebroke*') and the turn upwards towards Ryder's Hill via '*Dryeworke*'.

Two reaves meet.

As we climb we will notice the remains of ancient boundaries marked by reaves (low ruined walls).

If we look back down towards Combestone Tor and the light is right (here just after dawn) we will see more extensive patterns of reaves on the slopes below Sharp Tor.

Reaves on the hillside beyond Combestone Tor.

The reaves give some indication of the extent to which Dartmoor had been settled in the Bronze Age. If we plot all the known reaves on Dartmoor and the Forest Boundary as accepted by the Duchy, we can see that in the main the perambulators stayed away from these ancient settlements. Or it may just be that the ground on the higher parts of the moor was mostly unsuitable for possible settlement anyway.

EASTERN WHITE BARROW   WESTERN WHITE BARROW

Ryder's Hill is convex in shape and the summit never seems to near. When we eventually do reach the top we will note two granite markers and a Trig Point. Beyond we will see White Barrow Ridge that marked the furthest south the perambulators ventured. The Eastern Barrow looks rather like a surfacing submarine and was built up into this shape in the 1930s. The Western one, although cast down, probably holds more significance and has a stone cross.

To the southeast the top of the Wellabrook Girt is clearly visible – recorded by the perambulators as *'capud de Westerewelebrooke'*.

Having admired the view it is probably easiest to retrace our steps to Combestone Tor following one of the multiple sheep trails going northwards. The ground to the east and to the west of this summit is covered in large grass tussocks that make for uncomfortable walking.

Ryder's Hill.

Westerewelebrooke beyond Ryder's Hill.

SNOWDON   PUPERS HILL

WESTEREWELEBROOKE

Chapter 15

Excursion 8 – Wellabrook Girt to the White Barrows Ridge – from Lud Gate or Shipley Bridge

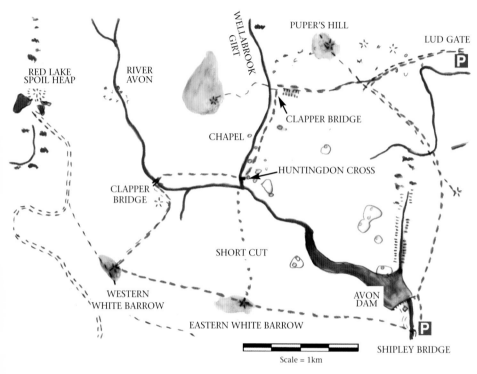

RED LAKE SPOIL HEAP

RIVER AVON

WELLABROOK GIRT

PUPER'S HILL

LUD GATE

CLAPPER BRIDGE

CHAPEL

HUNTINGDON CROSS

CLAPPER BRIDGE

SHORT CUT

WESTERN WHITE BARROW

EASTERN WHITE BARROW

AVON DAM

SHIPLEY BRIDGE

Scale = 1km

This walk is about 12km long but can be shortened if so wished *and* if the amount of water flowing down the River Avon near Huntingdon Cross makes crossing it by wading or rock-hopping possible. Starting from the parking spot near Lud Gate (SX692672) brings us most easily into the Wellabrook Girt. Alternatively we can park at Shipley Bridge (SX680629) below the Avon Dam and start from there: *'et sic per Westerewelebroke usque cadit in Avena. Et inde linealiter usque ad EstereWhyteburgh.'*

The major point of conjecture with this part of the route is whether or not the perambulators visited what is now called Eastern White Barrow or the cairn hosting Petre's Cross at Western White Barrow. Eastern White Barrow is a huge pile of rocks quite unlike any other on Dartmoor. It is like a submarine with its conning tower and its distinctive shape is visible from all directions. Here seen first on the horizon from a hilltop near South Brent and then closer up.

Eastern White Barrow.

Eastern White Barrow seen from South Brent.

Lane to Lud Gate.

Clapper bridge, Shipley Leat and Eastern White Barrow on the horizon.

Heron having been disturbed.

The walk from the lane near Lud Gate, where four or five cars can park on the grassy verge without blocking the road, starts up the tarmac road then continues along the stony track to the gate itself giving access to the open moor.

The climb up and to the south of the rocks on Pupers Hill is on a wide grassy track. After cresting the ridgeline, the track soon brings us to a granite stone bridge. The warreners (rabbit farmers) at Huntingdon Warren probably built this. Shipley Leat starts here and is full of fish – herons can often be seen here.

Below Left: *Chapel and (inset) the incised stone with a cross.*

Below: *Tinners' or warreners' buildings.*

Continuing down the stream brings us to a chapel, ruined, established by a group of young men between 1904 and 1914 guided by the Reverend Keble Martin. It has reportedly been used for weddings not so long ago. The cross etched into the upright stone, seen here in the centre of the grass bank, was made at the same time and is thus not ancient.

Further down we reach yet more ruined buildings standing in their own mini-quagmire.

Bear in mind that none of these signs of human activity would have been here in 1240 and the perambulators had probably been on the move all day to reach here and possibly getting tired.

At the bottom of the girt where the stream joins the Avon is Huntingdon Cross, probably erected around 1557 as a boundary stone of Brent Moor. It is also a marker on the east to west path known as the Abbot's Way. Although the Ordnance Survey map indicates that there are 'fords' hereabouts, if there are, they are uncomfortable to cross on foot and would be even more treacherous for a horse. A river crossing should not be attempted when it is full.

Huntingdon cross by the Avon.

Tussocks protect the barrow from the north.

Possible fords and medieval track beyond.

Clapper bridge over the Avon.

Western White Barrow and Petre's Cross.

If we can cross, we will then be faced with a most unpleasant struggle up through tussock grass almost all the way to Eastern White Barrow. Even the sheep seem to forsake this area, as there are no easily useable sheep trails through this ankle snapping ground.

Surely we are safe in making the assumption that knights on horseback would not wish to endanger one of their major assets, namely their mounts. I prefer to think that at this stream junction, they turned westwards along the Avon. It must have been late afternoon by now and the northern riverbank offers a much smoother passage. However, the Avon soon turns north and so I conjecture that the perambulators crossed the stream before this, there are easy crossing points just east of the clapper bridge, and then mounted the ridge beyond (the easiest ascent is up the track widened by subsequent medieval activity) towards Western White Barrow.

After crossing the river by either fording or using the bridge, we climb the first short rise and soon the slope eases. The path being followed passes to the north of the Barrow and as soon as we see it we just divert towards it.

The cross on Western White Barrow takes its name from Sir William Petre of Tor Brian who 'possessed certain rights over Brent Moor'. An important Devonian, he was Secretary of State in four reigns. He died in 1571. So, this cross would probably not have been here when the perambulators passed. I think that in fact this mete was chosen as it is nearest to the col over which we have just passed when leaving the river Avon and this collection of stones, probably from thrown down huts or a 'burgh', was the only other distinguishable feature here in 1240. The later work to dig china clay, create a railway track and raise the Red Lake spoil heap had simply not yet occurred.

The walk we will take now between the two White Barrows is relatively easy and just follows the ridgeline. It offers lovely views.

Above: *Looking north from White Barrows Ridge.* Above: *Wester Wellabrook from near Eastern White Barrow.*

Eastern White Barrow (left) and the barrow seen from Petre's Cross.

Looking to the north from the ridgeline, firstly the course of the Avon can be seen – the clapper bridge is just where it bears northwards. Later, as we progress, the course of the *'Westerewelebroke'* itself becomes clear.

Now it just remains for us to examine Eastern White Barrow, descend to the Avon Dam and then enjoy the views on the return to Lud Gate via Dean Moor.

Below left: *Riders on the Abbot's Way.*

Below: *Avon Dam.*

Avon reservoir and Eastern Whittaburrow from Dean Moor.

Chapter 16
Excursion 9 – Harford and Brent Moor

This excursion of about 10km starting near Harford is not on the perambulators' route. It is of interest in that it includes views of some of the features shown on the map described by Samuel Rowe and later re-examined by Spence Bate that is now held at the DHC, Exeter. It is a trip to the southern part of Dartmoor called Brent Moor. The walk will explore some of the objects described on both that early map and another held at the DHC.

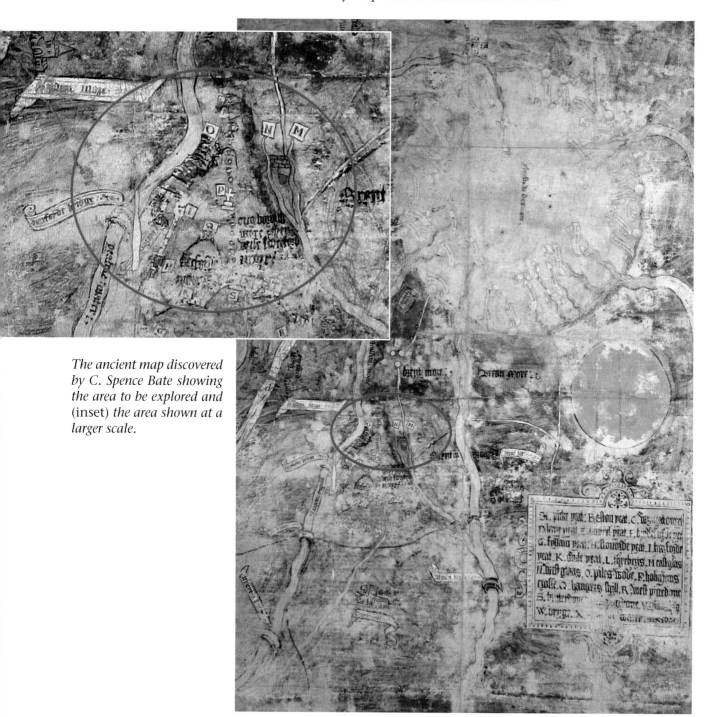

The ancient map discovered by C. Spence Bate showing the area to be explored and (inset) *the area shown at a larger scale.*

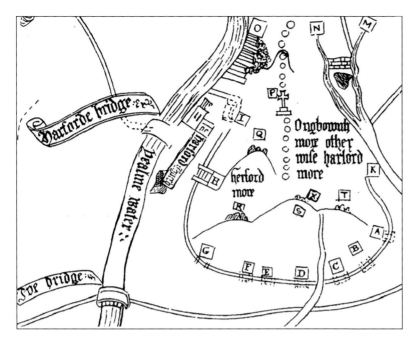

The enlarged area as sketched by C. Spence Bate.

Above is the same area sketched by Spence Bate and also on a map dated 1786 and held at the DHC – labelled "Copy of an antient Map of East Hartford Moore". Notice that only one cairn is shown on the White Barrow Ridge on the latter and that it is named 'Utter Whittborough' and it has a cross atop it – as at Western White Barrow.

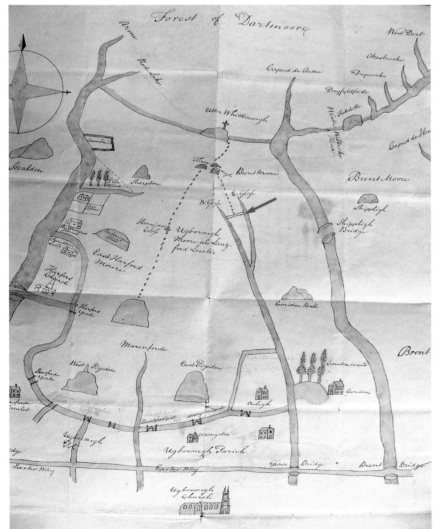

The 1786 map held at the Devon Heritage Centre, Exeter showing the wall built across the 'V' of the stream (arrowed).

Prrsent day view of the ancient wall across the 'V' of the valley (arrowed).

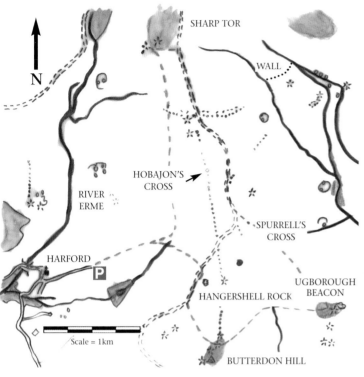

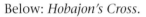

The start of the walk is from the car park above Harford church (SX643595). There are fairly obvious tracks leading through the undergrowth up and to the east. We can either go all the way up to the old tramway before bearing northwards to Sharp Tor, or at a slightly lower level follow the line of the underground pipes that run all the way from Red Lake to bring china clay off of the moor.

En route, we might encounter Hobajon's Cross – which is not a cross shaped piece of granite as shown on the old map or by Spence Bate but one of Dartmoor's incised crosses. It stands in a long stone row that leads all the way to Butterdon Hill to the south.

There is a good view from Sharp Tor down into the Erme Valley and across to the opposite hilltop where the remains of Hillson's House can be seen. Looking northwards we can see how steep sided is the Erme valley until past Erme Pound at Red Lake Foot.

We are now going to head for Ugborough Beacon, probably using the tramway as it is easier underfoot. Branching off westwards brings us to another ancient cross with one arm missing – Spurrell's Cross.

All the way from here to Ugborough Beacon, looking northwards towards Eastern White Barrow, in the foreground we will see a wall stretching between two streams. This is exactly as it is depicted on those maps from so long ago.

On leaving the moor, it is well worth also looking at two other items shown on those maps – namely Harford church and Harford bridge.

Below: *Hobajon's Cross.*

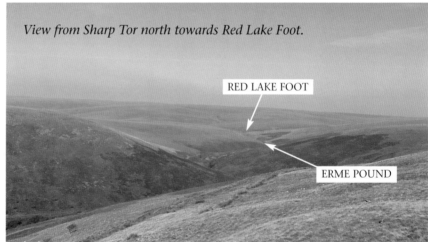

View from Sharp Tor north towards Red Lake Foot.

RED LAKE FOOT

ERME POUND

Spurrell's Cross looking towards Three Barrows.

Harford church.

Harford bridge.

Chapter 17

Excursion 10 – Plym Ford, Broad Rock, Erme Pits, Red Lake, Hortonsford Bottom and Grim's Grave – from the Scout Hut

This 15km excursion on the South Moor examines the possible routes that the perambulators might have taken between Red Lake and Eylesbarrow: *'ubi Rede Lake cadit in Erm Et inde ascendendo usque ad Grymesgrove. Et inde linealiter usque ad Elesburghe'*

There are varying ideas on how the perambulators might have travelled between Red Lake Foot and Eylesbarrow. A key to the puzzle would be to identify the possible form and location of *'Grymesgrove'*. We note that in four of the copies of the perambulation return, the perambulators 'ascended' to *'Grymesgrove'*; and in two they went 'linearly'. In one the scribe used both words! Another major factor is that the area of Erme Head, known in olden times as Arme Head, had not yet been mined and so would have been an unpleasant to cross boggy area – rather like Avon Head is today.

Three possible routes that the perambulators might have taken in 1240 have been suggested over the years. The northern route via Plym Head is direct but the ground approaching it from Erme Head is unsuitable for horsemen. The central route following the line of the medieval Abbot's Way can be ridden today but would have been very close to the Erme Head morass in 1240. And, both of these routes assume that *'Grymesgrove'* has disappeared, perhaps as a result of the mining that occurred later. A southern route via Hortonsford Bottom, Langcombe Head, Grim's Grave and Plym Steps is, I conjecture, more likely to have been the route taken. The Erme Head mire would have been avoided to the south; Hortonsford Bottom would have offered a suitable resting place at the end of the first day (its form has been altered by mining activity but not to too great an extent); the climb over Langcombe Head is certainly 'ascending'; Grim's Grave could easily be the *'Grymsgrove'* of old; the crossing of the Plym is easily accomplished at Plym Steps followed by a ride on firm ground up to Eylesbarrow.

The excursion proposed follows the central route described above to get to Red Lake Foot and then follows the southerly route back. Side trips can be made to explore other points of note. Parking is available at the ford (SX578673) short of the Scout Hut. The route starts and finishes on a hardened track but in places can get boggy if side explorations are undertaken.

Having crossed the ford and passed the Scout Hut follow the hardened track upwards. We will pass through the area of the old Eylesbarrow Mine and its ruined buildings. If we divert from the track and approach the Hartor Tors, we might be tempted to take a shortcut to

Map labels: EYLESBARROW, CRANE HILL, PLYM FORD, EYLESBARROW TIN MINE, PLYM HEAD, GREAT GNAT'S HEAD, SCOUT HUT, DITSWORTHY WARREN, DUCK'S POOL, GREEN HILL, ABBOT'S WAY, PLYM STEPS, BROAD ROCK, ERME HEAD, GRIM'S GRAVE, LANGCOMBE BROOK, LANGCOMBE HEAD, SHAVERCOMBE BROOK, WATERFALL, DITSWORTHY WARREN HOUSE, HORTONSFORD BOTTOM, RED LAKE, LANGCOMBE HILL, N, Scale = 1km

Mine building floating in the mist.

119

Broad Rock.

Floating morass on the banks of the Plym.

Rock incised 'A Head'.

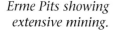

Erme Pits showing extensive mining.

Erme Head bog.

Broad Rock by crossing the river below the tors. Certainly the river is narrow enough to be jumped fairly easily but either side is made up of floating bogs that make this a treacherous passage.

By following the track up to Plym Ford we should be able both to cross the river easily and find the Abbot's Way – last met further east during Excursion 8. The track rises up the side of Great Gnats' Head and can be hard to distinguish in places. Eventually we will reach Broad Rock with its inscription. From here, the route of the Abbot's Way down to Red Lake starts to become more apparent. We might wish to divert to find the rock incised 'A Head' which is at the head of the Erme (Arme) – if we do so, note the boggy and treacherous ground still surrounding it.

Continuing downwards to Erme Pits, note both the ground underfoot and the view ahead.

As we leave Erme Pits, we might just climb a little to the northeast until we can see Hillson's House in the distance. From here we also get a view of the Erme valley and can see how wide it is. Imagine it full of bog – a place to avoid. Rising from the Erme valley to the south is the start of Hortonsford Bottom.

At Red Lake Foot, it is worth just climbing the ridge a little to the north again. Here we will see a stone row that is in fact the longest of its kind known, certainly the longest on Dartmoor and possibly in Europe. It runs some 3.5km from a cairn on Green Hill to the north to a circle of stones known as the 'Dancers' in the south. It passes the Erme Pound that featured on the ancient maps we looked at previously.

Erme Valley and Hortonsford Bottom.

RED LAKE FOOT

HILLSON'S HOUSE

HORTONSFORD BOTTOM

ERME VALLEY

Stone row looking northwards.

Stone row looking southwards.

Hortonsford Bottom from the stone row.

Having reached the furthest point of the planned walk, we might consider going just a little further for the view from the top of the spoil heap at Red Lake. We can just catch a glimpse of the Avon Reservoir and also Eastern and Western White Barrow – which we visited during Excursion 8.

Whilst at Red Lake Foot we might consider the route the 1240 perambulators took to get to the top of Langcombe Hill. The walk up through Hortonsford Bottom is relatively easy underfoot and although there has been mining activity here since 1240, it has been relatively shallow. As we leave to climb Langcombe Hill we can look back and see how protected the area is.

Having crossed Langcombe Hill, we now descend via Langcombe Brook to an ancient kistvaen, Grim's Grave – possibly the perambulators' 'Grymesgrove'. The route continues downwards to Plym Steps but if we wish to see one of the few waterfalls on Dartmoor, we should contour round southwards to the Shavercombe Brook. Contouring even further to Hen Tor leads to a good view of Ditsworthy Warren House used by Steven Spielberg in the making of the film 'War Horse'. There is now a good track from the farm to the car park at the ford.

Grazing in Hortonsford Bottom.

DITSWORTHY WARREN HOUSE

SCOUT HUT

Ditsworthy Warren and Scout Hut.

Grim's Grave.

Shavercombe Brook.

Chapter 18
Excursion 11 – Eylesbarrow to South Hessary Tor
via Siward's Cross

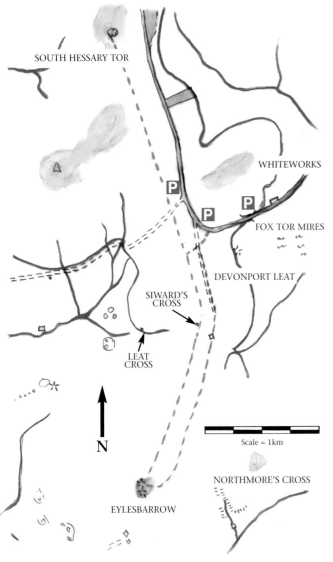

SOUTH HESSARY TOR

WHITEWORKS

P

P

P

FOX TOR MIRES

DEVONPORT LEAT

SIWARD'S
CROSS

LEAT
CROSS

N

Scale = 1km

NORTHMORE'S CROSS

EYLESBARROW

The route from Eylesbarrow to South Hessary Tor is easily traversed today, either on the turf following the modern Water Board boundary markers or on the nearby sandy bridleway. En route we will pass Siward's or Nun's cross, which was included in the return as a mete by the perambulators in 1240. This part of the boundary was described in the return as follows: *'ad Elesburghe Et inde linealiter usque ad crucem Syward. Et inde usque ad Ysfothere'*

The road from Princetown to Whiteworks is narrow and should thus be driven with care. There are several obvious parking places near the elbow in the road each of which has room for half a dozen cars or so.

If we start from the eastern most of the parking spots shown on the map here, parking by the bridge over the leat (SX608708), the easiest way to get to Nun's Cross Farm near Siward's Cross is along the path on the edge of the Devonport Leat. We will also see stones set in the leat as a sheep leap. From the leat, we get excellent views down over the Foxtor Mires that became the Grimpen Mire in Arthur Conan Doyle's Sherlock Holmes mystery – 'Hound of the Baskervilles'. The mires are just about impassable. It is possible to cross by just one partially reinforced path but such a crossing should not be undertaken without either a guide or a clear idea of the route and a very good set of boots.

The easiest route from Siward's Cross to Eylesbarrow is via a sandy track much favoured today by mountain bikers. The word 'sandy' on Dartmoor is often used to describe any fairly flat path or ford. The 'sand' of course

Fox Tor Mires and Fox Tor
in the distance.

Eylesbarrow boundary marker and cobra head.

is ground down granite and has to be treated with care as there are often larger lumps present and very often sharp quartz crystals.

I along with many other Ten Tors participants will remember this track well as it forms an easy route from the south moor to the north moor. I passed here in 1965 going north leading a team from my school to successfully complete a sixty mile Ten Tors trek. I still treasure that medal.

On the summit of Eylesbarrow is a ruined cairn. The site is strewn with rocks and is so spoilt as to be almost not worth visiting, except for one feature. It has the only remaining iron 'cobra' head on the moor. Four of these markers were erected in 1867 following a dispute over the line of the boundary between the Duchy and the Earl of Morley. They were installed on Great Mistor, North Hessary Tor, South Hessary Tor and here. They were described as iron 'crosses' but so resemble the head of a cobra snake that the name has stuck. The cobra head on South Hessary Tor disappeared in about 2013.

The author's Ten Tors medal.

To return to Nun's Cross Farm, we can either use the sandy track or stay on the turf and follow the line of Water Board markers. Alternatively, a short way away on Down Ridge is an excellent example of a stone row well worth a visit. It is some 350m in length with a menhir at each end. These stand proud today having been re-erected in the summer of 1894.

Down Tor stone row from the west.

Siward's or Nun's Cross.

Nun's Cross Farm.

Siward's or Nun's Cross was named as a mete in the perambulation return. It is the largest and oldest recorded cross on Dartmoor. It had to be repaired with its present iron splints in 1848. It probably dates from the reign of Edward the Confessor 1042–1066. William Crossing suggested that the present name is a corruption of 'nans' or 'nant', Cornu-Celtic for valley, dale or ravine. So when we are here, look around to see how apt this is. The cross stands surrounded by high ground beside the track above the now dilapidated farmhouse.

Leat (or Hutchinson's) Cross.

Passing underneath us here in a tunnel is the Devonport Leat. We cannot enter the tunnel because of the fear of the dangers from accumulations of radon gas in the granite. The eastern entrance to the tunnel is not very attractive but the western end of the tunnel 600m away is worth a visit. Another new cross, Leat Cross, erected in 1968, stands close to the tunnel mouth. Although the cross is new, the socket in which it has been placed is of an unknown age.

The route from Nun's Cross to South Hessary Tor is straightforward. If we climb to the top of the tor, being careful as it is a bit of a scramble, the remains of the missing 'cobra' head can be seen. This has disappeared relatively recently. Whilst here, we can puzzle over a part of the 1240 perambulation return. Not once did the perambulators name what we now call a tor as a mete. This mete, if it is this tor, is named in the return as *'Ysfother'*. North Hessary Tor was named just as 'another' Ysfother – *'aliam Ysfother'*. Could the word *'Ysfother'* possibly not be a name but mean a large blockhouse-like rock – which both of these are?

South Hessary Tor at Dawn – stump of cobra head.

Looking ahead to North Hessary Tor, the sandy track goes via Princetown that of course did not exist at all in 1240. The boundary follows the greener path now marked by Water Board marker stones.

Track to South Hesssary Tor.

Looking back to South Hessary Tor from a modern stone marker near Princetown.

Towards North Hessary Tor.

Chapter 19

Excursion 12 – North Hessary Tor, Rundlestone and Great Mis Tor

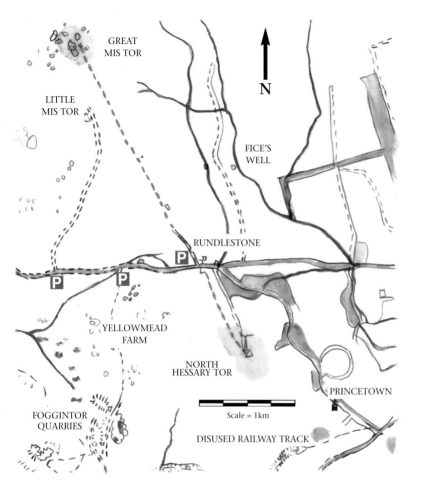

It is worth ascending both North Hessary Tor and Great Mis Tor on clear days as they afford great views in all directions. The perambulators of course would have seen the same horizon but the nearby sights would have been very different – as Princetown and the turnpike roads crossing the moor simply did not exist in 1240. The route was described in the return as follows: *'et sic ad aliam Ysfothere Et inde per mediam Mystmore'*.

There are several parking sites beside the road from Princetown to Tavistock. The one nearest to the site of the Rundlestone is small and takes two to three cars, the one at the entrance to Yellowmeade Farm can take five to six and the car park near the old school below Little Mis Tor takes several dozen. If we are so inclined, some of the area can be explored by bicycle. Having ridden through Princetown, an easy ride is accomplished if we take the course of the old railway track to Foggintor quarries before returning via the Yellowmeade Farm track.

The Rundlestone itself, which William Crossing measured as 7ft tall in 1881, has long since disappeared, probably having been broken up when the nearby wall was built. It was named as a marker on the Forest Boundary in 1702, but was not mentioned in the returns of the 1240 or 1609 perambulations.

We use the stile beside the road to climb over the wall to begin the ascent to North Hessary Tor. It is best to pick a clear day as from the summit dozens of other tors can be seen. It can be hard to find a day of good weather, as Princetown is known to have its own wet microclimate and its own

North Hessary Tor from the west.

Great Mis Tor from North Hessary Tor.

clouds! I once climbed the tor on a day of low cloud and could not see the 700ft mast from the tor top, which was quite eerie.

From the top of the tor, where it is assumed that the modern Trig Point has engulfed the old 'cobra' head boundary marker, we can look towards Great Mis Tor and the next part of the perambulators' route. Looking north, beyond Great Mis Tor we can see Great Links Tor and the High Willhays ridgeline, which mark the perambulators' way back to their start point. As we survey the view we must bear in mind that in 1240 they would not have seen the nearby stone walls, any buildings, no plantations, the town of Princetown with its prison and associated fields nor of course the transmitter mast. It would have been quite an isolated spot.

Returning and crossing the road, we head up the track to Great Mis Tor (not crossing into the military range if the red flag is flying).

Great Mis Tor.

'Mistorpann' looking to North Hessary Tor.

'Mistorpann'.

Although Great Mis Tor is large and prominent, the 1240 perambulators only mentioned it as a place they passed through – *'per mediam Mystmore'*. It was not taken as a mete. They were on their way into the valley beyond to *'Menweburghe'*, which we take to be an ancient settlement somewhere short of White Barrow on Cocks Hill.

The 1609 perambulation return mentions a rock called *'Mistorpann'* as a mete. Many suppose this to be the weathered sculpture atop the tor itself.

From the top of the tor, looking ahead, we can see that the next obstacle to be crossed is the river Walkham. If we wish, we could take a walk down to the river and then follow it upstream. There are many places where it can be forded easily. The climb up the start of Cocks Hill is most easily undertaken by following one of the shallow valleys, such as the one named Dead Lake. We then return to our start point.

Walkham River valley and beyond to Great Links Tor.

Walkham river valley.

Bottom of Dead Lake.

Chapter 20
Excursion 13 – White Barrow, Lynch Tor
and Head of Western Red Lake – from Bagga Tor

Having passed through the middle of the rocks making up Great Mis Tor, the perambulators descended to the Walkham River and then on northwards to the foot of the Rattlebrook. It has generally been accepted that the route taken, and hence the boundary, passes by what we now call White Barrow on Cocks Hill, then along the top of the ridge past Limsboro Cairn adjacent to Lynch Tor before descending to Rattlebrook Foot via Western Red Lake. One 19th century scholar offered a rather different interpretation based on his study of the ancient Celtic language. He supposed that *'Menweburghe'* was the greater entrenchment on White Tor and that what we take as *'Lullyngessete'* was in fact *'Lullingsfote'* or foot. Hence it could be where Bagga Tor farm now stands. Thus he supposed, in summary, based upon a study of language that the perambulators left Great Mis Tor, visited White Tor then passed Bagga Tor before climbing Standon Hill and then descended to Rattlebrook Foot. I doubt he was right and we can judge for ourselves on this 9km walk.

This part of the route is quickly described in the return as: *'Et inde per mediam Mystmore usque ad MenWeburghe Et inde usque ad Lullyngessete Et inde usque ad Rakernebrokefote'*

Parking is available for half a dozen cars beyond the gate at Bagga Tor (SX546805). The track upwards follows a wall and fence for a while before they diverge. A medieval track rises to the left below Lynch Tor going northwards looking almost like a dried up stream. Keeping to the right hand track we are on the Lich Way that has led all the way from the centre of the moor near Bellever. The new take walls on the right of the track are, of course, relatively new.

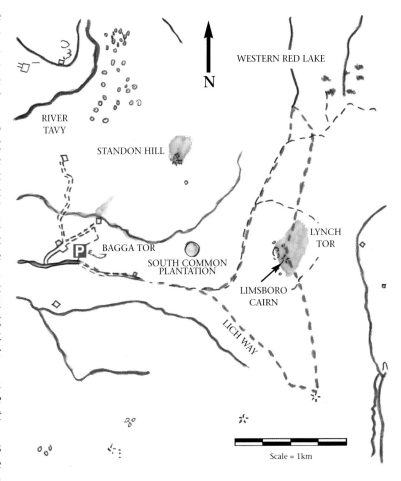

Lynch Tor on the skyline.

White Barrow (arrowed) with Limsboro Cairn beyond.

Looking south to Great Mis Tor from White Barrow.

Limsboro Cairn.

Passing over the ridgeline, we soon reach White Barrow. It is immediately apparent that this is a misnomer as the remains of the cairn are now grassed over completely and it is green.

Looking southwards, we can appreciate the route choices that are open between Great Mis Tor and the foot of Dead Lake.

Turning northwards, the ground is open (albeit a little boggy most of the time) between the White Barrow and Limsboro Cairn, marked today by the military range pole. We can contrast this easy passage with the much more gruelling route for the perambulators via White Tor, Bagga Tor and Standon Hill suggested by one earlier writer.

Having passed Lynch Tor, which is very insignificant from the east, we can continue across the plain of cotton grass. Often this is a sign of a boggy area to be bypassed but here is so widespread that it cannot be avoided.

The head of Western Red Lake is not too far from the 'fat' range pole that marks the conjunction of three military range areas. We head over the horizon towards this until we cross the medieval pack animal track we noted earlier (known locally as Black Lane North) and this time follow it back below Lynch Tor to Bagga Tor.

If we did continue on a little further, the next part of the perambulators' route, up the course of the Rattlebrook, would open before us.

During the return to the car, we should keep looking westwards in order to appreciate better how difficult it would have been to pass from White Tor through the valley bottom (now a working farm) and up the slopes on to Standon Hill. Most have agreed that this one interpretation of the boundary is flawed. From a scholarship point of view, perhaps this highlights clearly the need to approach the interpretation of the perambulators' return, and hence meanings and intentions, using many factors rather than just one – here, linguistics.

If the season is right, we may be lucky enough to be able to admire the acres of bluebells carpeting the lower slopes of Standon Hill.

Lynch Tor above the cotton grass.

Bagga Tor farmland, Ger Tor, Hare Tor and entrance to Tavy Cleave.

Looking north into the Rattlebrook Valley with Great Links Tor to the left.

Chapter 21

Excursion 14 – Tavy Cleave, Rattlebrook Foot and Watern Oke – from Lane End

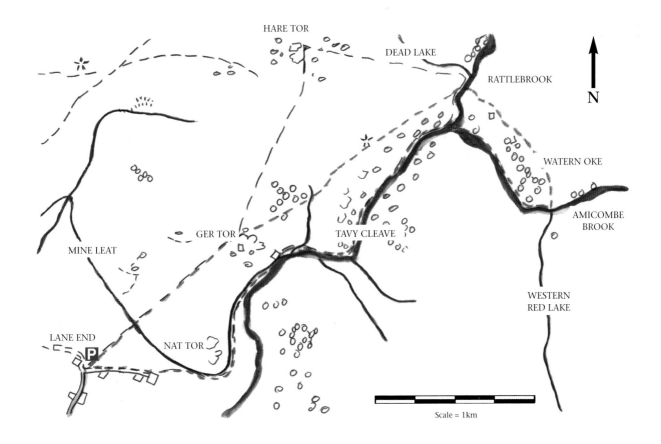

HARE TOR

DEAD LAKE

RATTLEBROOK

WATERN OKE

AMICOMBE BROOK

GER TOR

TAVY CLEAVE

MINE LEAT

WESTERN RED LAKE

LANE END

NAT TOR

N

Scale = 1km

This 9km excursion takes in the spectacular Tavy Cleave (which the perambulators did not traverse but which is well worth visiting) and explores the area around the prehistoric remains of a village on Watern Oke at the foot of the Rattlebrook, which in the return is called '*Rakernebrokefote*'. The aim of the excursion is to demonstrate that, in places, the perambulators must have been unable to actually ride along the whole Forest boundary, as here even walking the boundary is difficult.

Parking for quite a few vehicles is available at Lane End (SX537823). This can be a popular spot in summer as many come here to walk up into the Tavy Cleave or to the heights of Hare Tor.

Our route takes us through the Tavy Cleave starting out along the footpath beside Mine Leat (which eventually ends in the Wheal Jewell Reservoir).

After reaching the head of the Mine Leat, we follow the river upstream trying to keep to the narrowing path along increasingly steep sided valley sides.

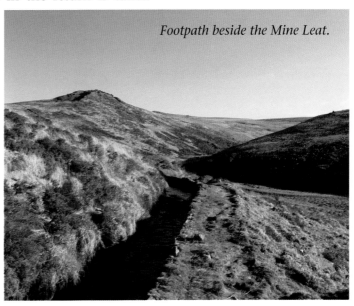

Footpath beside the Mine Leat.

Lower part of Tavy Cleave.

Above right: *Looking back down the Cleave.*

Above: *The route now involves rock hopping.*

Having reached the junction of the Tavy and the Rattlebrook, we now follow the Tavy upstream.

RIVER TAVY

RATTLEBROOK

Foot of the Rattlebrook.

Watern Oke side of the Tavy.

As we make our way upstream, we can see that crossing the brook on horseback would be pretty much impossible for most of its first five or six hundred metres. Yet this is the boundary. Just coming down to the brook having followed the ridge along from Lynch Tor leaves us with a steep rocky downhill climb.

The conclusion we must surely draw from this is that it is most probable that the perambulators would have descended to the Tavy following the line of Western Red Lake, crossed it and then climbed again to skirt the upper limit of Watern Oke.

The foot of Western Red Lake from the Watern Oke side of the valley.

Descending to the Tavy from the South.

The ford and stepping stones across the Tavy at the foot of Western Red Lake (hopefully not so icy as here).

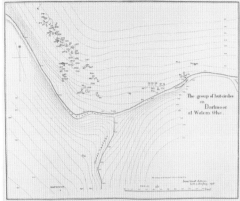

Above: *Map of some of the hut circles.*

Right: *Local hunt riding along below Hare Tor.*

Below: *Typical jumble of rocks at Watern Oke.*

Only about six of the supposed sixty-to-ninety or so Watern Oke hut circles are clearly discernible and they have to be sought out amongst the jumble of rocks. To find them, it might be worth sourcing a map such as shown above left to use as a guide.

There is a rather ugly military range hut near Watern Oke but its location does afford a lovely view down into the Cleave we ascended. Having crossed the Rattle Brook and ascended the ridge beyond, Hare Tor offers excellent views right into Cornwall and also back across the valley to Watern Oke. We can note once again how difficult it would have been to ride down the slope off the northern edge of Standon Hill. To return to the car park, we simply follow the ridgeline past the sites of several pre-historic settlements. There are good views into the Cleave but beware going too close as the sides are very steep.

Looking back to Watern Oke across Rattlebrook Foot from near Ger Tor.

Chapter 22

Excursion 15 – Rattlebrook, Bleak House, Hunt Tor, Stenga Tor, Kitty Tor, Great Links Tor and Widgery Cross – from the Dartmoor Inn

This 14km excursion takes us up the length of the Rattlebrook, which is clearly identifiable as a bound in the perambulation return – *'Et inde usque ad Rakernebrokefote et sic ad capud ejusdem aque'*. It also allows us to examine the beginning of the next bound. From the head of the Rattlebrook, there have been several interpretations of the next part of the route recorded in the perambulation return simply as *'Et deinde usque ad la Westsolle'*.

Most scholars have suggested that *'Westsolle'* is an object such as a tor – for example Stenga Tor or even the Sourton Tors. Perhaps we should interpret it not as a point but rather as a line feature. The *'la'* in front of *'Westsolle'* could be a contraction of the Latin word *'linea'*, meaning 'line of', and *'Westsolle'* could in fact be read as *'Westfolle'* – shorthand for West Flu(vio), i.e. the West Okement river. Thus this part of the return could merely be saying that the route was via or to (and across) the line of the West Okement river.

It is very noticeable in the last 8km of the perambulation that the distance between metes increases. Perhaps this was because the perambulators were more familiar with this part of the boundary, which bordered land in Okehampton held by the Sheriff, or were just plain tired. The West Okement valley hereabouts is called 'the valley of doom' by the youngsters undertaking the annual Ten Tors expedition as it is so steep-sided and scattered with rocks.

From a practical point, the only good direct route down to and across the river between Shelstone Tor in the north and Kneeset Nose to the south leaves the ridgeline near Kitty Tor.

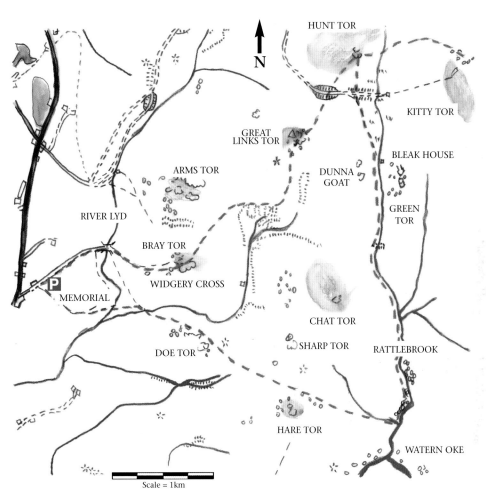

Scale = 1km

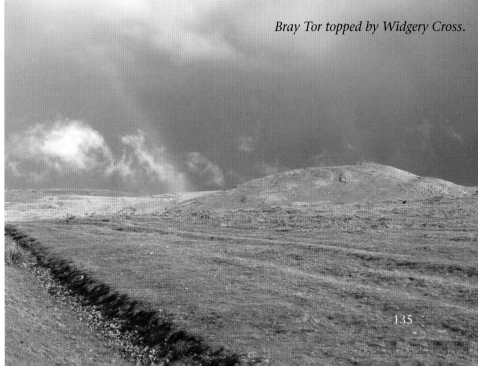

Bray Tor topped by Widgery Cross.

135

Footbridge and stepping stones with Arms Tor beyond.

Our start point is the car park just east of Lydford where we can see Widgery Cross on Bray Tor. Parking is available for lots of cars beyond the gate at SX525853. The approach lane to the car park starts beside the inn opposite the road to Lydford.

We can cross the river Lyd using the ford, stepping-stones or footbridge (SX532857) or take a more direct route via the memorial to a soldier lost in the First World War (SX532851). Then we follow the hardened track NNE to Doe Tor past the enclosed fields.

From either river crossing, we head for Hare Tor rising diagonally across the hillside via Doe Tor, picking our way through the various fields of rocks that are strewn about here. Having crossed the ridgeline, we drop down to the foot of the Rattle Brook near Watern Oke.

It is easiest to walk upstream on the western bank of the Rattle Brook and so there is no need to cross the stream. If we do choose to cross the water and climb a little way up onto Amicombe Hill, the course of the brook to the north is clear.

Rattlebrook from Amicombe Hill.

Lower reaches of the Rattlebrook near the stream bank.

Tussocks and foxgloves ('cowflops' to the locals) further up the slope.

Many moorland streams have paths that run parallel to them but not necessarily at the water's edge. It is worth making the effort to find the best path by exploring at right angles to the stream. The east bank of the Rattlebrook is quite marshy with tussock grass that makes passage awkward. On the west bank, close to the water it can be rocky or boggy, while slightly higher up firm tracks have been carved over the centuries. As we climb, we will pass Bleak House, once home to the supervisor of the local peat cutting works and might possibly meet a modern herdsman.

Looking south to Great Mis Tor along a firm track.

Remains of Bleak House.

Bleak House and Green Tor, showing scars left by peat cutters.

Modern herdsman on harder ground almost out of the valley.

Hunt Tor.

Yes Tor, High Willhays and Ford-sland Ledge.

As we approach the mire at the head of the Rattle Brook, rearing to our left is Great Links Tor, to our right on the ridge is Kitty Tor and ahead is Hunt Tor truly at the head of the Rattle Brook on the side of Woodcock Hill. We make for it keeping to the western side of the mire and avoiding the fenced off areas containing holes of an unknown depth.

We will stop and take a look around from Hunt Tor. Looking back from whence we came, we might be able to see as far as North Hessary Tor and Great Mis Tor.

Looking around from Hunt Tor gives us clues about the likely boundary. Whilst we can see Yes Tor and High Willhays, we cannot see Stenga Tor that many have supposed to be the *'Westsolle'* named as a mete in the perambulation return. Additionally there is no real path, ridge, stream or any other linear feature that leads a traveller to the tor. Indeed to find it, we need to get out a compass to plot the course! This is one reason for supposing that Stenga Tor was not a mete added to which is the sheer awkwardness of the grass tussocks on the direct route.

Looking towards the east, Kitty Tor is visible mainly because today it has a military range flagpole on it. More interestingly, to the north of the tor is a shallow col scarred today by a man made track. For anyone wishing to head east, this col is the most natural point of aim.

Looking south over Rattlebrook Head Mire to Green Tor and Higher Dunna Goat.

Kitty Tor and its col above Rattle-brook Head Mire.

Kitty Tor and Great Links Tor.

We will now head to Kitty Tor, a rather unassuming tor only really noticeable because of the flagpole on top.

From here we can examine the routes into and out of the West Okement valley. Downwards there is one obvious path used by most walkers, which leads down to Sandy Ford. From there it is clear that the easiest route eastwards from the ford rises diagonally across the hillside north of Lints Tor to Dinger Tor.

Path down from Kitty Tor Col to Sandy Ford, now used regularly by those undertaking the annual Ten Tors expedition. Inset: Route up from Sandy Ford to Dinger Tor.

Towards Black Tor.

Towards Fordsland Ledge.

To Sandy Ford, Dinger Tor, Lints Tor.

Sandy Ford.

If we remain unconvinced that Stenga Tor should be dismissed as a mete, let us now go there. Stenga Tor means 'tor in a bog' so we must be prepared to get wet feet.

Having already noted that it is hard to get to directly from Hunt Tor and not on any natural line, let us now look at what the perambulators would have faced to get into and out of the West Okement valley. From the tor, the routes both nearby and up from the far side of the river do not look at all pleasant all the way from Black Tor to the north to High Willhays to the northeast. As seen before, the route eastwards to Dinger looks the most likely and yet we would now have to backtrack to Kitty Tor to get down to the river safely. Do we imagine this would be popular after over forty miles of riding!

If we need more convincing and have the energy, we could now make our way down to the West Okement river.

There we can see that an easy passage is afforded at Sandy Ford (assuming water levels are low). Also, whilst here in the valley bottom, it can be seen just how awkward it is to cross the river on horseback downstream from Sandy Ford. Also, from such a crossing one would have to climb the scree covered slope.

If you are really feeling energetic, it is worth climbing to Fordsland Ledge and looking back to view the difficulty of the routes directly down from Stenga Tor.

On our way back to the car park, Widgery Cross on top of Bray Tor is a good signpost. The route directly down from the cross is steep and easier routes down can be found to the north and south of Bray Tor. The views into Cornwall from here are to be appreciated, as can be the sight of any approaching weather front!

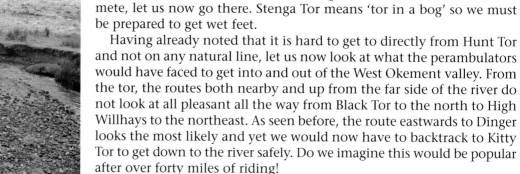

West Okement river downstream from Sandy Ford, with Lints Tor beyond.

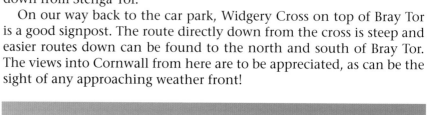

Widgery Cross on Bray Tor.

Scree on lower slopes of High Willhays after a crossing downstream from Sandy Ford.

Chapter 23
Excursion 16 – High Willhays to Row Tor – from Anthony's Stile

This 12km excursion takes us from a parking spot near Anthony's Stile by Okehampton Camp (SX587926) to the highest point on Dartmoor, High Willhays. It is very noticeable that the 1240 return offers few clues as to the route taken in the last stretch of the perambulation. Therefore we should examine the going underfoot carefully. If we assume that the perambulators crossed the West Okement river ('*Westfolle*') at Sandy Ford, then the next mete named is '*Ernestorre*'. This could refer to a tor but if so it would be the only tor named in the whole return. Or it could refer to an area where the local people collected summer ('*erne*') matting ('*storre*'). This could have been the wet but firm ground beside the Black-a-Ven brook above, around and below New Bridge. We may conclude that it is unlikely that the perambulators ascended the heights of High Willhays and Yes Tor, as the going is not horse friendly, but we will do so to admire the views and to check the going: '*Et inde linealiter ad Ernestorre Et inde Linealiter usque ad Vadum Proximum in Orientali parte Capelle Sancti Michaelis*'

It is best if we follow the military tracks to Black Down and then the col between West Mill Tor and Yes Tor. Beware, this latter track attracts water and can either resemble a stream or in mid-winter becomes like a skating rink.

As we approach the col we meet a track crossing ours and can either turn left for West Mill Tor or right for Yes Tor.

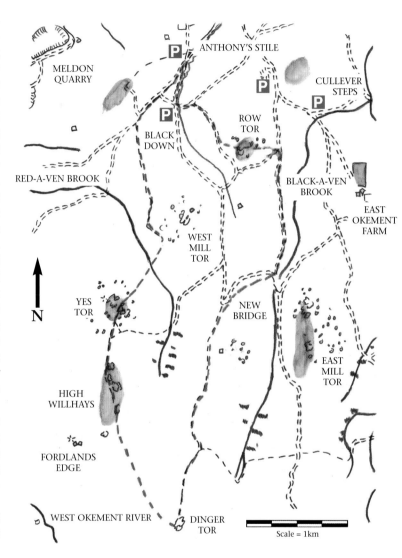

Yes Tor from near Anthony's Stile.

Frozen track.

West Mill Tor from the col.

Yes Tor from West Mill Tor.

Yes Tor one frozen morning.

Whilst on the top of Yes Tor, we should look eastwards towards Cosdon Hill. Surely it is clear that nobody on horseback would risk such a rock-strewn descent as from here.

The path from Yes Tor to High Willhays is well worn and easy to follow. The highest point on Dartmoor is marked with a cairn to which we might care to add an extra rock.

Cosdon Hill from Yes Tor.

From the cairn on High Willhays back towards Yes Tor.

Stenga Tor and Kitty Tor from Fordsland Ledge.

If we now descend to Fordsland Ledge, looking across the West Okement valley we can appreciate once again how unlikely it is that Stenga Tor would have been used as a mete. It is truly isolated and stands above a large clitter field.

Turning now towards Dinger Tor, we can either contour along to it easily or drop down a few hundred feet towards Lints Tor – better to appreciate the going from Sandy Ford to Dinger Tor.

As we cross this area, we should look out for the boundary stones between the Forest and Okehampton parish. This modern boundary crosses our route about halfway to Dinger Tor.

Whilst picking our way down, we can once again appreciate the rocky nature of the ground on this approach from Sandy Ford to High Willhays and lower down the boggy unpleasantness of the ground. The line of the boundary stones carefully bisects these two challenges to a rider.

Rocks on southern slopoes of High Willhays.

The going just above the line of boundary stones with Lints Tor beyond.

Lints Tor and the West Okement valley.

143

Above: *New Bridge and East Mill Tor – Cosdon Hill Beyond.*

Below: *Boundary stone and East Mill Tor.*

We pass Dinger Tor and follow the military track for a few hundred metres until East Mill Tor appears. If we then cut diagonally downhill across the slope we will appreciate both how easy it would be to ride along here and also, lower down, the abundance of reeds that grow along the line of the Black-a-Ven brook.

We need to leave the brook and return to the car park at Anthony's Stile and the road is probably the most obvious route choice. However, it is worth diverting to the top of Row Tor from where we can see the line of the brook we have followed and also the difficulties riders would face if trying to go directly from Yes Tor to West Mill Tor to here.

Of course, I hope you will persevere and press on to Cullever Steps as this, after all, was the start and finish of the whole perambulation.

Above: *Line of the Black-a-Ven brook from Row Tor.*

Below: *Cullever Steps and Irishman's Wall beyond.*

145

APPENDICES

Appendix 1

RETURN ONE – 1335 FEODARY AND CHARTULARY OF THE COURTENAY FAMILY, EARLS OF DEVON (BL)

This copy is to be found in the Harleian Collection in the British Library (BL) in London. It is in a volume entitled the "Feodary and Chartulary of the Courtenay Family, Earls of Devon" (ref. Add. 49359). This volume, which consists of documents stuck onto paper pages, was probably originally compiled in connection with the recognition of Hugh de Courtenay as 9th Earl of Devon (1st creation, de jure) in 1335. The copy of the return is written on vellum and is now stuck onto a paper page at folio 54.

As the volume itself is dated to 1335, it is most probable that the copy of the return was created earlier. It is a beautifully presented volume and the copy itself has red highlighting of some of the key letters. It is however rather indistinct to the naked eye and difficult to decipher in places.

As was the practice at the time when vellum was very expensive, there is a note on an unrelated matter at the bottom of this page. This has been ignored here.

Each copy will be presented in the form of one line per bound after the shorthand has been expanded.

1335 - Feodary and Chartulary of the Courtenay Family, Earls of Devon (British Library)

1	Qui	incipiunt perambulationem		*ad*	hogam de Costdonne
2	et	inde	linealiter	usque	*ad*	parvam hogam que vocatur parva Houndetorre
3	et	inde		usque	*ad*	Theurlestone
4	et	inde	linealiter	usque	*ad*	Wotysbrokelakysfote que cadit in Teng
5	et	inde	linealiter	usque	*ad*	Hengheston
6	et	inde	linealiter	usque	*ad*	Yestetone
7	et	inde	linealiter	usque	per	mediam turbarium de Alberesheved
8	et	sic	in longem			Walebrokum
9	et	inde	linealiter	usque	*ad*	Furnem Regum
10	et	inde	linealiter	usque	*ad*	Walebrokehenyd
11	et	sic	in longem Walebrokum	usque		cadit in Derta
12	et	sic	per Dertam	usque		aliam Dertam
13		sic	per aliam Dertam ascendendo	usque		Okbrokysfote
14	et	sic	ascendo Okbroke	usque	*ad*	*linea Dryeworke*
15	et	ita	ascendendo	usque	*ad*	*linea Dryefeldford*
16	et	inde	linealiter	usque	*ad*	Cattyshill
17	et	inde	linealiter	usque	*ad*	capud de Westerewelebroke
18	et	sic	per Westerewelebroke	usque		cadit in Avena
19	et	inde	linealiter	usque	*ad*	EstereWhyteburgh
20	et	inde	linealiter	ubi		*linea Rode Lake cadit in Erm*
21	et	inde	ascendendo	usque	*ad*	Grymesgrove
22	et	inde	linealiter	usque	*ad*	Elesburghe
23	et	inde	linealiter	usque	*ad*	crucem Syward
24	et	inde		usque	*ad*	Ysfothere
25	et	sic			*ad*	aliam Ysfothere
26	et	inde	per mediam Mystmore	usque	*ad*	Menweburghe
27	et	inde		usque	*ad*	Lullyngessete
28	et	inde		usque	*ad*	Rakernebrokefote
29	et	sic			*ad*	capud ejusdem aque
30	et	deinde		usque	*ad*	*linea Westfolle*
31	et	inde	linealiter	usque	*ad*	Ernestorre
32	et	inde	linealiter	usque	*ad*	vadum proximum in orientali parte Capelle Sancti Michaelis De Halghestoke
33	et	inde	linealiter	usque	*ad*	predictam Hogam de Costodone in orientali parte

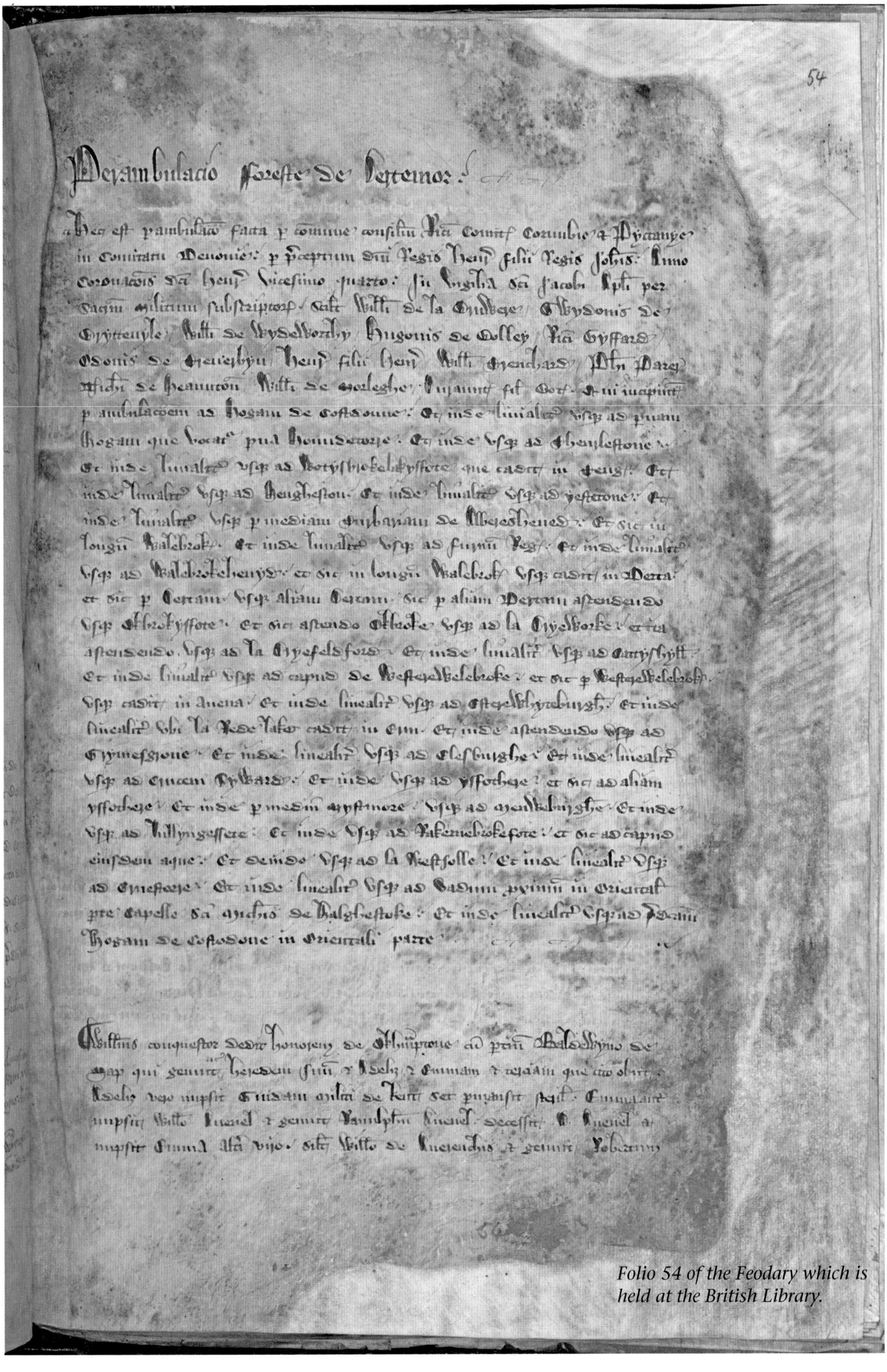

Folio 54 of the Feodary which is held at the British Library.

Appendix 2

RETURN TWO – 1478 – VERSO OF COLOURED MAP (DHC)

A large coloured map showing the Forest of Dartmoor dated somewhere as late 15th or early 16th century was presented to the Albert (now Royal Albert) Memorial Museum in 1877. It was mentioned in the 1896 re-issue of Samuel Rowe's book – "A Perambulation of the Antient and Royal Forest of Dartmoor and the Venville Precincts" first published in 1848. The map is now in the Devon Heritage Centre (DHC) at Sowton in Exeter. It was called the Devon Record Office until 2012 when it was renamed on the arrival of all the material from the Westcountry Study Centre that was previously in the centre of Exeter. The map will be described in more detail elsewhere. Of interest here is the copy of the 1240 perambulation return that is on the back of the map.

It is of interest to try to relate the creation of a copy of the return, a not inexpensive project, to the lives of the Earls of Devon and the Duke of Cornwall. During the period 1470 to 1510 there were multiple events. There was no Earl of Devon from 1471 to 1485. Edward Courtenay 1st Earl of Devon, Third Creation was the earl from 1485 until his death in 1509. The Earldom was forfeited at his death by his son's attainder but restored to his grandson in 1512. Dukes of Cornwall during this period were numerous: Edward Plantagenet (later Edward V) 1470–1483; Edward of Middleham 1483–1484(d); Arthur Tudor 1486(b)–1502(d); Henry Tudor (later Henry VIII) 1502–1509. Linking any of these occurrences to this copy of the Forest return is not possible.

One suggestion made in 1941 by R Hansford Worth at a Devonshire Association meeting was that the map and copy of the return could have been written to support suits made when 'claims of the Abbot of Buckfast were challenged by the men of Devonshire, probably in 1478'. As the map shows far more detail of the southern Moor, beyond the Forest boundary, this could well be the case. Of course, we shall never know for certain.

1478 – Verso of Coloured Map (Devon Heritage Centre)						
1		Qui incipiunt perambulationem			*ad*	Hogam de Cosdonne
2	et	inde	linealiter	usque	*ad*	parvam hogam que vocatur parva Houndetorre
3	et	inde	linealiter	usque	*ad*	Thurlestone
4	et	inde	linealiter	usque	*ad*	Wotysbrokelakysfote que cadit in Teing
5	et	inde	linealiter	usque	*ad*	Hengystone
6	et	inde	linealiter	usque	*ad*	Langstone
7	et	inde	linealiter	usque	per	mediam Turbarium de Alberyshede
8	et	sic	in longem			Wallebroke
9	et	inde	linealiter	usque	*ad*	ffurnem Regis
10	et	inde	linealiter	usque	*ad*	Wallebrokesheed
11	et	sic	in longum Wallebroke	usque		cadit in Darta
12	et	sic	per Dartam	usque		aliam Dartam
13	et	sic	per aliam Dartam ascendendo	usque		Okbrokysfote
14	et	sic	ascendo Okebroke	usque	*ad*	*linea Dryaworke*
15	et	ita	ascendendo	usque	*ad*	Dryefeldford
16	et	inde	linealiter	usque	*ad*	Cattishille
17	et	inde	linealiter	usque	*ad*	capud de Westerewallebroke
18	et	sic	per Westerwalbroke	usque		cadit in Avena
19	et	inde	linealiter	usque	*ad*	Estere Whyteburgh
20	et	inde	linealiter	usque		*linea Rode Lake ubi cadit in Erme*
21	et	ita	linealiter	usque	*ad*	Grymesgrove
22	et	inde	linealiter	usque	*ad*	Elysborough
23	et	sic	linealiter	usque	*ad*	crucem Sywardi
24	et	inde		usque	*ad*	Ysfothere
25	et	sic			*ad*	aliam Ysfothere
26	et	inde	per mediam Mystor	usque	*ad*	Menweburghe
27	et	inde		usque	*ad*	Lullingesfote
28	et	inde		usque	*ad*	Rakernebrokesfote
29	et	sic			*ad*	capud ejusdem aque
30	et	deinde		usque	*ad*	*linea Westfolle*
31	et	inde	linealiter	usque	*ad*	Ernestorre
32	et	inde	linealiter	usque	*ad*	vadum proximum in orientali parte Capelle Sancti Michaelis De Halstorke
33	et	inde	linealiter	usque	*ad*	predictam Hogam de Costonne in Orientali parte

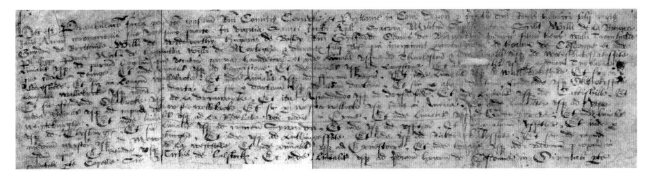

1478 copy of the perambulation return on the back of the map.

Appendix 3

RETURN THREE – 1502 – HENRY (LATER HENRY VIII) BECOMES DUKE OF CORNWALL (KEW)

This copy of the perambulation return is on a single scrap of what feels like paper. It is held at the National Archives at Kew, London. It appears not to have been known by previous scholars in the 19th Century. It has been badly damaged at some time – its right hand side has suffered in particular.

The type of paper and script used lead the records' specialists to date it to the time of Henry VII or Henry VIII. It could well have been made as Henry Tudor (later Henry VIII), became Duke of Cornwall.

The 1502 text seen under ultra violet light.

1502 - Henry (later Henry VIII) becomes Prince of Wales (National Archives Kew)
[right hand side spoilt]

1	Qui incipiunt perambulationem				*ad*	hogam de ?
2	Faded					que vocatur parva Hundetorr
3	Faded or Missing					
4	Faded					
5	et	inde	linealiter	usque	*ad*	Hoghston
6	et	inde	linealiter	usque	*ad*	Yestone
7	et	inde	?	?	?	
8	?	?	?			
9	et	inde	linealiter	usque	*ad*	furnem Regis
10	et	inde	linealiter	usque	*ad*	Walebrokehenyd
11	et	sic	in longum ?			
12	Missing		Dertam	usque	*ad*	aliam Dertam
13	et	sic	per aliam Dertam ascendendo	usque		Okbrokysfote
14	et	sic	ascendo	?	?	?
15	?	?	ascendendo	usque	*ad*	*linea Driefilforde*
16	et	inde	linealiter	usque	*ad*	Gnattyshull
17	et	inde	linealiter	usque	*ad*	capud de West????
18						
19	?	?	?	?	?	?
20	et	inde	linealiter	ubi		*linea ? Cadit in Erm*
21	?	?	ascendendo	usque	*ad*	GrymesGroseve
22	et	inde	linealiter	usque	*ad*	Eleborough
23	et	inde	linealiter	usque	*ad*	crucem Sywarde
24	et	inde	?	?		
25	?	?	?	?		Hysfother
26	et	inde	usque		*ad*	Mystmore
26a	et	inde	usque		*ad*	Meweborough
27	et	inde	usque		*ad*	Lullyngessete
28	Missing					
29	Missing					
30	et	deinde	usque			ejusdem aque
31	et	inde	linealiter	usque	*ad*	yornestorr
32	et	inde	linealiter	usque	*ad*	vadum proximum in orientali parte
33						Hogam de Costondone in orientali parte

Appendix 4

Before his death in 1601, John Hooker (Hoker or Vowell), who was an English writer, solicitor, antiquary and civic administrator (he was chamberlain of Exeter from 1555 to his death), wrote his last and probably uncompleted work – the first topographical description of the county of Devon. Two copies have been found. One in the Devon Heritage Centre, regrettably missing four bounds of the perambulation, and another in the British Library which is so indistinct as to be virtually unreadable. This work concentrated on describing the major families in Devon and so perhaps inclusion of the perambulation return was for completeness sake but of little importance.

Second page of Hooker copy.

1599 - The Hooker Manuscript held in Exeter (Devon Heritage Centre)					
1			Qui incipiunt perambulationem		*ad* hogam de East Donne
2	et	inde	linealiter	usque	*ad* parvam hogam que vocatur hountore
3	et	inde		usque	*ad* Thurlestone
4	et	inde	linealiter	usque	*ad* Wotesbrokelackesfoote et cadit in Albercheves
5	et	inde	linealiter	usque	*ad* hengeston
6	et	inde	linealiter	usque	*ad* Eastestone
7	et	inde	linealiter	usque	per mediam turbariam de albercheved
8	et	sic	in longam		Walbrooke
9	et	sic	linealiter		*ad* furnem Regis
10	et	sic	linealiter	usque	*ad* Walbrooke hed
11	et	sic	in longa Walbrooke	et inde	cadit in derta
12	et	sic	per derta	usque	aliam dertam
13			ascendendo	usque	*ad* oke broad
14	et	sic	ascendo Okebrooke	usque	*ad* *linea dryewoke*
15			These 3 bounds were missed out by Hooker in this version!		
16					
17					
18	et	sic	per wasterwelbroke	usque	cadit in avena
19	et	inde	linealiter	usque	*ad* Easterwhitborough
20	et	inde	linealiter	usque	*ad* *linea redd lake et cadit in Erme*
21	et	inde	ascendend	usque	*ad* Grymesgrove
22	et	inde	linealiter	usque	*ad* Englyshborough
23	et	inde	linealiter	usque	*ad* crucem Sywarde
24	et	inde		usque	*ad* Esfother
25			This bound was missed out by Hooker!		
26	et	inde	per mediam mistmore	usque	*ad* memborough
27	et	inde		usque	lullinge
28	et	inde			*ad* Rakebrokefoote
29	et	sic			*ad* capud ejusdem aque
30	et	deinde		usque	*ad* Westall
31	et	inde	linealiter	usque	*ad* Grenestone
32	et	inde	linealiter	usque	*ad* vadum proximum in orientali parte capell Sancti Michaelis de Haughstoke
33	et	inde	linealiter	usque	*ad* predictam hogam de East Donne in orientali parte

1599 - The Hooker Manuscript held in London (British Library)

#						
1		Qui incipiunt perambulationem			*ad*	hogam de Costdonne
2	et	inde	linealiter		*ad*	Parvam hogam que vocatur Houndetorre
3	et	inde		usque	*ad*	Theurlestone
4	et	inde	linealiter	usque	*ad*	Wotesbrokelackesfoote que cadit in Teng
5	et	inde	linealiter	usque		Hengheston
6	et	inde	linealiter	usque	*ad*	Yestestone
7	et	inde	linealiter	usque	per	mediam turbariam de Aberesheved
8	et	sic	in longem Walbrooke			
9	et	sic	linealiter	usque	*ad*	Furnem Regis
10	et	inde	linealiter	usque	*ad*	Walbrokehenyd
11	et	sic	in longem Walbrook	usque		cadit in Derta
12	et	sic	per Derta	usque	*ad*	aliam Dertam
13			ascendendo	usque		Okbrookesfoote
14	et	sic	ascendo Okebroke	usque	*ad*	*linea Dryeworke*
15	et	ita	ascendendo	usque	*ad*	*linea Dryefeldford*
16	et	inde	linealiter	usque		Battyshall
17	et	inde	linealiter	usque	*ad*	capud de Westerwelebrooke
18	et	sic	per Westerwelbrooke	usque		cadit in Avena
19	et	inde	linealiter	usque	*ad*	Easterwhitborough
20	et	inde	linealiter	usque		*linea Rode lake que cadit in erme*
21	et	inde	ascendendo	usque	*ad*	Grymesgrove
22	et	inde	linealiter	usque	*ad*	Elesburghe
23	et	inde	linealiter	usque	*ad*	crucem Sylward
24	et	inde	usque		*ad*	Ysfothere
25	et	sic	per			aliam Ysfothere
26	et	inde	per mediam Mystmore	usque	*ad*	memborough
27	et	inde	usq...			Lulling…
28	et	inde			*ad*	Rakernebrokefoote
29	et	sic			*ad*	caput ejusdem aque
30	et	deinde	usque		*ad*	Westall
31	et	inde	linealiter	usque	*ad*	Ernestorre
32	et	inde	linealiter	usque	*ad*	vadam proximum in orientali parte capell Sancti Michaelis de Haughstoke
33	et	inde	linealiter	usque	*ad*	predictam Hogam de Costdonne in orientali parte

Appendix 5

Included here are notes taken from a copy held by the British Library but which is too difficult to photograph without damage.

1624 - Buckfastleigh Abbey Record of Brent Moor (British Library)

1			unt perambulationem		*ad*	hogam de Costdonne
2	et	inde	linealiter	usque	*ad*	parvam hogam que vocatur parva Houndetor
3	Missing					
4	Missing					
5	et	inde	linealiter	usque	*ad*	Hengheston
6	et	inde	linealiter	usque	*ad*	Yestetone
7	et	inde	linealiter	usque	*ad*	mediam turbarium de Alberesheved
8	Missing					
9	et	inde	linealiter	usque	*ad*	Furnem Regum
10	et	inde	linealiter	usque	*ad*	Walebrokehenyd
11	et	sic	in longem Walebroke	usque		cadit in Dartam
12	et	sic	per Darta	usque	*ad*	aliam Dartam
13	et	sic	per aliam Darta ascendendo	usque	*ad*	Okbrokysfote
14	et	sic	ascendo Okbroke	usque	*ad*	*linea Driwork*
15	et	sic	ascendendo	usque	*ad*	Dryefeldford
16	et	inde	linealiter	usque	*ad*	Cattyshill
17	et	inde	linealiter	usque	*ad*	capud Westerewelebroke
18	et	sic	per Westerewelebroke	usque		cadit in Aven
19	et	inde	linealiter		*ad*	EstereWhyteburgh
20	et	inde	linealiter	usque	*ad*	Rode Lake cadit in Erme
21	et	inde	ascendendo	usque	*ad*	Grymesgrove
22	et	inde		usque	*ad*	Elesburghe
23	et	inde	linealiter	usque	*ad*	crucem Silward
24	et	inde		usque	*ad*	hisfother
25	et	sic			*ad*	aliam hisfother
26	et	inde	usque ad Mystmore et inde	usque	*ad*	Menweburghe
27	et	deinde		usque	*ad*	Lullingefoot
28	et	inde		usque	*ad*	Rakernebrokefote
29	et	sic	per			capud ejusdem aquae
30	et	inde		usque	*ad*	*linea Westfolle*
31	et	inde	linealiter	usque	*ad*	Ernestore
32	et	inde	linealiter	usque	*ad*	vadum proximum per orientali parte Capelle De Halghestoke
33	et	inde	linealiter	usque	*ad*	predictam Hogam de Costendonne in orientali parte

Appendix 6

RETURN SEVEN – 1650 – SERJEANT MAYNARD (INNS OF COURT)

A copy of the return previously seen in the 19th century by members of the Devonshire Association still resides in the same location as then – the library at the Inns of Court in London.

Reportedly created by Serjeant Maynard – the 'king's serjeant' Sir John Maynard (1602–1690) – this copy was stated to be have been copied verbatim from a parchment manuscript of the date of Edward II (1307–1327), contained in a 'Leiger Book of my Lord B', meaning probably the Earl of Bedford's Leiger Book or Cartulary of Tavistock Abbey. This could well have occurred during the time that Oliver Cromwell ran the country (1649–1658). With the removal of Charles (later Charles II) as Duke of Cornwall in 1649, the Lords Protector would surely have wanted an account of what had now to be supervised. It is assumed that might have been in 1650, we will never be certain.

Above: *Serjeant Maynard's copy.*

1650 - Serjeant Maynard's Version (Inns of Court)					
1		Qui incipiunt perambulationem		ad	hogam de Costdonne
2	et inde	linealiter	usque	ad	parvam hogam que vocatur parva houndtor
3	et inde		usque	ad	Theurlestone
4	et inde	linealiter	usque	ad	Wotysbrokelakysfote que cadit in Tenge
5	et inde	linealiter	usque	ad	hengheston
6	et inde	linealiter	usque	ad	Yestetone
7	et inde	linealiter	usque	per	mediam turbariam de Alberesheved
8	et sic	in longem			Walebroke
9	et inde	linealiter	usque	ad	furnem Regis
10	et inde	linealiter	usque	ad	Walesbroke?
11	et sic	in longem walebrok	usque		cadit in derta
12	et sic	per dertam	usque		aliam dertam
13	et sic	per aliam dertam ascendendo	usque		Okbrokysfote
14	et sic	ascendo Okbroke	usque	ad	?
15	et ita	ascendendo	usque	ad	*linea dryefeyldford*
16	et inde	linealiter	usque	ad	Cattyshyll
17	et inde	linealiter	usque	ad	capud de Westerewelebroke
18	et sic	per Westerewelebroke	usque		cadit in ?
19	et inde	linealiter	usque	ad	EstereWhiteburgh
20	et inde	linealiter	ubi		*linea Rede Lake cadit in Erm*
21	et inde	ascendendo	usque	ad	grymesgrove
22	et inde	linealiter	usque	ad	Elesburghe
23	et inde	linealiter	usque	ad	crucem Syward
24	et inde		usque	ad	ysfothere
25	et sic			ad	?? Ysfothere
26	et inde	per mediam Mistmore	usque	ad	Meuweburghe
27	et inde		usque	ad	lulling?
28	et inde		usque	ad	Rakernebrokefote
29	et sic			ad	capud ejusdem aque
30	et deinde		usque	ad	*linea Westfolle*
31	et inde	linealiter	usque	ad	Ernestorre
32	et inde	linealiter	usque	ad	vadum proximum in orientali parte capelle Sancti Michaelis de halghestoke
33	et inde	linealiter	usque	ad	predictam Hogam de Costodone in orientali parte

Appendix 7

RETURN EIGHT – 1699 – CHARTER OF EARL MORETON (PLYMOUTH AND WEST DEVON RECORD OFFICE)

The part of the National Archives in Plymouth holds a scroll wherein are details of the disafforestation of Devon and Cornwall (1204), confirmation of the same for King Henry III (original dated 1252) and a copy of the return from the first perambulation (1240). Archivists believe the roll was created in the 17th century.

The scroll is marked as 'Charter of Earl Moreton'. Perhaps this referred to a title King John had from 1189 to 1199 when Mortain was lost to France, namely 'Count of Mortain'.

Of course, the seventeenth century was a turbulent one for the whole country. In the midst of the century, Oliver Cromwell ran the country having deposed and seen Charles I beheaded. Charles II reassumed the throne in 1660 following the death of Cromwell and the restoration of the monarchy. Prince James Edward Francis was Duke of Cornwall from birth (1688) until attainted in 1702. So there should well have been Royal interest in the Duchy's holdings in this period and the creation date assumed for this record is 1699.

Above: *The 1699 perambulation return held at the West Devon Record Office.*

1699 - Plymouth Record Office					
1a Qui incipiunt perambulationem				ad	hogam de Costdowne
2	et	inde	linealiter	usque	ad	parvam hogam que vocatur parva Hountorre
3	et	inde		usque	ad	Thurleston
4	et	inde	linealiter	usque	ad	Wotesbrokefote que cadit in Teng
5	et	inde	linealiter	usque	ad	Hengstone
6	et	inde	linealiter	usque	ad	yestone
7	et	inde	linealiter	usque	per	mediam turbarium de Aberesheved
8	et	sic	in longem			Walebroke
9	et	inde	linealiter	usque	ad	furnem regis
10	et	inde	linealiter	usque	?	?
11	et	sic	in longum Walbroke	usque		cadit in Darta
12	et	sic	per Dertam	usque		aliam Dertam
13	et	sic	per aliam Dertam ascendendo	usque	ad	Okesbroke fote
14	et	sic	ascendendo Okebrok	usque	ad	*linea Dryaworke*
15	et	ita	ascendendo	usque	ad	*linea Dryefelford*
16	et	inde	linealiter	usque	ad	Cattyshill
17	et	inde	linealiter	usque	ad	capud de Wester Welbroke
18	et	sic	per Westerewelebroke	usque		cadit in Avena
19	et	inde	linealiter	usque		Eoster Whyteburg
20	et	inde	linealiter	ubi		*linea RedLake cadit in Erme*
21	et	inde	linealiter/ascendendo	usque	ad	Grmysgrove
22	et	inde	linealiter	usque	ad	Elysburgh
23	et	inde	linealiter	usque	ad	crucem Syward
24	et	inde		usque	ad	Ysfother
25	et	sic			ad	aliam Ysfother
26	et	inde	per mediam mystmore	usque	ad	Mewyburghe
27	et	inde		usque	ad	Lullingysfote
28	et	inde		usque	ad	Rakernebrokefote
29	et	sic			ad	capud ejusdem aque
30	et	deinde		usque	ad	*linea Westfolle*
31	et	inde	linealiter	usque		Ernystorre
32	et	inde	linealiter	usque	ad	vadum proximum in orientali parte capelle Sancti Michaelis de Halghestoke
33	et	inde	linealiter	usque	ad	predictam Hogam de ? ? Orientali parte

Appendix 8

The Duchy of Cornwall was first created in 1337. It holds a volume containing transcriptions from earlier archival documents that was put together over a number of years and prepared for binding in 1793. It is entitled 'Lidford (sic) Manor and Castle and Dartmore Forest: collections of Records and Office Papers etc from 1203 to 1735 by Richard Gray and Robert Gray Dated 1793'

This volume contains one short document that it says has been transcribed from the papers of Thomas Lane. Quite which Thomas Lane this was is not known.

The Duchy perambulation return.
© HRH The Duke of Cornwall 2014

		1793 - Held by the Duchy of Cornwall				
1	Hic incipiunt perambulationem				*ad*	Hogam de Cosdonne
2	et inde	linialiter		usque	*ad*	Parva Hogam que vocatur Parva Houndetorr
3	et inde	linialiter		usque	*ad*	Thurleston
4	et inde	linialiter		usque	*ad*	Wotesbrokeslakesfote que cadit in Teinge
5	et inde	linialiter		usque	*ad*	Heighestone
6	et inde	linialiter		usque	*ad*	Langstone
7	et inde	linialiter		usque	per	Mediam Turbarium de Alberyshede
8	et sic	in Longu				Wallebroke
9	et inde	linialiter		usque	*ad*	Furnum Regis
10	et inde	linialiter		usque	*ad*	Wallebrokeshede
11	et sic	in Longum Wallebroke		usque		cadit in Darta
12	et sic	per Dartam		usque		aliam Dartam
13	et sic	per aliam Dartam ascendendo		usque		Okebrokysfote
14	et sic	ascendendo Okebroke		usque	*ad*	*linea Dryaworke*
15	et ita	ascendendo		usque	*ad*	Dryfeldforde
16	et sic	inde linealiter		usque	*ad*	Cattishille
17	et inde	linialiter		usque	*ad*	Caput de Wester Wellebroke
18	et sic	per Wester Welbroke		usque		cadit in Avena
19	et inde	linialiter		usque	*ad*	Yester Whyteburghe
20	et inde	linialiter		usque	*ad*	*linea Rodelake ubi cadit in Erme*
21	et inde	linialiter		usque	*ad*	Grymesgreve
22	et inde	linialiter		usque	*ad*	Elysburghe
23	et sic	linialiter		usque	*ad*	Crucem Sywardi
24	et inde	usque			*ad*	Ysfother
25	et sic	per				aliam Ysfother
26	et inde	per Mediam Mystor		usque	*ad*	Mewyburghe
27	et inde			usque	*ad*	Lullingesfote
28	et inde			usque	*ad*	Rakernebrokysfote
29	et sic				*ad*	caput ejusdem Aque
30	et deinde			usque	*ad*	*linea Westfolle*
31	et inde	linialiter		usque	*ad*	Ernestorre
32	et inde	linialiter		usque	*ad*	Vadum proximum in orientali parte Capelle Sancti Michaelis de Halstock
33	et inde	linialiter		usque	*ad*	predictam Hogam de Cosdonne in orientali parte

Appendix 9

In 1848, Samuel Rowe published his book containing a 'compilation' from several copies of the return. As this version is quoted so often, it is shown here for the sake of completeness.

1848 - Rowe Second Edition (not a handwritten document per se but a compilation of knowledge in the 19th century)						
1		Qui incipiunt perambulationem			*ad*	hogam de Cossdonne
2	et	inde	linealiter	usque	*ad*	parvam hogam que vocatur parva Hundetorre
3	et	inde	linealiter	usque	*ad*	Thurlestone
4	et	inde	linealiter	usque	*ad*	Wotesbrokelakesfote que cadit in Tyng
5	et	inde	linealiter	usque	*ad*	Heigheston
6	et	inde	linealiter	usque	*ad*	Langestone
7	et	inde	linealiter	usque	per	mediam turbarium de Alberysheved
8	et	sic	in longum			Wallebroke
9	et	inde	linealiter	usque	*ad*	Furnum regis
10	et	inde	linealiter	usque	*ad*	Wallebrokeshede
11	et	sic	in longum Wallebroke	usque		cadit in Dertam
12	et	sic	per Dertam	usque	**ad**	aliam Dertam
13	et	sic	per aliam Dertam ascendendo	usque		Okebrokysfote
14	et	sic	ascendendo Okebroke	usque	*ad*	la Dryeworke
15	et	ita	ascendendo	usque	*ad*	la Dryefeld ford
16	et	sic	inde linealiter	usque	*ad*	Battyshull
17	et	inde	linealiter	usque	*ad*	caput de Wester Wellabroke
18	et	sic	per Wester Wellabroke	usque		cadit in Avenam
19	et	inde	linealiter	usque	*ad*	Ester Whyteburgh
20	et	inde	linealiter	usque	*ad*	la RedeLake que cadit in Erme
21	et	inde	linealiter	usque	*ad*	Grymsgrove
22	et	inde	linealiter	usque	*ad*	Elysburghe
23	et	sic	linealiter	usque	*ad*	crucem Sywardi
24	et	inde	usque		*ad*	Ysfother
25	et	sic	per			aliam Ysfother
26	et	inde	per mediam Mystor	usque	*ad*	Mewyburghe
27	et	inde	usque		*ad*	Lullingesfote
28	et	inde	usque		*ad*	Rakernesbrokysfote
29	et	sic			*ad*	caput ejusdem aque
30	et	deinde	usque		*ad*	la Westfolle
31	et	inde	linealiter	usque	*ad*	Ernestorre
32	et	inde	linealiter	usque	*ad*	vadum proximum in orientali parte capelle Sancti Michaelis de Halgestoke
33	et	inde	linealiter	usque	*ad*	predictum hogam de Cossdonne in orientali parte

INDEX

159